Unions and
Public Schools

Lexington Books Politics of Education Series
Frederick M. Wirt, Editor

John C. Hogan, *The Schools, the Courts, and the Public Interest*

James Hottois, Neal A. Milner, *The Sex Education Controversy: A Study of Politics, Education, and Morality*

Frederick M. Wirt, Ed., *The Polity of the School: New Research in Educational Politics*

Lawrence E. Gladieux, Thomas R. Wolanin, *Congress and the Colleges: The National Politics of Higher Education*

Dale Mann, *The Politics of Administrative Representation: School Administrators and Local Democracy*

Harrell R. Rodgers, Jr., Charles S. Bullock III, *Coercion to Compliance*

Richard A. Dershimer, *The Federal Government and Education R&D*

Tyll van Geel, *Authority to Control the School Program*

Andrew Fishel, Janice Pottker, *National Politics and Sex Discrimination in Education*

Chester E. Finn, Jr., *Education and the Presidency*

Frank W. Lutz, Laurence Iannoccone, *Public Participation in Local School Districts*

Paul Goldstein, *Changing the American Schoolbook*

Everett F. Cataldo, Micheal W. Giles, Douglas S. Gatlin, *School Desegregation Policy: Compliance, Avoidance, and the Metropolitan Remedy*

William J. Grimshaw, *Union Rule in the Schools: Big-City Politics in Transformation*

David K. Wiles, *Energy, Winter, and Schools: Crisis and Decision Theory*

Robert H. Salisbury, *Citizen Participation in the Public Schools*

Douglas E. Mitchell, *Shaping Legislative Decisions: Education Policy and the Social Sciences*

Emmett H. Buell, Jr., *School Desegregation and Defended Neighborhoods: The Boston Controversy*

David L. Colton, Edith E. Graber, *Teacher Strikes and the Courts*

Hawley, Willis D., et al., *Strategies for Effective Desegregation*

Randall W. Eberts and Joe A. Stone, *Unions and Public Schools: The Effects of Collective Bargaining on American Education*

Unions and Public Schools

The Effect of Collective Bargaining on American Education

Randall W. Eberts
Joe A. Stone
University of Oregon

LexingtonBooks
D.C. Heath and Company
Lexington, Massachusetts
Toronto

Library of Congress Cataloging in Publication Data

Eberts, Randall W.
  Unions and public schools.

  (Lexington Books politics of education series)
  Bibliography: p.
  Includes index.
  1. Collective bargaining—Teachers—United States. 2. Teachers' unions—United States. 3. School personnel management—United States. 4. Academic achievement. I. Stone, Joe A. II. Title. III. Series.
LB2844.59.U6E23 1983   331.89'041371100973   82–48862
ISBN 0–669–06372–x

Copyright © 1984 by D.C. Heath and Company

Published simultaneously in Canada

Printed in the United States of America

International Standard Book Number: 0–669–06372–x

Library of Congress Catalog Card Number: 82–48862

To
Diane and Crystal,
who never question why we
engage in such activity

Contents

Figures and Tables   ix

Foreword *Lawrence C. Pierce*   xiii

Preface and Acknowledgments   xv

Chapter 1   **Introduction**   1

Previous Research on Teacher Collective
   Bargaining   2
The Educational Process and Collective
   Bargaining   4
Organization of the Book   10

Chapter 2   **The Collective-Bargaining Contract**   13

Why Do Teachers Organize?   14
Major Trends in the Scope of Bargaining   20
Bargaining Outcomes   30
Conclusions   38

Chapter 3   **A Model of Student Achievement**   41

Measuring the Effects of Collective
   Bargaining On Student Achievement   43
Analysis of the Determinants of
   Mathematical Skills   52
Conclusions   60

Chapter 4   **Teachers and Collective Bargaining**   63

Labor Contracts, Compensation, and
   Working Conditions   63
The Union-Nonunion Salary Differential   73
Teacher Attitudes, District Policies, and
   Collective Bargaining   81
Teacher Labor Markets   86
Conclusions   120
Appendix 4A: Formal Derivation of
   Contract-Curve Model   127

Chapter 5   **Administrators and Collective Bargaining**   131

                 Resource Allocation and Teacher Contracts   132
                 Educational Policy and Practice and
                     Teacher Contracts   148
                 Conclusions   151

Chapter 6   **Student Achievement and Collective Bargaining** 157

                 Resources, Student Achievement, and
                     Collective Bargaining   157
                 Costs, Student Achievement, and Collective
                     Bargaining   166
                 Conclusions   170

Chapter 7   **Conclusion**   173

                 Overall Assessment of Collective Bargaining   173
                 Detailed Effects of Collective Bargaining   174
                 Where Does This Leave Us?   176

                 References   179

                 Index   189

                 About the Authors   197

Figures and Tables

Figures

1-1	Path Diagram of Factors Determining Student Achievement	5
4-1	Diagram of Contract-Curve Model	64
5-1	Definitions of District Financial Categories	135
6-1	Difference between Predicted Posttest Scores in Union and Nonunion Districts by Pretest Score	164

Tables

1-1	Determinants of Student Achievement and the Hypothesized Effects of Collective Bargaining	7
2-1	Trends in Attainment of Key Provisions for a National Sample of Public-School Districts: 1970 and 1975	23
2-2	Trends in Selected Contract Provisions for Michigan Public-School Teachers: 1972 and 1976	25
2-3	Trends in Selected Contract Provisions for New York Public-School Teachers: 1972 and 1976	28
2-4	Means and Standard Deviations of Variables by Subsample	34
2-5	Estimates of the Determinants of the Appearance or Disappearance of Reduction-in-force Provisions in New York Teachers' Contracts	36
2-6	The Effects of RIF Provisions on Estimates of Total-Operating-Expenditure Equations for New York School Districts	37
3-1	Effect of Student Background Measures and Pretest Scores on Fourth-Grade Mathematics Scores	55
3-2	Effect of Teacher Measures and Teacher Time-Allocation on Fourth-Grade Mathematics Scores	56

3-3	Effect of Principal Measures and Staff Size on Fourth Grade Mathematics Scores	57
3-4	Effect of Attitudes of Principals and Teachers about Principal's Instructional Leadership on Fourth-Grade Mathematics Scores	58
3-5	Ranking of Important Inputs into the Educational Production Function	61
4-1	Estimates of Hedonic Wage Equation	69
4-2	Wage-Level Regressions of 1974 and 1977	76
4-3	Wage-Change Regression for 1974-75 and 1977-78	78
4-4	Difference in Means of Responses of Union and Nonunion Teachers	83
4-5	Regression Analysis of Determinants of Selected Teacher Attitudes, by Union Affiliation vs. Nonaffiliation	84
4-6	Comparison of Rates of Teacher Quits and Transfers from Selected Studies	90
4-7	Wage-Level Regressions (CPS Data)	93
4-8	Determinants of Occupation Change for Educators (CPS Data)	95
4-9	Wage-Change Regressions for Educators (CPS Data)	97
4-10	Wage-Level Regressions for Educators (Oregon Data)	99
4-11	Determinants of Interdistrict Mobility of Educators (Oregon Data)	101
4-12	Wage-Change Regressions for Educators (Orgeon Data)	104
4-13	Interdistrict Mobility by Enrollment Trend	106
4-14	Distribution of Principal and Teacher Responses to Questions about Teacher Personnel Decisions	109
4-15	Distribution of Teacher Responses to Questions Concerning Teacher Assignments and Personnel Decisions	110
4-16	Distribution of Teacher Responses to Questions Concerning Teacher Assignment	111

4-17   Logit Estimation of the Odds That an Individual
        Teacher Chose to Work in Present Assignment   112

4-18   Logit Analysis of Teacher Turnover, by Union
        Affiliation vs. Nonaffiliation   114

4-19   Logit Analysis of Teacher Turnover, by Class Size
        and Staffing Provision   115

4-20   Estimates of the Odds of Transferring   117

4-21   Estimates of the Odds of Terminating Employment   119

5-1   Nonunion Determinants of the Allocation of
        District Expenditures   137

5-2   Hierarchy of New York Public-School Contract
        Provisions   140

5-3   Impact of Individual Contract Provisions on the
        Allocation of District Expenditures   143

5-4   Estimates of the Effect of the Number of Contract
        Provisions, and other Determinants, on Budget
        Allocation in New York Public Schools, 1967–1977   146

5-5   Determinants of the Propensity of Districts in New
        York to use Various Class Arrangements, 1976–77   149

5-6   Teacher Participation by Contract Status (SDC Data)   150

5-7   Regressions for Teacher Participation and Contract
        Status (SDC Data)   152

6-1   Means of Education Inputs by Union Status
        (SDC Data)   159

6-2   Education Production Functions by Union Status
        (SDC Data)   160

6-3   Effects of Student Achievement of Differences
        between Union and Nonunion Districts in
        Education Inputs   162

6-4   Instructional Modes and Resources for Mathematics
        in Union and Nonunion Districts   165

6-5   Estimates of the Effect of Teachers' Collective
        Bargaining and Student Achievement on District
        Operating Expenditures   169

Foreword

Public schools are being scrutinized as never before. The listing of school failures has become a litany in numerous committee and commission reports. Each has its explanations of what is wrong with schools and suggestions for restoring excellence or quality to public education.

The National Commission on Excellence in Education's report, *A Nation at Risk,* received widespread attention. Its proposals for a return to the basics, higher standards, more discipline, longer school days, longer school year, and higher teacher salaries are not new. For the past twenty years, commissions, critics, councils, consumers, and Congress have offered advice by the carload. The range of proposals extends from space-age technology to stone-age discipline. The striking thing is that reformers and reforms come and go, yet public schools seem impervious to significant and positive change. Not only can public schools absorb change and resume their original form, but they are frequently able to resist change altogether. What is it that makes them so resilient? The National Commission's proposals for restoring excellence to education and beating back the "rising tide of mediocrity that threatens our very future as a nation and a people," have little chance of success unless we can answer this question.

A weakness of most reform proposals is that they are not based on a clear understanding of how schools operate. We do not know very much about how to package educational inputs to guarantee that students learn. As the authors of this book point out, "a combination of inputs works with some students, while the same combination fails with others. Attempts to measure the impact of an event or occurrence, such as collective bargaining, on a process that itself is not well understood, necessarily produce uncertain results. . . . ''

The nineteenth-century political economist Knut Wicksell noted that the task of social theory is not to dictate what is equitable and efficient policy, but to specify the institutional framework in which equitable and efficient policies are likely to be chosen. In public education, we need to know more, not only about the process through which education occurs, but also about the process through which decisions are made about the operation of schools. Schools are resilient to change because reformers have not been able to change the institutional mechanisms through which decisions about change in schools take place.

That is why this book is so important. Professors Eberts and Stone have written a book that unveils some of the mysteries surrounding the effects of unionization and collective bargaining on public schools. Collec-

tive bargaining has become a principal mechanism for making decisions affecting public education. School teachers not only control much of what goes on in their classrooms, but collectively influence the choices of management. The collective bargaining contract acts as a constraint upon the choices available to management for operating public schools. This book provides an excellent description and analysis of the effects unions and collective bargaining have on public education in the United States.

Contrary to much conventional wisdom about collective bargaining in public schools, Professors Eberts and Stone show that teacher collective bargaining does affect the way public schools operate. Unionized teachers receive higher salaries, teach smaller classes, spend less time instructing students, and have more time for classroom preparation. These and other differences between unionized and nonunionized districts do not seem to affect the average performance of students on standardized tests. As the authors point out, "the major difference detected between union and nonunion districts is the cost of education—for the same level of educational quality, the annual operating costs per pupil in union districts is 15 percent higher than in similar nonunion districts."

While the book assiduously avoids any judgments about unions or collective bargaining, it provides the kind of information policymakers need to make their own judgments. School board members can learn much about the effects of particular contract items and combination of contract items on the behavior of teachers, the operation of classrooms, and the performance of students. The book provides information which will help state legislators evaluate proposed changes in employee relations statutes.

In summary, the book is one of the most extensive efforts to describe the actual effects of collective bargaining in public schools. With this knowledge, reformers will be better able to devise reforms that can actually improve the quality of American education.

Lawrence C. Pierce
Professor of Political Science
University of Oregon

Preface and Acknowledgments

Research on the influence of teacher collective bargaining in public schools has been primarily anecdotal. Studies of the bargaining process and its effect on the operation of schools typically look at as few as six or seven school districts and rarely more than twelve. The picture that researchers construct of the way teacher unions influence the operation of schools has been sketchy. In reading accounts of how a handful of districts or teachers respond to collective bargaining, one may come across descriptions of behavior that are familiar from personal experience, but one must ask whether such behavior is the rule or the exception.

The purpose of this book is to begin to uncover trends in the effects of teacher collective bargaining. One reason researchers have confined themselves to limited samples when trying to piece together a comprehensive picture of the response of teachers, administrators, and students to collective bargaining is because of the tremendous amount of data required to complete the picture. The task of collecting information is obviously much simpler if only isolated effects of collective bargaining, such as differences in wages, budget allocation, or personnel procedures, are examined. Data requirements for exploring a more complete list of effects are much greater.

We choose to address basic issues of how collective bargaining affects teachers and administrators and, ultimately, how it affects the achievement of students. More specifically, we consider the effects of teacher collective bargaining on the mobility of teachers, the allocation of resources, wage differentials, working conditions, teacher attitudes and job satisfaction, teacher-administrator interactions, administrative discretion, educational policy and practice, the determinants of student achievement, and district operating costs.

The work reported in this book represents four years of research, much of which was supported by the National Institute of Education (NIE), through the Center for Educational Policy and Management (CEPM) at the University of Oregon. Jane Arends, Wynn DeBevoise, and Robert Mattson of CEPM were instrumental in guiding our research through its various stages. Amassing data from a broad cross-section of districts requires a tremendous amount of time and effort, and the scope of the project would not have been possible without the financial support of the NIE. Needless to say, however, the opinions expressed in this book do not necessarily reflect the positions or policies of the NIE or the U.S. Department of Education.

We are indebted to numerous individuals across the country who made

the data available. For the Michigan data, we owe thanks to June Olsen of the Michigan State Department of Education and to the staff of the Michigan Education Association. For the New York data, we are grateful to William Keleher of the New York State United Teachers (NYSUT), who was also instrumental in helping us interpret the myriad of provisions included in each contract; to other members of the NYSUT staff, who were very helpful in providing information regarding bargaining processes and issues in New York State; and to Leonard Powell of the New York State Department of Education, who provided the basic information on teachers and school finance. For the Oregon data, we appreciate the help of the Oregon Department of Education, as well as the assistance of Robert Dahlman of the Oregon Education Association. For the national data for students, teachers, and schools, we owe thanks to Jan Anderson of the U.S. Department of Education and Ralph Hoepfner of the Systems Development Corporation. For the national labor force data from the Current Population Survey, we owe thanks to the late Wesley Mellow of the U.S. Bureau of Labor Statistics.

When we began our study, we were joined by a third colleague, Lawrence C. Pierce. Dr. Pierce was instrumental in getting the project underway, and without his initial involvement the project might not have begun. Unfortunately for us, other commitments forced him to leave the project before it was finished.

No study of this magnitude can be completed without the talents, energy, and dedication of research assistants. We owe a very special thanks indeed to Patricia Beeson, Bruce Bowers, David Hedrick, Shogo Ishii, Robin Pyle, and Alphons van de Kragt. We are keenly aware of the importance of their individual contributions to our work.

We have been extremely fortunate in having a number of colleagues concerned enough about our work to read drafts, offer criticism and suggestions, discuss problems, and the like. No list is likely to be complete, but we do wish to thank Joseph Antos, William Baugh, Jay Chambers, W.W. Charters, Edward Dean, Ronald Ehrenberg, James Fox, Daniel Hamermesh, Stephen Haynes, Duane Leigh, and Richard Murnane. We owe special gratitude to the late Wesley Mellow of the U.S. Bureau of Labor Statistics.

For typing drafts of some of the chapters and countless tables, we appreciate the skill and patience of Dorothy Van Cleef and Sandra Pestka; for typing the final book manuscript under impossible circumstances, we thank Terri Williams, whose dedication was well beyond the call of duty. For the actual publication process, we thank Jaime Welch and Nancy Herndon of Lexington Books; and for the decision to publish the study, we thank the Series Editor Frederick Wirt.

 **Introduction**

Teachers' unions have become crucial forces in deciding how public education should be run in the U.S. —Wall Street Journal[1]

One need look no further than the headlines or editorial pages of local newspapers to see concern over what unions are supposedly doing to public education. Aside from obvious concerns over the disruptions caused by teacher strikes, there is growing public concern that teacher unions increase the costs and decrease the quality of education, not only by demanding what many taxpayers believe to be unwarranted salary increases, but also by increasing nonsalary compensation and by diverting the attention of teachers and administrators away from the classroom and into the bargaining room. Indeed, in the relatively short period of time that public-sector bargaining has been recognized as a legal counterpart to private-sector bargaining, teacher unions appear to have made major strides in advancing the interests of their members.

Along with the expansion of their influence into what were once administrative prerogatives, however, teachers have raised the ire of the public. For every advocate of teacher collective bargaining, whether it be a teacher union member or a sympathetic parent, there appears to be a staunch opponent of teacher unionism declaring that teachers have abandoned their sense of duty and professionalism and have lost sight of the goals of education. The debate can be wild and furious at times with rhetoric shouted across the chasm separating the opposing views.

We want to leave the front lines of this battle and retreat to the quieter, more objective domain of the researcher who asks relatively simple, yet important, questions about the actual effects of teacher collective bargaining. What does collective bargaining do for teachers? Does it increase salaries, improve working conditions, increase teachers' sense of professionalism? Does it provide better job security? Does it give teachers greater voice in the operation of schools? How does it affect administrators? Does it reduce their discretion in making decisions or increase their leadership? How does collective bargaining affect the students? Does it reduce the quality of education they receive? And what about taxpayers? Do teachers' unions increase the cost of providing a given quality and quantity of education?

1

By answering such questions as these, we seek to assess the influence that collective bargaining has on public schools in America. We are certainly not alone in this endeavor. A tremendous amount of work has been generated on this particular topic. The analysis reported in this book is unique in three ways. First, the book marks the first attempt to gauge the impact of collective bargaining on the teaching and learning process by examining the various responses of teachers and administrators to the bargaining environment. Second, using an educational production-function framework, we are able to assess the net effect of collective bargaining on educational quality, as measured by student achievement on standardized tests. Third, we calculate the difference in what it costs union and nonunion districts to provide the same quality of education.[2]

By concentrating entirely on the task of measuring the actual effects of collective bargaining on education, we claim only one niche in the literature on teacher unionism. We do not purport to span all of the issues related to teachers' unions. We do not ask if public-sector bargaining is consistent with democratic institutions; we simply accept the quite obvious fact that collective bargaining is well established and that it appears to play a significant role in public education. We also do not consider the bargaining process in any detail. We do report empirical analysis of the determinants of bargaining outcomes, but only to provide a brief background of the negotiation process and to test if bargaining activity can be considered independently of its effect on the behavior of teachers and administrators. Furthermore, we seek to examine the long-run effects of collective bargaining as an institutional change, not the effects of collective bargaining when negotiations lead to strikes.

Finally, we should make clear that we are by profession labor economists. Although in some instances we are forced to deal with issues of educational process that might best be explained by educational researchers, we view public schools as economic institutions—they use resources to produce a valuable product, take the largest percentage of local taxes, employ a large proportion of the public labor force, and provide services that affect the operation of the entire economy. From this standpoint we are interested in the effects that collective bargaining may have on the allocation of resources both to and within the district and the productivity of school-based inputs. We believe that we bring a valuable perspective, though certainly not the only perspective, to the issue of collective bargaining in public schools.

Previous Research on Teacher Collective Bargaining

The literature on teacher collective bargaining has moved in at least three directions. The first body of literature asks the normative question, "What

should be the relationship between management and labor in the public sector?'' The second asks the positive question, ''What is the nature of the bargaining process in public schools?'' The third ponders the actual effects of collective bargaining on the educational process. The first two questions dominate the collective-bargaining literature. Cresswell and Spargo (1980), in a survey of the literature on teacher collective bargaining, find that a disproportionately small amount of research addresses the direct impact of collective bargaining on either costs or student achievement.

The normative literature typically asks whether public-sector bargaining is consistent with democratic institutions. Such questions are important, and the insights gained in considering these issues are valuable. Even so, they do not provide a direct understanding of how collective bargaining alters the pattern of public education, if it actually does. In many respects, answers to these normative questions depend upon understanding the nature of the interactions between teacher unions and school districts.

The positive strand of literature looks at the bargaining process but falls short of measuring the effect of bargaining activity on schools. Many of these studies examine the scope of bargaining and the determinants of the appearance of certain provisions in contracts. Conclusions are drawn about the impact of bargaining by examining the content of contracts. However, measuring the impact of collective bargaining simply by the presence or absence of particular contract provisions has at least two major drawbacks. First, the presence of a contract provision may not induce its intended effects. Economic and political factors and administrative resistance may weaken its impact. Second, important trade-offs between contract provisions, or between provisions and wage and employment decisions, cannot be detected by examining contracts alone. For example, what effect do job-security provisions teachers have gained have on compensation or staffing arrangements? Two outcomes are possible: teachers may be forced to accept lower compensation, or they may be able to achieve both job security provisions and higher wages. The latter could occur as a result of increased bargaining power or other trade-offs, such as larger classes. The point is that such intricate substitutions on the part of administrators, teachers, students, and district taxpayers cannot be detected by examining only the intended effects. The actual link between collective-bargaining agreements and the educational process must be established.

Empirical investigations typically show that collective bargaining significantly influences the compensation and working conditions of teachers. However, McDonnell and Pascal (1979) find that teachers' unions have gone far beyond the traditional role of negotiating wages and working conditions. Unions take the stance that terms and conditions of employment encompass educational policy and personnel decisions. Analyzing teachers contracts, McDonnell and Pascal detect a distinct pattern in teacher negotiations; after teachers' organizations bargain over and obtain in-

creases in salaries and fringe benefits, they quickly move on to consider working conditions, job security, and finally issues of educational policy. McDonnell and Pascal conclude that teachers influence school and classroom operations, regulate class size, and play a major role in educational policy and personnel decisions.

Kerchner and others (1981), looking at selected districts in two states, find that the scope of bargaining has changed the overall pattern of public education. They report that collective bargaining has substantially altered definitions of teachers' work responsibilities, has induced basic changes in the mechanisms that control how teachers perform their duties, and has modified the authority of principals and other administrators.

After examining nine school districts' lengthy experience with collective bargaining, Perry (1979) reaches similar conclusions: the primary effect of collective bargaining is on salaries and working conditions. Organized teachers have been able to get taxpayers to pay them more for their services, and working conditions have been improved by increasing teacher/student ratio. In addition, teachers have gained rights, through protection from arbitrary treatment, and a role in educational decision-making.

All these pieces of research create a mosaic of effects that leads to the conclusion that teachers' collective bargaining does affect the way public education is run in the United States. The problem with arriving at such a conclusion based upon scattered pieces of research is just that. The research is drawn from different samples of school districts, at different times in their bargaining history, and using different methods of analysis. Researchers have considered the effects of collective bargaining on various inputs into the educational process, but no one has attempted to assess directly the overall effect of collective bargaining on the cost and quality of education. Moreover, research that concentrates upon a small domain of factors cannot provide an assessment of the overall effect of collective bargaining on schools.

The Educational Process and Collective Bargaining

Collective bargaining takes place basically at the school-district level; the student's education takes place in the classroom. For collective bargaining to affect student achievement, its effects must enter the classroom. The obvious primary carrier of these effects is the teacher. The educational process is sufficiently complex that concentrating only upon the teacher, or aspects of the interaction between teacher and student, is not sufficient to assess the overall effect of collective bargaining. Hence we posit a simple model of the educational process that identifies five basic groups of determinants of student outcomes: (1) student characteristics, (2) teacher characteristics, (3)

time spent by teachers and students performing various tasks, (4) modes of instruction, and (5) administrator characteristics. Figure 1-1 depicts the paths of influence between major inputs and student achievement.

The student receives resources or is influenced by resource decisions at various levels of the district organization. In the classroom the student interacts with a teacher by spending time on various instructional activities. Thus at the classroom level the important determinants are student and teacher characteristics, including attitudes and motivation, the time devoted to instructional activities, and the mode of instruction. These factors are influenced by activities at the school and district levels. Building administrators coordinate instructional programs and determine the assignment of students to various classes. Principals also determine, to some extent, the amount of equipment and other resources available to teachers. The degree to which teachers are able to influence these decisions depends upon the level of participation given teachers in each school.

At the district level, salaries are determined, teacher hiring and transfer decisions are made, and budgets are allocated to various functions. Consequently, decisions at both the school and district level can affect the composition of the teaching staff, the attitudes and motivation of the teaching staff, class and school size, and the organization of the instructional process. These factors in turn affect the interaction between student and teacher and the quality of education. Thus it becomes obvious that one must model the behavioral responses of teachers, students, and administrators to account fully for the effects of major factors on student achievement.

By affecting a variety of these inputs into the educational process, collective bargaining can influence student achievement through a number of channels. Table 1-1 provides a more detailed breakdown of the basic ingredients for the educational process and provides some preliminary hypotheses about how these ingredients may be affected by collective bargaining. We briefly discuss some of these possible effects as a preface for the more detailed analyses of the subsequent chapters.

Student Achievement

It is well documented that the abilities and motivation that students bring to the classroom are important determinants of academic success. Many of these characteristics are related to home environment, as measured by childhood experience, parental involvement, economic status, and the importance parents place on education. The influence of social norms, as applied to children of different sex and ethnic backgrounds, is also a critical factor in the student's achievement.

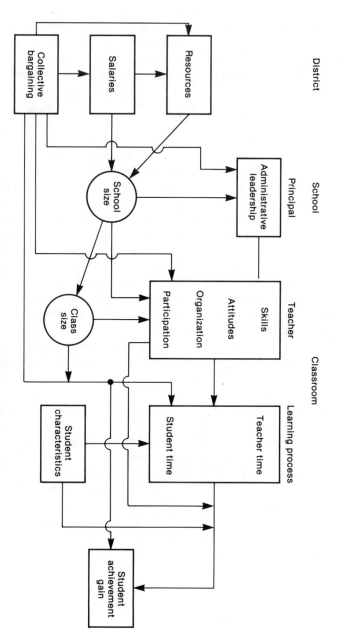

Figure 1-1. Path Diagram of Factors Determining Student Achievement

District

School

Principal

Classroom

Teacher

Learning process

Collective bargaining

Salaries

Resources

School size

Administrative leadership

Class size

Participation

Organization

Attitudes

Skills

Student characteristics

Student time

Teacher time

Student achievement gain

Table 1-1
Determinants of Student Achievement and the Hypothesized Effects of Collective Bargaining

	Student Characteristics	Time	Mode of Instruction	Teacher Characteristics	Administrative Leadership
Determinants of student achievement	Age	Instruction (interaction of time in instruction with characteristics and modes)	Individualized	Experience (inside and outside school and district)	Maintenance of order
	Sex		Size of instructional unit		Introducing change
	Race		21+	Degree	Setting clear objectives
	Childhood experience	Preparation	14–21	Inservice programs	Supporting teachers
	Parental involvement	Administration	7–13	Type of instructor	Providing rewards and incentives
	Exact grade level	Parents	2–6	Classroom	Observing classrooms
	Economic status		Other	Aide	Allocating resources
	Pretest score			Specialist	
	Attitudes			Attitudes	
	Attendance			Degree of participation	
Effects of collective bargaining	No hypothesized effect	Has been shown to affect all items. Now must show the influence on the effectiveness of time	Size of instructional unit is influenced by staff size, which is influenced by bargained wages	Has been shown to affect all items except degree of participation	Hypothesized constraints on flexibility and on formality of interactions with teachers. Possible "voice" effect

We assume that collective bargaining has no influence on these factors, although the reverse may be true. There may be some instances in which families who have strong preferences about teacher unionism or who have experienced an especially disruptive teacher strike, may send their children to a different district or to private schools, but for our analysis we consider the composition of the student body attending a particular school district to be unaffected by the level of bargaining activity.

Student characteristics may also affect test scores through the composition of peer groups. Evidence provided by Henderson and others (1978) and Summers and Wolfe (1977) suggests that elementary-school children with low initial skill levels make greater progress in schools where the average achievement level is already high than in schools where the achievement level is relatively low. Both studies find the effect on individual achievement of improvements in average class achievement to be greater at the low end of the achievement distribution than at the high end. Collective bargaining, by determining the assignment of students to classes, may have a significant effect on student achievement.

Teacher Characteristics

Teachers are the primary school-based input into the educational process. They are the primary medium through which the student acquires educational skills and academic ideals. Thus it is only fitting that the role of teachers has been the central focus of quantitative research on school effectiveness. We consider the role of teachers in two ways: as a stock of attributes and as flow of services. Murnane (1981) reports that virtually every study of school effectiveness finds that some stock of teacher attributes is significantly related to student achievement. Teachers' attitudes toward their working conditions and toward the ability of students are also considered important determinants of student achievement (Murnane 1975).

Collective bargaining can influence teachers' characteristics in several ways. The first is through mobility. Teachers, either by their own preference or administrative action, may enter or leave a district and, in so doing, change the composition of the teaching staff. A second avenue of influence is through the structure of salary schedules. Since experience and education are given a premium, teachers have some salary incentives to remain with the district and to obtain additional education.

The collective-bargaining environment may also influence the attitudes of teachers, especially those attitudes related to working conditions and to their relationship with principals. The formation of certain attitudes may be related to the degree of participation given teachers on policy matters, such as class assignment, student assignment, and curriculum development. Col-

lective bargaining may provide teachers with a greater level of participation but at the same time may cast the administration in an adversarial role.

Teacher and Student Time

The flow of teacher services can be measured by the amount of time teachers spend in various activities and by the amount of time students spend on various supervised tasks. As we report in chapter 3, time spent by teachers on instruction and preparation is positively correlated with gains in student achievement.

We report in chapter 4 how collective bargaining affects the amount of time teachers spend on various activities. Our results indicate that teachers in districts covered by collective bargaining spend less time on instruction, but more time on preparation and administration, than teachers in districts not covered by collective bargaining. The effect of collective bargaining on student achievement through the allocation of teacher time cannot be assessed without first knowing the importance of instructional time to student achievement.

Mode of Instruction

The primary factor in this group is class size. Most studies report that class size has an effect on student achievement. Collective bargaining can affect class size through the internal allocation of resources brought about by salary negotiations or constraints placed on administrators by provisions that limit class size. We also consider a variety of specialized instructional modes and resources.

Administrators

Administrators perform at least two functions that affect student outcomes. The first is the internal allocation of resources. The effect of collective bargaining on this function has already been discussed. The second function is to provide instructional leadership. This is a rather complex issue, and there are debates about the effectiveness of principals in this role. Even so, we do consider this function, both in its relationship to student achievement and in its relationship to collective bargaining. Of course the effectiveness of principals is closely tied to the posture that teachers and principals are forced to take during difficult negotiations. As one might expect, there is no consensus on the effect of collective bargaining on principals' leadership.

Methodology

The primary tool of analysis we use throughout the book is multivariate regression, applied both to cross-sectional and to time-series data. Critics of this approach would argue that the use of statistical techniques with secondary data sources removes the researcher from the nuts and bolts of what is actually taking place in the district. We defend our approach on a number of grounds. First, we wish to be removed to some degree from the activities of the district. That is to say, we wish to perform a natural experiment in which we observe the behavior of teachers, administrators, and students in their daily routines, undisturbed by the watchful and sometimes intrusive eye of the researcher. Certainly, we wish to avoid the Hawthorne effect, where any experimental change has significant consequences simply because people are aware they are engaged in an experiment. Second, the use of secondary data sources does not mean that we are uninformed about what takes place within the district. In fact, given the tremendously detailed data we have amassed, we may be in a better position to obtain an objective picture of the school environment than researchers who conduct only on-site visits. Third, we seek to report more than effects observed in isolated districts. We would like to discern any general trends in the effects of collective bargaining on schools. However, we do not deny the importance of case studies. Indeed, both case studies and cross-sectional analyses are essential. Nonetheless, for our professed purpose of examining general trends, the latter method is more appropriate.

Organization of the Book

In this book we attempt to provide a comprehensive assessment of collective bargaining by amassing and analyzing data covering the important characteristics of the educational process and the bargaining process. With these data, we can trace the influence of collective bargaining to its effects on student performance on standardized tests, and to its effects on the cost of providing educational services. Tracing the effects of collective bargaining from the bargaining table into the classroom requires a detailed examination of the influence of collective bargaining on all levels of the educational process. In the remainder of the book, we concentrate on two major inputs into the educational process, teachers and administrators, and consider how they respond to the collective-bargaining environment. Since our goal is to show the effect of collective bargaining on both the level and cost of student achievement, we need a substantial amount of groundwork.

The chapters are organized in the following way. Chapter 2 provides a brief sketch of the bargaining process. It discusses why teachers organize,

explores the nature of the bargaining process, examines determinants of the content of contracts, and analyzes trends in bargaining over the last decade. Chapter 3 models the educational process through the use of educational production functions. The model links inputs that can be affected by collective bargaining to student test scores. Estimates of the educational production are obtained based on the same data we use to assess the impact of collective bargaining on education inputs. By ranking the importance of the various inputs, we can discover which inputs, if affected by collective bargaining, will have the largest impact on student achievement.

Our analysis of the effects of collective bargaining begins in chapter 4 with an examination of what it has done for teachers. We provide evidence on the effect of collective bargaining on teachers' salaries and fringe benefits, on the trade-off between compensation and noncompensation provisions in contracts, on the attitudes of teachers about the operation of the school, on the relationship between teachers and administrators, and on teacher mobility. Chapter 5 explores the response of administrators to the constraints imposed by bargaining agreements. We look at the effect of bargaining activity on the internal allocation of resources, the level of district spending, and district personnel practices. Chapter 6 brings all the myriad effects of collective bargaining to bear on gains in students' test scores and district operating expenditures. Using the educational production function developed in chapter 3, we explore the differences in student achievement between union and nonunion districts. In addition, we assess the difference in cost of providing the same quantity and quality of education in the two district types. The final chapter summarizes our findings and provides an overall assessment of the effect of collective bargaining on public schools.

Notes

1. Gilbert T. Sewall, "Teachers' Unions and the Issue of Academic Standards," *Wall Street Journal,* January 6, 1983.
2. The phrases *union member* and *covered by collective-bargaining agreement* are not necessarily synonymous. Teachers may be members of a teachers' group, such as a local affiliate of the National Education Association (NEA) or of the American Federation of Teachers (AFT) but not covered by a collective-bargaining agreement. This may occur either because public-sector bargaining is not recognized in the state or because local interest is not sufficient to organize the required number of teachers into a recognized bargaining unit. When the distinction is not crucial, the two phrases are used interchangeably.

2

The Collective-
Bargaining Contract

Teacher contracts contain rules that regulate the interaction between teachers and administrators. Dunlop (1958) and Kerr and Siegel (1955) view the relationship between workers and managers as being governed by what they call a "web of rules." This network of rules, established through the bargaining process, provides substantive guidelines that can affect nearly every dimension of the workplace. In the context of public schools, rules exist that define the rights and duties of teachers to particular assignments, govern the compensation of teachers, establish disciplinary sanctions for failure of teachers to achieve certain standards; and provide for teacher participation in structuring the workplace. Naturally, not all contracts contain the same rules or delineate teacher and administrator rights along the same lines. The evolution of teacher contracts is determined by a number of factors: the preferences and attitudes of teachers, the attitudes of school boards and administrators, state bargaining legislation, and the national affiliation of the local teacher organization, to mention a few.

Before we examine the effect of collective bargaining on the operation and effectiveness of schools, we need to look at the structure and scope of contracts. The purpose of this chapter, then, is to describe the nature of bargaining and the content of contracts. Much of the chapter summarizes the work of other authors, although some of our own analysis of contracts at the state level is included. More detailed discussion of the bargaining process and bargaining outcomes is found in fine surveys by Cresswell and Spargo (1980) and Cooper (1982). Before we can explore the actual effects of contracts, we must set down the reasons why teachers bargain collectively and describe the environment within which bargaining takes place and the nature of the contracts.

The first section of the chapter considers the reasons why teachers organize. Knowledge of the motivation for teachers to organize provides insight into the scope of issues negotiated at the bargaining table. Trends in bargaining are discussed next. We present a brief history of bargaining in New York and Michigan and look at the scope of bargaining in these two states. In addition, we consider major trends in a national sample of districts analyzed by McDonnell and Pascal (1979). We next explore the determinants of bargaining outcomes. Of primary interest in bargaining out-

comes is the simultaneity, or feedback, issue: Are certain provisions placed in contracts in response to the internal conditions of the school district, or are they influenced by factors outside the district? This is an important question when using regression to study the impact of certain policies. If the latter holds, contract provisions can be considered exogenous to the internal operation of the district and consequently can be treated as exogenous variables in determining the effects of collective bargaining on the operation of schools. If the latter does not hold, then simultaneity bias plagues the results. Understanding the bargaining process also can provide insight into whether unions improve relations between administrators and teachers.

Why Do Teachers Organize?

There is no simple answer to the question of why teachers organize. The establishment of teachers organizations as recognized bargaining units is a relatively recent phenomenon in the history of education. Understanding the motivations behind this movement requires knowledge of the history of the labor movement and of the recent events affecting public education, as well as an appreciation for the needs of teachers as professionals. A comprehensive analysis of the determinants of the organization of teachers would require psychological inquiries and historical treatises far beyond the intent of this chapter. Our major purpose for exploring this question is to gain insight into the range of issues negotiated at the bargaining table and included in teacher contracts. We therefore provide a brief description of the basic reasons for the growth of teacher collective bargaining.

Four general reasons for the growth of collective bargaining are cited in the literature (Cooper 1982; Goldschmidt 1982). The first is the passage of state laws that protect the rights of teachers to seek bargaining recognition. One of the most important changes in the legal structure to accommodate public-sector bargaining was modification of the doctrine of sovereign immunity. The second reason is concern by teachers for their own economic and professional well-being. In addition to their concern about their economic position, teachers also are concerned about their access to and influence over educational policy and their ability to maintain a sense of professionalism. Declining enrollments, skyrocketing inflation in the 1970s, and general public discontent with public schools has threatened teachers' job security, has eroded their purchasing power, and has diminished their self-esteem. The third reason often cited for teacher bargaining is changes in social conditions and workforce demographics. By the mid-1970s, the teaching force was younger, with a greater proportion of males, and with teachers who had grown up during a decade of protest. The increased militancy and the awareness of change provided fertile ground for the growth of

unionism. The fourth reason is related to the labor movement in general. Unionism in the private sector has been declining, partly because industrial work is becoming increasingly capital-intensive. Education, on the other hand, is highly labor-intensive. As teachers became less resistent to the idea of unionizing, the unions were ready to move. Rivalry between the American Federation of Teachers (AFT) and the National Education Association (NEA) increased their militancy and their fervor to organize.

Legal Structure of Teacher Collective Bargaining

Legal provisions for the conduct of public-sector collective bargaining have come almost exlusively from state governments. Although Congress has considered possible federal legislation to regulate negotiations of public employees, states have assumed the leadership in this matter. Meaningful legislation giving public employees a voice in determining the conditions of their employment was enacted first in the 1960s. Before that time only two states, New Hampshire and Alaska, had statutes that allowed local governments to negotiate with groups representing public employees. Neither state extended to public employees the same rights granted to private employees, however. The National Labor Relations Act (NLRA) of 1935, later amended in 1947, requires employers to meet and confer in good faith with respect to wages, hours, and other terms and conditions of employment. New Hampshire's law of 1955 and Alaska's law of 1959 did not require or ensure bargaining; local governments were allowed to negotiate only under specified conditions. Permitting public employees to bargain, nonetheless, was a major step in treating private and public employees equally in the bargaining arena. Before this time contracts between school boards and teacher unions were seen as an illegal delegation to school boards of local citizens' sovereign constitutional powers.

Wisconsin was the first state to pass legislation for public employee bargaining that resembled in any way the language found in the NLRA. In 1962 a statute was enacted requiring local governments to bargain in good faith with employee groups. This statute also created administrative machinery to enforce the law. The Wisconsin Public Employee Relations Board was charged with determination of appropriate bargaining units, prevention of prohibited practices, fact-finding, and mediation of disputes.

The enabling legislation passed in Wisconsin marked the beginning of widespread recognition of the rights of public employees to bargain collectively. New York and Michigan passed similar laws within the next five years. By 1974, thirty-seven states had passed some legislation regulating the bargaining of public employees, although statutes varied considerably. Altogether, twenty-seven states provided for exclusive representation of

nonsupervisory personnel by an employee group, and mediation or fact-finding were mandatory in twenty-three states. Strong state administrative agencies oversaw negotiations of public employees in twenty-two states, while the same number of states prohibited unfair labor practices and provided some means of enforcement. In addition to such provisions, seven states had impasse procedures that allowed teachers' organizations to go on strike or force compulsory binding arbitration. Four years later an additional seven states had legislation permitting explicit bargaining; seven more states had assigned roles to public-employee-relations boards and permitted strikes by teachers. Thus by 1978, 61 percent of classroom teachers resided in states that permitted formal collective bargaining in education (Ross 1978).

Even with the widespread passage of enabling legislation by states, teachers faced barriers to the expansion of the scope of bargaining not shared by their private sector counterparts. Kay (1973) cites three basic restraints on the scope of bargaining for public employees and for teachers in particular. The first is the express language of the enabling legislation. Many of the state legislatures, in drafting the collective-bargaining law, chose to employ language other than that set forth by the National Labor Relations Act. As of 1978 some states, for example Minnesota, Nevada, Montana, and Pennsylvania, did not allow bargaining on managerial policy issues such as hiring, promotions, assignments, class size, or instructional policy (Ross 1978).

The second major limitation to collective bargaining, cited by Kay, originates with the limited authority of the public employer. As mentioned earlier, the public employer, in our case the school board, is a representative body whose power is delegated by local citizens. In many cases, as in Michigan and Oregon, the school board does not have fiscal authority but must gain budget approval from the voters. Final approval by a third party makes negotiations between the school board and teachers "in good faith" strained and has resulted in a number of allegations of unfair labor practices (Brodie and Williams 1981).

The third barrier to a broad scope of bargaining originates because public employment is governed by rules and regulations apart from those related to collective bargaining. Teachers are covered by state tenure laws, which often come into conflict with employment provisions negotiated in district contracts, for example. In some states, notably Michigan and New York, the problems of dealing with preexisting labor laws have been dealt with by labor boards and courts. The private-sector standards eventually have found acceptance in these decisions as the prebargaining maze of employment rules has been circumvented to a large degree, discounted, or ruled to be superseded by the collective-bargaining statutes.

In spite of these difficulties, the legal status of collective bargaining

for teachers has advanced considerably since 1965. The extent of collective bargaining now exceeds considerably the legal specifications provided by state statutes. Contractual agreements have been reached in many cases where no statutory requirements are specified, and some school boards have set up bargaining procedures more favorable to teachers than the law requires. What is most important, the range of bargaining issues extends far beyond the legal requirements specified in the statutes (Pierce 1975).

Attitudes and Needs of Teachers

Teachers long have carried the banner of professionalism and have resisted the idea of organizing as a bargaining unit. In the early years of the NEA, members felt that the organization's role should be one of promoting the professional side of teaching. Although NEA members were sensitive to their financial needs, the official posture of NEA was one of debate, not collective action (Cooper 1982:22)

The metamorphosis of teachers from passive professionals to union activists can be understood partially by considering how they see themselves as teachers. A number of studies have been conducted to assess the attitudes of teachers toward their jobs. The picture that emerges shows teachers wanting both respect from the public for their dedication to their profession (Herndon 1976; Strom 1979; Lortie 1977) and the financial rewards they feel should come to skilled professionals (Steele 1976; Donley 1976; McDonnell and Pascal 1979). Teachers' self-concept on both these counts reached a low point during the 1960s. Educators came to realize that they were underpaid and that their lagging prestige as professionals had suffered even more because of their low wages and limited control over conditions of employment. In addition, as school districts became larger and the number of teachers and administrative personnel increased, teachers felt they were left with little control over their teaching activities. As Guthrie points out, "Bureaucracy and bigness . . . severely curtailed teachers' feelings of efficacy. As school systems grew and came under the dominance of expert managers, teachers lost their ability to communicate freely with their employers, school trustees, or even with the superintendent and his staff" (1974:3).

Thus teachers saw bargaining as a way to increase their professional discretion through rules to insulate them from external control (Kerchner and others 1980). Some of the rules embodied in contracts, however, have produced a somewhat undesirable by-product. Bargaining leads to greater participation by teachers in decision-making in school affairs (Belasco and Alluto 1969; Eberts 1982). Yet participation does not seem to be their objective. In fact Belasco and Alluto found that too much participation can lead

to dissatisfaction, and Eberts (1982) showed that it takes away from instructional time. Nonetheless, the means to greater autonomy, regardless of the increased participation, appears to be a goal of most bargaining units.

The second motivation for teachers to organize is their desire for increased compensation and improved working conditions. Wages and hours were the first mandatory items bargained by public employees. McDonnell and Pascal (1979:vii) found that teacher organizations bargain over and obtain increases in salary and fringe benefits before they move on to working conditions and job security and then to issues of educational policy. Therefore it is reasonable to accept Cooper's conclusion that "the growth of educator collective bargaining stems from the same needs voiced by other white-collar, public-sector employees, and private industrial sector unionists" (1982:8).

Changes in Social Conditions and Workforce Demographics

Numerous events during the 1960s affected the educational process, the working conditions of teachers, and the attitudes of teachers about their role in education. The 1960s saw tension mount in major cities across the country. City schools became more populated by children from low-income households and minority groups as the more middle-class families fled to the suburbs. The transition of urban and suburban schools put considerable stress on administrators, teachers, and parents. Administrators, especially in the central cities, were faced with financial problems that accompanied the overall erosion of the cities' tax base. Teachers were frustrated because they had to work with children whose backgrounds and values were frequently at odds with their own middle-class values. Parents and citizens became dissatisfied because they found the public schools too bureaucratic and unresponsive to their demands and preferences (Guthrie 1974).

Added to these events was a change in the composition of the teaching force. By the mid-1960s the average teacher age had declined, the proportion of males had increased, and more men and women from varied occupational, racial, and ethnic backgrounds had become public-school teachers. They entered the profession during a decade of protest and came away with less reverence for existing institutions and a new appreciation for how change is to take place in society (Corwin 1968). Teachers saw, in the civil rights movement and the protest against the Vietnam War, that public demonstrations could be an effective force and that picketing need not be confined to the working-class labor groups. In addition bureaucratic authority structures of the schools were seen as obstacles to improvement and not vulnerable to anything less than a strong and militant teacher organization.

Set against this background of increased militancy and acceptance of change, teachers found themselves losing control over their workplace. The 1950s and 1960s witnessed a massive movement to consolidate and centralize school districts. Furthermore, local, state, and federal regulation of schools increased regimentation and uniformity of instructional policy and procedure. In effect, as Cooper (1982) summarizes, centralized employment leads to unified employee responses, and teachers proved to be no exception.

The Labor Movement and the NEA and AFT

By 1960 organized labor was on the decline. The mechanization of the workplace and the shift in manufacturing away from the prounion states of the Northeast and Midwest had reduced the membership of the major labor groups. At the same time the rapid expansion of the labor-intensive service sector made this group of employees an attractive target for union organizers.

Since its inception in the early part of this century, the American Federation of Teachers had tried to bring teachers into the mainstream of organized labor. Unlike their considerably more powerful rival, the NEA, the AFT advocated collective action as the best way to promote the interests of teachers. NEA, on the other hand, preferred what they called a "professional" approach to employee relations, avoiding the strike and supporting devices such as blacklisting schools that failed to treat teachers properly (Cooper 1982).

Since NEA membership dwarfed AFT membership during the 1950s by thirteen to one, a general nonunion posture of teachers prevailed (*NEA Handbook* 1979). In 1961, however, a major victory for the AFT in organizing New York City teachers changed the course of teacher collective bargaining. Donley describes the AFT victory in New York City as "probably the biggest single success in the history of teacher organizing in the United States" (1976:46). Indeed the victory in New York City had a profound effect on NEA's attitude toward collective bargaining. Feeling threatened by the sudden popularity of AFT-style labor relations, NEA officially urged bargaining but tempered its support within the bounds of professionalism. Burton attributes the shift in NEA's posture to the "organizing success of the AFT, which began to grow rapidly in the 1960s largely at the expense of the NEA" (1979:30). Within a few years, competition for members rendered the efforts of AFT and NEA indistinguishable. As McDonnell and Pascal (1979) found, one can no longer differentiate between the content of AFT and NEA contracts.

Major Trends in the Scope of Bargaining

Teachers organize for specific purposes: to increase wages, to improve their working conditions, and to increase their professional status. The ability to achieve these goals lies in the range of provisions that teachers are able to place in contracts. Scope of bargaining therefore is the main instrument by which teachers affect school operations and policy (Cresswell and others 1978). Establishing scope means drawing the line that is the demarcation between management prerogatives and teacher involvement in decision-making.

The scope of bargaining laid down in state statutes is classified into three areas. Although federal legislation does not cover public-sector bargaining, most state statutes follow to varying degrees the guidelines established by the National Labor Relations Act. The first area is termed "mandatory" since it lists subjects that must be negotiated upon request of *either* party. Although mandatory items differ according to the various state laws, these usually include hours, wages, and certain working conditions. The second area of bargaining, termed "permissive" includes those subjects that may be negotiated only upon agreement of *both* parties (Cresswell and Spargo 1980:41). In this case a second level of bargaining is required to determine whether or not a specific subject is to be negotiated. The third area describes items that may not be negotiated into the contract regardless of the requests or concurrence of the parties (Zirkel 1975:4).

The guidelines set down by state laws provide only the basic framework for negotiations; they do not dictate the actual content of the contract, except in what they prohibit. The actual scope of bargaining is determined by economic, political, and social forces. Indeed the forces that determine the content of contracts reflect the motivations for teachers to organize. Needless to say, the complex interactions between the parties engaged in negotiation and the changing conditions to which they respond make analysis of scope very difficult.

Quantitative work done on this subject has resulted in some interesting insights, however. Before embarking on the subject of the determinants of bargaining scope, it is instructive to consider the major trends in bargaining. We examine trends first at the national level, considering a national sample of district contracts analyzed by McDonnell and Pascal (1979). Next we consider trends found in contracts of school districts situated within two states, Michigan and New York. State-level analysis is undertaken for two reasons. First, since the terms of scope are articulated on a state-by-state basis, it is important to consider contracts that have been negotiated within the same legal environment. Second, recognizing the need to control for legal constraints on bargaining, much of the analysis reported in later chapters is based on the behavior of districts in Michigan and New York,

and it is useful at this time to describe the district contracts within these two states.

National Trends

Mandatory and permissive bargaining issues go far beyond the basic concerns of hours and wages. In their study of outcomes of teachers' bargaining, McDonnell and Pascal (1979) found that teachers bargain over issues related to instructional policy, personnel decisions, and resource allocation. McDonnell and Pascal developed a list of fourteen separate domains of bargaining provisions. The choice of provisions within these domains was governed by two criteria: (1) provisions address working conditions, job security, and the professional autonomy of public school teachers; and (2) they are linked to the way educational services are delivered and schools governed. Given these concerns of teachers, the following list was compiled:

Working conditions
    School calendar and working hours
    Class size
    Supplementary classroom personnel (e.g., aides)

Student discipline and teacher safety

Job security
    Assignment
    Transfers
    Promotion
    Reductions in force

Professional issues
    Inservice and professional development
    Instructional policy committees
    Student grading and promotion
    Teacher evaluation

Other
    Grievance procedure
    Federal programs

The various contract provisions listed have the potential to affect most of the aspects of a teacher's workplace, including the classroom. For example, limits on class size and hours influence the amount of contact between individual students and their teachers. Teachers' input into grading, assignment, and instructional policy as well as the inclusion of disciplinary

provisions increases their control over the classroom. The use of supplementary personnel (aides) can increase the staff/child ratio in the classroom and may free teachers for instructional duties. In addition, having a voice in their own evaluation and in establishing promotion criteria increases teachers' autonomy and sense of professionalism.

Contracts, on the other hand, if they do indeed increase teachers' autonomy, reduce the discretion of administrators, which may in turn reduce the coordination and efficacy of the educational process. For instance, disciplinary power may increase the orderliness of classrooms but carries with it the potential for abuse by teachers who are disinclined to work with the hard to educate. The regulation of teacher evaluation may make it more difficult to identify the less competent teachers. Incorporation of personnel policies into the contract standardizes procedures, which offers administrators less flexibility to meet changing conditions.

The content of a national sample of contracts compiled by McDonnell and Pascal, displayed in table 2-1, shows a wide-ranging distribution of provisions. The order of frequency in which certain provisions appear in contracts reflects to some extent teachers' preferences for and administrators' resistance to these provisions. The most frequent provision is the grievance procedure. McDonnell and Pascal quote negotiators as saying that grievance procedures are the "heart of the contract," without which other provisions would be unenforceable (1979:9). With the exception of school hours, the ranking of the rest of the provisions shows that teachers have gained control over instructional matters, whereas administrators have retained discretion over certain personnel policies. Pupil exclusion, assignment refusal, teacher evaluation, and class size all affect the management of the classroom. Promotion rules, transfer criteria, and reduction-in-force procedures are personnel matters, traditionally the prerogative of administrators. McDonnell and Pascal offer a more formal analysis of the determinants of bargaining outcomes, which we present subsequently.

A comparison of the content of contracts for 1970 and 1975 reveals distinct patterns in the gains in collective bargaining. Regulation of class size may be the most dramatic gain, although given the relatively small percentage of districts that have bargained about this provision, it still remains a costly item to include in the contract. Equally important from management's point of view is the increased say that teachers have over who will work in schools (transfer, assignment, and evaluation provisions) and for how long each day (class-hours provision). Organized teachers also have more influence over the kinds of people who will supervise them (promotion criteria). Furthermore, teachers have gained a significant increase in influence in the classroom by receiving a voice in the numbers (and functions) of aides and over curricular and disciplinary matters.

Table 2-1

Trends in Attainment of Key Provisions for a National Sample of Public-School Districts: 1970 and 1975

	Percentage of Contracts Exhibiting Provision (n = 151)		Districts that Lacked Provision in 1970 but Had Attained It by 1975	
Provision	1970	1975	Number	Percent
Grievances	70	83	20	44
Teacher evaluation	42	65	35	40
School hours	39	58	29	32
Pupil exclusion	28	46	26	24
Assignment refusal	21	27	9	8
Class size	20	34	20	17
Promotion rules	20	32	19	15
Transfer criteria	19	29	16	13
Instructional committee	16	31	15	18
Reduction-in-force procedures	11	37	21	30
Aides	11	29	13	21

Source: Lorraine McDonnell and Anthony Pascal, "Organized Teachers in American Schools," Rand Corporation, Santa Monica, Calif., 1979. Reprinted with permission.

Michigan Contracts

We have examined contracts for districts in Michigan for roughly the same period as covered by McDonnell and Pascal's analysis. Before examining the trends, it is useful to describe in more detail the legal environment for bargaining in Michigan.

The Michigan Public Employee Relations Act (PERA) was signed into law on July 23, 1965, as an amendment to the 1947 Hutchinson Act. The earlier act "gave public employees the right to organize and bargain collectively" but "did not provide the administrative machinery to effectuate these provisions" (Steiber and Wolkinson 1977:89). The 1965 PERA provided the necessary guidelines. PERA provides for employee organization, representation procedures, employee and unfair labor practices, mediation, and fact-finding (Steiber and Wolkinson 1977:89). The PERA also explicitly deals with the issue of strikes. Although strikes by public employees are prohibited, the legislation failed to specify penalties for such strikes. In addition, the administrative agency for PERA, the Michigan Employment Relations Commission (MERC), and the Michigan courts have weakened

the prohibition of public-employee strikes, especially teacher strikes (Steiber and Wolkinson 1977).

The duty to bargain under PERA is described in language that closely approximates section 8(d) of the National Labor Relations Act. Section 15 of PERA reads in part:

> For the purposes of this section, to bargain collectively is the performance of the mutual obligation of the employer and the representative of the employees to meet at reasonable times and confer in good faith with respect to wages, hours, and other terms and conditions of employment, or the negotiation of an agreement, or any question arising thereunder, and the execution of a written contract, . . . but such obligation does not compel either party to agree to a proposal or require the making of a concession. (Public Employee Relations Act: paragraphs 423.201–423.216)

The public-school teachers in Michigan have been particularly successful in establishing what is apparently a relatively broad scope of duty to bargain. In 1972, in a landmark opinion (7 MERC Lab. Op. 313 (1972— *Westwood Community Schools*), MERC adopted the position that, since strikes by public employees are prohibited, there is no reason to restrict severely the subjects that may be brought up in negotiations. This position was reinforced in subsequent court decisions, such as the Van Buren case, which stated that only by "requiring mandatory bargaining on a wide range of subjects are public employees rights protected since, pursuant to section 2, public employees are forbidden to strike" (*Van Buren Public School District* vs. *Wayne County Circuit Judge,* 51 Mich App6, 232 Nwzd 728).

The decisions just cited refer to public employees in general but, as a matter of history, they were spawned in large part by teachers' disputes, and teachers' unions appear to be the only public unions exhibiting interest in establishing a broader spectrum of bargainable issues. This perhaps is due, as stated earlier, to teachers' self-identification as professionals for whom conditions of employment include areas that management traditionally has viewed as falling exclusively in its domain.

From the time teacher bargaining became recognized legally in Michigan, teachers there have negotiated some of the most comprehensive contracts in the country. The wide range of subjects negotiated by Michigan teachers is documented by two studies that compare state bargaining laws. Kochan (1973) classified the comprehensiveness of the bargaining laws of the fifty states as they stood in 1971. Using a twelve-item index developed by the U.S. Department of Labor (1971), the scale provides numerical values for each state based on provisions related to (1) administrative body, (2) bargaining rights, (3) unit determination, (4) rules of procedure, (5) recognition procedures, (6) impasse procedures, (7) strike policy, (8) management rights, (9) scope of bargaining, (10) unfair labor practices, (11)

grievance procedures, and (12) union security. A total score of 48 points is possible. Michigan ranked ninth with a score of 17 on this index. The highest score, a 24, was received by Pennsylvania. A 1977 study of the scope of teacher bargaining in fourteen states conducted by the Academic Collective Bargaining Information Service showed Michigan to be third (after New York and Orgeon) in the number of mandatory bargaining issues, and to be tied with Nevada and South Dakota for the lowest number (1) of non-permissive subjects of bargaining (Academic Collective Bargaining Information Service 1977). Although the indexes used in the two studies are not comparable, both studies place Michigan in the same relative position with respect to the other states.

The extent to which Michigan teachers have negotiated nonwage items can be seen in the analysis performed by the Michigan Education Association (MEA). Its 1973–74 *Summary of Selected Contract Provisions,* parts of which are tabulated in table 2–2, shows the frequency with which districts negotiated various items. An important aspect of bargaining gleened from this table is the high percentage of districts that have negotiated items related to instructional and professional concerns. Items such as limitations

Table 2–2
Trends in Selected Contract Provisions for Michigan Public-School Teachers: 1972 and 1976

Contract Provision	Percentage of Contracts Exhibiting Provision n = 454		Districts that Lacked (Had) Provision in 1972 and Had (Lacked) It by 1976	
	1972	*1976*	*Number*	*Percent*
Bargaining unit includes teachers	60	74	64	35
Class size	84	67	(77)[a]	(51)
Class size grievable	65	50	(68)	(30)
Teacher evaluation	40	79	177	65
Staff reduction by seniority	70	83	59	43
Joint instructional policy committee	62	42	(91)	(34)
Inservice	50	60	45	20
Professional days	73	70	(14)	(10)
Aides	35	24	(50)	(14) –

Source: Data are from *Summary of Selected Contract Provisions,* Michigan Education Association, selected years.
[a]Numbers in parentheses indicate number or percentage of districts that lost provision, whichever is appropriate.

on class size, inservice program, reduction in force, instructional council, and regulation of teacher evaluations and teacher aides were negotiated in at least 25 percent of the contracts by 1976.

In summary, it appears that teachers in Michigan have maintained one of the strongest bargaining positions in the country. The legal prohibition on public-employee strikes has provided a rationale for MERC and the courts to be lenient on the issue of scope of duty to bargain. On the other hand, since the law provides no explicit sanctions for public employee strikes, strikes have occurred, especially by teachers and have gone virtually unpunished. This has had the effect of broadening the scope of bargaining beyond even what might have occurred had public-employee strikes not been permitted.

New York Contracts

On April 21, 1967, Governor Nelson Rockefeller signed into law the New York State Public Employees Fair Employment Act, more commonly known as the Taylor Law, after George Taylor, chairman of the Governor's Committee on Public Employee Relations. This law was designed to make up for the defects of its predecessor, the Condon-Wadlin Act of 1947, which not only provided no public-employee bargaining rights, but also carried harsh, although largely ineffective, penalties against strikers (Yaffe and Goldblatt 1971).

The intended purpose of the Taylor Law was to "promote harmonious and cooperative relationships between government and its employees and to protect the public by assuring, at all times, the orderly and uninterrupted operations and functions of government" (Lipsky and Drotning 1977). The law gave bargaining rights to representative units of all public employees and created impasse procedures intended to avoid the need for strikes. It also prohibited public-employee strikes and invoked severe penalties on violators of the no-strike provision.

The impasse procedures under the Taylor Law included mediation, fact-finding, and "superconciliation" (a higher level mediation process, usually administered by a staff member of the Public Employees Relations Board (PERB) and, until 1974, a legislative hearing). This last step was really a hearing before the board of education, which had the absolute final authority to resolve the dispute. Teacher organizations opposed this step as being biased in favor of management, and they succeeded in 1974 in having amendments passed that eliminated this step. The board, however, still has the final authority to resolve disputes (Lipsky and Drotning 1977).

In 1969 an amendment was passed providing PERB the jurisdiction to consider unfair labor practices. The joint legislative committee that

reported on this amendment states that under these revised statutes: "PERB has been given the power to require the parties to negotiate in good faith. The most significant aspect of this authority is in the determination of the proper scope of bargaining" (Select Joint Legislative Committee on Public Employee Relations, Legislative Document (1968) Number 14, p. 19).

PERB officials have stated the following conditions for matters that are to be considered "mandatory subjects of bargaining": (1) The matter must be a term and condition of employment; (2) it must be within the discretion of the employer; and (3) it may not deal with the mission of the employer (Helsby 1977). If a subject is deemed nonmandatory, PERB has ruled that bargaining on that subject either may be prohibited (nonpermissive) or permitted (permissive). An example of the former is the agency shop, which the Taylor Law explicitly prohibits. An example of a permissive subject is class size, which PERB has held to be a nonmandatory subject of bargaining, but which still can be negotiated. If a subject is deemed permissive, a party may press for negotiations on that subject only through the mediation stage. If the other party has not agreed to negotiate by that time, it must be dropped before submitting the dispute to a fact finder (Helsby 1977: 61)

The basic criterion for establishing the mandatory-nonmandatory nature of a bargaining issue was established in a 1972 court of appeals case, *Board of Education, Town of Huntington* vs. *Associated Teachers of Huntington,* which reads

> Public employees must, therefore, be presumed to possess the broad powers needed to negotiate with employees as to all terms and conditions of employment. The presumption may, of course, be rebutted by showing statutory provisions which expressly prohibit collective bargaining as to a particular term or condition [of employment] but, [i]n the absence of an express legislative restriction against bargaining for that term of an employment contract between a public employer and its employees, the authority to provide for such [term] resides in the [school board] under the broad powers and duties delegated by statutes [citation omitted]. It is hardly necessary to say that, if the Board asserts a lack of power to agree to any particular term or condition of employment, it has the burden to demonstrate the existence of a specific statutory provision which circumscribes the exercise of such power. It has failed to meet this burden in the present case. (30 N.Y. 2d 122 (1972), 5 PERB 7507)

This ruling established an extremely broad scope of bargaining for all public employees, teachers in particular. The increased scope of bargaining can be documented by comparing Kochan's ranking of states according to bargaining provisions in 1971 with the separate 1977 study performed by the Academic Collective Bargaining Information Service. In 1971 Kochan found New York to rank eleventh according to the indexing scheme described earlier. By 1977 New York held a solid number-one position as the

state with the greatest number of demands that were considered either mandatory or permissive subjects of bargaining (New York, 54; New Jersey, 43; Michigan and Oregon, 34). Items that are rarely mandatory in most states, but are in New York, are

1. Impact of change in class size
2. Work rules
3. Reimbursement of tuition for continuing education
4. Rules and regulations governing teachers' powers and duties
5. Paid or unpaid time off for union activities

The New York State United Teachers (NYSUT), an affiliate of the AFT, has analyzed 455 contracts of the 549 public school districts with grades K–12 in New York state.[1] The NYSUT analysis contains *yes-no* responses to a list of eighty-six items. If a contract contains a provision of a certain kind, such as reduction in force or class-size limitation, then a *yes* is recorded. The absence of such a provision in the contract is recorded by a *no*. The percentages of New York school districts with selected contract items are shown in table 2–3. Tabulations show that by 1976 a relatively large percentage of the districts in the state contained provisions that regulate the operation of the schools, especially with regard to personnel

Table 2–3
Trends in Selected Contract Provisions for New York Public-School Teachers: 1972 and 1976

Contract Provision	Percentage of Contracts Exhibiting Provision n = 455		Districts that Lacked (Had) Provision in 1972 and Had (Lacked) it by 1976	
	1972	*1976*	*Number*	*Percent*
Bargaining unit defined	65	89	120	69
Class size	62	56	(30)[a]	(14)
Grievances	96	99	15	75
Teacher evaluation	67	87	100	61
Length of school year	32	49	85	25
Staff reduction	12	40	140	32
Education committees	37	39	10	3
Preparation time	55	72	85	38
Inservice	51	39	(60)	(20)

Data are from Teacher Contract Analysis, New York State United Teachers, selected years.
[a]Numbers in parentheses indicate number or percentage of districts that lost provision, whichever is appropriate.

and instructional decisions. Over half the districts had provisions that restrict class size. Close to 40 percent of the districts had reduction-in-force provisions, educational-curriculum committees, and contractually provided inservice programs. Eighty-seven percent of the negotiated contracts had provisions that gave teachers some input in and control over their evaluations.

In summary, the Taylor Law is relatively broad and vague in defining scope of bargaining. It does not provide a specific listing of mandatory or prohibited subjects of bargaining, nor does it include a management-rights clause. Subsequent PERB and court decisions, however, have clarified significantly the scope-of-bargaining question. As shown in various contract analyses, the bargaining environment created by the Taylor Law has allowed New York teachers, on the whole, to negotiate some of the most comprehensive contracts in the country.

Comparing National Trends with Trends in
Michigan and New York

Although the contract provisions included in analyses of Michigan and New York are not identical to those used in the national sample, it is instructive to compare the relative rankings of the three samples. As found for the nation by McDonnell and Pascal, grievance procedures were the most frequent provisions in New York and Michigan districts. A marked difference emerged, however, when looking at the next most frequent items. Districts in New York followed the national trend, with items related to classroom autonomy occupying the next highest priority. The next most frequent items for the Michigan districts on the other hand were items related to personnel matters—class size and reduction in force. For New York, although class size was a close fourth, only 12 percent of the districts, compared with 76 percent for Michigan, had a reduction-in-force provision. The frequency with which the rest of the provisions were found in contracts were comparable across the two states.

It is interesting to examine the change in the status of contracts for Michigan and New York between 1972 and 1976. The most dramatic change is the considerable reduction in the number of district contracts that contained class-size provisions. For Michigan 77 of the 382 districts with this provision in 1972 lost it by 1976. For New York 30 of the 310 districts that had the provision lost it by 1977. Provisions gained also differed across the two states. For New York, the largest gainer was the reduction-in-force provision. For Michigan the largest gainer was teacher evaluations.

The change in the scope of bargaining during this short period reflects two aspects of the nature of negotiations. First, by trading class-size provi-

sions for reduction-in-force provisions, teachers in New York appeared to be responding to the decline in student enrollments that affected many districts during this period.[2] Although class size, if enforced as a lower bound on the teacher/student ratio, also serves as a job-security measure, it is apparent that teachers preferred the more explicit language of a reduction-in-force provision, perhaps because it protects more senior teachers over more junior ones. Second, districts apparently attempted to add provisions in which they were "deficient." Relatively few Michigan districts negotiated teacher-evaluation provisions by 1972. But, being one of the least frequent provisions, it experienced the widest acceptance by 1976. The next section discusses in more detail the determinants of these trends.

Bargaining Outcomes

Although each collective bargaining relation is unique, the uniqueness of the agreement is not a random event and, consequently, variations in the bargaining outcomes can be related to the environment. Teachers respond to their environment and use collective bargaining to control or shape their workplace. When faced with declining enrollments and the fear of losing jobs, for example, teachers endeavor through collective negotiations to implement policy that will address the issue of staff reduction. Teachers in increasing-enrollment districts, on the other hand, may be less concerned with job security than with overcrowded classes, and they may seek to negotiate policy that limits the number of students in the class.

The view that bargaining and the internal operation of schools are intimately related poses a serious problem for studies of the impact of union policy. The classic multivariate regression approach to analyzing the effects of policy relates policy variables (and other factors entered as controls) to observed behavior, such as budget changes or teacher mobility. Certain policy variables may not be exogenous, but they may depend upon the behavior of teachers or the operation of schools. If this feedback is not taken into consideration, then single-equation estimation of the bargaining impact may lead to biased results. The extent to which the results are biased depends upon the degree of feedback in the system: that is, how endogenous the contract provisions actually are.

The concern with the determinants of bargaining outcomes is more basic than the problems it causes in estimating the impact of teacher contracts on the operation of schools. Understanding the bargaining process can provide insight into whether unions improve relations between administrators and teachers. Freeman and Medoff (1979) suggest that the extent to which unions can be a positive force in labor relations depends, in part, upon the receptiveness of both parties to their respective policies, demands, and conditions. They contend that managerial efficiency, and consequently

the performance of the school district, can be improved if administrators use the collective-bargaining process to learn about and to enhance the operation of the workplace. Thus the basic premise that unions can be a vehicle to promote coordination and cooperation among teachers and administrators rests, in part, with the responsiveness of unions and administrators to each other's actions and concerns.

Considering the determinants of bargaining outcomes therefore entails considering simultaneity. The basic question is whether contract provisions are related to the internal operation of school districts (budgets, enrollment changes, school policy changes) and teacher behavior or whether they are related only to factors exogenous to these decisions.

To explore these issues, we follow two routes. First, we review the bargaining-outcome literature to inventory the various factors shown to be significantly related to the presence of selected contract provisions. This approach is not very satisfactory, since most of these studies assume that the chain of causation is from background and policy variables to contract provisions without considering the possibility of feedback. The second approach, then, examines the simultaneous nature of the bargaining process. Simultaneity is examined in a study that used a simultaneous system of equations to capture both the bargaining and budgeting processes. Although we consider the bargaining process to some degree, the major emphasis in this section is bargaining outcomes; the budgeting process is discussed extensively in chapter 5.

Our conclusion, based upon a limited sample, is that the presence of provisions in district contracts is not endogenous to the district decision-making process but is determined by factors outside the district. This conclusion is based on two facts. First, the variables that most consistently explain the presence of contract provisions appear to be outside the control of district administrators. Second, the simultaneous-equation study reveals that causation is in one direction: contract items influence resource allocation. Although there may be exceptions to the cases cited, the results of this section provide some justification for pursuing the single-equation estimation procedures employed in subsequent chapters.

Literature on Bargaining Outcomes

The most definitive analysis to date on the determinants of teacher contract outcomes is the study by McDonnell and Pascal (1979). In addition to providing an overview of the general trends in collective bargaining for a national sample of 152 school districts, which we reported in the previous section, McDonnell and Pascal also attempt to explain factors that contributed to the presence of certain provisions in the contracts they observed.

McDonnell and Pascal consider two basic classifications of explanatory

variables that from their own fieldwork and the writings of other researchers may affect the content of teachers' contracts. The first type are background variables such as school district characteristics and locational attributes, which include enrollments, county demographics, percentage of state
labor force unionized, and regional variables. The second group of factors
center around policy variables relating to organizational and legal characteristics. Variables include union affiliation (AFT or NEA), proportion of
teachers represented in district, starting salaries, propensity to strike, and
legality of bargaining on specific items. Only one variable can be considered
endogenous to the operation of the school system: teachers' starting salaries, which are negotiated concurrently with nonwage provisions. The contract provisions included in the analysis are grievances, school hours, pupil
exclusion, assignment refusal, class size, promotion rules, instructional
committee, and transfer criteria. Using logit analysis, a form of multivariate regression, only a handful of explanatory variables were found to be
statistically significant. Teachers' starting salary was not found to be significant at a reasonable confidence level for any of the contract provisions.
The strongest predictors of bargaining outcomes were union affiliation and
the state's statutory environment. Both variables are clearly exogenous to
the local district's decision process.

Kochan and Wheeler (1975), in a study of municipal-employee collective bargaining, also found background variables to be the most significant
predictors of bargaining outcomes. As in the McDonnell and Pascal study,
Kochan and Wheeler included only a handful of variables that can be considered endogenous. Only one of these variables, the degree of decision-
making power of the management negotiator, was found to be significant.

The weakness of using these studies to determine the exogeneity of contract formations is that they include very few variables that can be considered endogenous to the district decision-making process. We have considered the issue of simultaneity directly by explicitly modeling the bargaining and budgeting processes in a simultaneous-equation framework. The
analysis focuses on the effect of reduction-in-force provisions on budget
allocations in school districts in New York during the 1970s. The reduction-
in-force (RIF) provision is chosen as the representative contract provision
since it gives teachers partial control over employment, which in turn puts
them directly in a position to affect the allocation of district resources.[3]

Estimating the Bargaining and Budgeting Processes

The study models the behavior of three parties that play important roles in
allocating budgets and negotiating contracts in public school districts. The
stylized behavior of the three parties can be summarized as follows: local

taxpayers determine the total district operating levy; district administrators allocate the total operating levy to various budget categories; and teachers' unions negotiate contract provisions that provide teachers with benefits ranging from insurance coverage and class-size-limitation provisions to RIF provisions. The model is based on a number of simplifying features. (1) Three budget categories are considered in the analysis: instruction, employee benefits, and student services, with instruction broken into teacher/ student ratio and average teacher salary. (2) It is assumed that local taxpayers determine a budget commensurate with that chosen by the median voter. (3) Budget decisions of district administrators also are assumed to reflect community preferences. (4) The RIF provision is a concern of both the taxpayers and the administrators, since it is assumed that some of the costs of negotiations can be passed on to taxpayers. (5) Because the implementation of a RIF provision is contingent on budget allocations and district conditions, it is hypothesized that these conditions affect the presence of a RIF provision, whereas other provisions unrelated to employment are considered exogenous to the decision process. The behavior of each of the three parties is described by a separate equation (Eberts 1982).

The system of equations is estimated using data from public school districts in the state of New York for the 1972–73 and 1976–77 school years. Having data available for two years permits us to look at changes instead of levels, which makes us better able to record the intricacies of the processes. District financial and student characteristics were obtained from the New York Department of Education, and an analysis of contract provisions was provided by the state office of the New York State United Teachers. The NYSUT analysis included NEA affiliated districts as well as their own affiliates. Since all but a handful of districts in New York State had formal bargaining units while the data was being collected, the sample contained only unionized districts. The New York City public-school system was purposely excluded from the sample because of its unusual size and unique behavior.

Estimation of the system of equations is performed on two subsamples of school districts. The first subsample contains districts that lost the reduction-in-force provision between 1972 and 1976 and districts that retained the provision during the period. The second subsample includes districts that gained the reduction-in-force provision during the five-year period and those that never possessed it. Thus, in the first sample, the impact of the contract item on the growth of resources is measured by comparing the growth rate of districts that had a reduction-in-force provision in both years to the growth rate of districts that possessed the provision in 1972 but did not possess it in 1976. The impact of the contract item in the second sample is measured by comparing districts that did not possess the contract items in either year to those that did not have it in 1972 but gained it in 1976.

As indicated by the means and standard deviations of the variables

Table 2-4
Means and Standard Deviations of Variables by Subsample

	Districts that Lost RIF Provision 1972–1976 (n = 59)		Districts that Gained RIF Provision 1972–1976 (n = 441)	
	μ	σ	μ	σ
Endogenous[a]				
Instruction	.32	.08	.32	.08
Benefits	.43	.07	.43	.09
Student services	.27	.22	.36	.44
Total operating expense	.33	.07	.33	.09
Teacher/student ratio	.023	.094	.036	.085
Salaries	.203	.129	.183	.119
Exogenous				
SMSA dummy	.71	.46	.51	.50
Change in real assessed valuation	55.92	55.61	49.71	46.23
Change in tax rate	− .07	.06	− .06	.04
Change in state aid	228.21	85.20	253.15	139.89
Change in federal aid	2.99	29.03	− .15	12.58
Percentage change in total enrollment	− .04	.10	− .04	.09
Percentage change in enrollment, K–6	− .11	.13	− .10	.11
Change in dropout rate	.71	3.73	.20	3.08
Change in graduates/pupils attending four-year college	− .01	.01	− .01	.01
School closure dummy	.37	.48	.33	.47
Log (budget/pupil) in 1972	7.41	.23	7.33	.21
Percentage of districts in county with RIF	.51	.19	.39	.22
Number of items gained or lost/number same status	.36	.24	.20	.13
Enrollment 1972	4589	4176	3230	4702

[a]Endogenous variables are the percentage change in the various categories listed and are expressed in per-student values.

shown in table 2-4, the two samples are very similar. The only significant difference is in the locations and sizes of the districts. Seventy-one percent of the districts in the first sample are located in Standard Metropolitan Statistical Areas (SMSAs), whereas only 51 percent of the districts in the

second sample are in SMSAs. In addition, districts in the first sample are larger and spent more per pupil in 1972 than districts in the second group. It should be noted, however, that the sample of districts that lost the provision contains the largest and smallest districts in the state, excluding New York City.

The most striking result of the analysis, displayed in table 2-5, is that none of the coefficients of the budget variable in the bargaining outcome equations is statistically significant. In other words the appearance or disappearance of reduction-in-force provisions cannot be explained by budget changes. The estimates also show that neither enrollment changes nor school closures significantly affect bargaining outcomes. These findings are consistent with those of Kochan and Wheeler (1975), who found that economic events did not significantly affect bargaining outcomes.

The primary determinants of bargaining outcomes are found in factors that lie outside the realm of the local district administrator. This is evidenced by the significance of the neighborhood effect variable and the district negotiating variable. The neighborhood effect variable is the percentage of districts within the county that possesses a reduction-in-force provision. The district negotiating variable is an index of the trend in negotiations of each district. It is constructed by calculating the ratio of the change in the number of contract items between 1972 and 1976 to the number of items unchanged throughout the period. Selection of the appropriate base depends upon the subsample of districts analyzed. The denominator is either the number of items of the eighty possible included in the analysis that were never obtained or the number of items possessed in both years. The signs of the coefficients of the neighborhood effect variable suggest that a district located in a county with a higher than average percentage of districts possessing a reduction-in-force provision is less inclined to lose the item and more inclined to gain. The positive coefficient on the district negotiating trend variable indicates that the appearance or disappearance of that provision follows the general trend of negotiation of other items in the district contract. Thus it appears that teacher unions place more emphasis on factors outside the district's control than they do on factors, such as resource allocation and hiring decisions, that are determined by district administrators.

The reduction-in-force provision, on the other hand, does have some impact on the internal allocation of resources. Districts that lost the provision experienced a reduction in the growth rate of instructional expenditures, while districts that gained the provision experienced a slight increase in this category. Although reduction-in-force provisions do have a varying degree of impact on the internal budget allocation, the major impact is on total operating expenditures. Districts that gained the provision experience an annual growth rate in total expenditures of 3 percent above the mean

Table 2-5
Estimates of the Determinants of the Appearance or Disappearance of Reduction-in-Force Provisions in New York Teachers' Contracts

	Districts that Lost RIF Provision between 1972 and 1976 (Dependent Variable: Odds of Item Disappearing)			Districts that Gained RIF Provision between 1972 and 1976 (Dependent Variable: Odds of Item Appearing)		
	Instruction	*Benefits*	*Services*	*Instruction*	*Benefits*	*Services*
Constant	-.094 (.04)	-1.52 (.36)	.128 (.12)	-2.83 (2.39)	-2.32 (1.63)	-3.48 (6.25)
Budget item (corsponding to column heading)	1.54 (.18)	4.98 (.43)	1.11 (.25)	-2.62 (.64)	-3.36 (.90)	-.714 (.17)
Percentage change in enrollment	-.081 (.03)	.246 (.08)	-.127 (.04)	-.683 (.35)	-1.16 (.56)	.202 (.15)
Number of items changed/items unchanged	3.53 (2.16)	3.44 (2.11)	3.37 (1.77)	4.24 (4.50)	4.30 (4.53)	4.15 (4.42)
Change in tax rate	-2.06 (.28)	-.078 (.01)	-2.24 (.33)	-2.37 (.85)	-2.45 (.90)	-1.89 (.66)
School-closure dummy	-.332 (.41)	-.339 (.43)	-.333 (.42)	-.412 (1.52)	-.358 (1.34)	-.383 (1.44)
Neighborhood	-5.54 (2.28)	-5.67 (2.42)	-5.49 (2.41)	5.26 (7.46)	5.38 (7.34)	5.11 (7.34)
Miller's M^2	.13	.13	.13	.15	.15	.15

Note: t-ratios in parentheses.

Table 2–6
The Effect of RIF Provisions on Estimates of Total-Operating-Expenditure Equations for New York School Districts

	Lost RIF Provision, 1972–1976	Gained RIF Provision, 1972–1976
	(Dependent Variable: Growth Rate of Total Operating Expenditures)	
Constant	.176	.158
	(5.24)	(13.26)
RIF dummy	−.103	.054
	(2.49)	(3.07)
Change in assessed valuation	.001	.001
	(2.79)	(8.59)
Change in state aid	.001	.001
	(2.93)	(16.02)
Change in federal aid	−.001	.001
	(1.23)	(2.01)
Percentage change in enrollment, K–6	−.053	−.136
	(.77)	(4.45)
SMSA dummy	.023	.001
	(1.19)	(.174)
Number of items changed/items	.101	−.013
	(2.27)	(.43)
R^2	.44	.46
F	4.88	46.21

Note: t-ratios in parentheses.

(table 2–6). Districts that lost the provision experience an annual growth rate of 6 percent below the mean. Apparently the costs or savings due to contract agreements of this sort are passed on the taxpayers and are not internalized by the districts through budget reallocations. Chapter 5 concentrates on the effect of bargaining on resource allocation and the budgeting process.

Given the insignificant effects of budget changes on bargaining outcomes and the significant effect of reduction-in-force provisions on budget changes, there is evidence to support the notion that causation is basically in one direction: contract items influence resource allocation.

The results also provide insight into the interaction between administrators and teachers' unions. The observation that the impact of reduction-in-force provisions on total expenditures is much greater when unions lose the provision than when they gain it suggests that with regard to this provision, administrators exercise greater bargaining strength than teachers.

Teacher unions, on the other hand, appear to base negotiations more on factors outside the district than on internal conditions. It follows, therefore, that if neither party is attentive to the actions of the other, then contrary to the arguments of Freeman and Medoff (1979), collective bargaining may not contribute to efficiency gains through improved communication.

Conclusions

While public education experienced general enrollment declines during the 1970s, organizations representing public-school teachers experienced phenomenal growth. Spearheading the growth of public-sector bargaining, the two major teacher unions, NEA and AFT, increased their ranks from 770,150 members in 1960 to 2,196,469 by 1978. The total membership represents nearly 60 percent of the teaching force. Four reasons are generally cited for the growth in teacher collective bargaining. The first is the recognition by many states that public-sector bargaining should be given the same legal status, with some exceptions, as private-sector bargaining. The second reason basically is economics. Teachers, feeling underpaid and overworked in relation to employees in other sectors, sought to increase their salaries by organizing. Declining enrollments also prompted teachers to use collective bargaining to promote job security. In addition, teachers turned to collective bargaining to maintain a sense of professionalism and some degree of autonomy. Finally, a change in the demographics of teachers and a change in the national mood after the turmoil of the late 1960s provided fertile soil for growth of unionism among professional groups.

Teacher contracts have matured very quickly in the two decades of recognized bargaining. From the simple beginnings of negotiating only salary and certain working conditions, the scope of bargaining agreements has expanded into areas that traditionally have been administrative prerogatives. Teachers now set educational policy; control, to various degrees, personnel matters, including layoffs and promotions; participate in decisions regarding student assignment; and negotiate teacher/student ratios. Although most of these provisions address teachers' concerns about working conditions, empirical analysis reveals very little significant relationship between district conditions and the presence of contract provisions. In fact, most studies, including our own, show that factors exogenous to district decision-making are the best predictors of bargaining outcomes. Our analysis also reveals that gains in contract provisions are not achieved without costs to the unions. In both Michigan and New York, for example, districts that gained reduction-in-force provisions are more likely to lose class-size-limitation provisions than are districts that have not recently gained such provisions.

Nonetheless teachers have acquired a number of noncompensation items that have the potential to limit the flexibility of school management and to increase the costs of public education. At this point in the analysis, we cannot assert that collective bargaining has actually reduced management discretion and increased costs. Such an evaluation cannot be based on the content of contracts alone, since there may be factors that cause these provisions to be ineffective. Chapters 4 and 5 are concerned with measuring the actual effects of these provisions by analyzing how these rules affect the operation of schools and the behavior of teachers and administrators.

Notes

1. The NEA conducts a similar analysis but with less detail. Both analyses contain information on contracts of bargaining units not affiliated with the respective organizations performing the analysis. The NEA data show that of the 736 public school districts listed by state education department, 84 are affiliated with NEA, 54 are nonaffiliated or have no formal bargaining unit, and the remainder are affiliated with the AFT. In comparing the content of contracts reported by both analyses, we found them to be surprisingly close. Since the NYSUT analysis was more comprehensive, we preferred to use it over the NEA analysis.

2. An interview with staff members of NYSUT revealed that job security was one of the major bargaining issues during that time, and it still is. (Interview conducted June 1981, Albany, N.Y.)

3. The variable indicates whether a provision is present in a district contract that addresses reduction in force. The variable does not record the nature of the adopted procedure, however, although we do know that the majority of districts in New York base reduction in force on seniority.

3

A Model of
Student Achievement

Most Americans believe that the success or failure of their children's education lies with the classroom teacher. It is not surprising, therefore, that when teachers unionize and are perceived by some to switch from the role of a dedicated classroom teacher to that of a dedicated union member, concern is expressed about how this will affect the quality of education. Although much energy has been devoted to debating the issue of the effects of collective bargaining on American education and to speculating about its effects, most of the research has looked at the effects that are more directly related to the immediate consequences of the bargaining process. Studies have examined the effect of collective bargaining on class size, teachers' salaries and fringes, teachers' attitudes, teachers' time, administrative leadership, and district organization. In addition, research has examined the dynamics of the bargaining process and the characteristics of the participants involved in shaping the agreements.[1] Nonetheless, nowhere in this volume of work is a study that relates collective bargaining directly to student outcomes.[2]

The absence of such a study does not reflect a lack of interest in the overall effects of teacher collective bargaining on the effectiveness of teachers. On the contrary, most studies that deal with one of the various immediate consequences of collective bargaining try to make some link to student achievement. Furthermore, in critiquing the various studies on collective bargaining, most of the noted researchers acknowledge the importance of making the link between collective bargaining and student achievement.

The obvious question then is why we are still waiting for such a study to be performed. We offer two answers. First, since the effects of collective bargaining on student achievement are by-products of negotiations over teacher salaries and working conditions, many researchers dismiss the significance of the ultimate effects on student achievement. Mitchell and Kerchner (1981) together with their colleagues, for example, contend that bargainers for both sides are so concerned with the immediate problems and consequences of the negotiations that they fail to gain a perspective on the effect of their decisions on the overall pattern of public education. It also is argued that since the issues considered at the bargaining table do not explicitly address teacher effectiveness, such matters are not in fact affected by the bargaining outcomes. Both observations lead to the conclusion that,

since the consequences of collective bargaining on student outcomes are neither immediately apparent nor addressed during bargaining, the incidental effects should be ignored.

Other researchers take a different stand on the incidental effects of collective bargaining. McDonnell and Pascal, for example, accept the premise that teacher collective bargaining can affect students, but they recognize the complex task of linking bargaining outcomes to student outcomes. They report that

> Students experience the effects of bargaining only indirectly and occasionally. They may attend somewhat smaller classes, but for fewer hours per day and fewer days per year. Rising personnel costs may result in less supplementary learning resources for students, but at the same time teachers may be happier and aides and specialists more plentiful. An older and more highly credentialed teacher force may mean more expertise in instruction, but perhaps less flexibility and energy. How any of these consequences of collective bargaining influence the rate of learning or other student interests remains largely unknown. (1979:xii)

In a more recent statement about linking bargaining to students, McDonnell states that "it is much too early to try to tie collective bargaining outcomes to the effective school research" (CEPM Conference Proceedings 1982:41).

McDonnell's statement leads us to our second answer. Research on teacher effectiveness is not sufficiently refined to detect the intricate and subtle effects collective bargaining may have on the education process. The past two decades of research have revealed very little consensus regarding the contribution of school resources to student achievement. Educational production functions have been plagued by three problems. First and foremost is that the models did not address the question of how resources are allocated in school systems. Without this specification, behavioral responses of teachers, students, and administrators were not taken into account properly. Second, the time teachers and students spend on learning activities only recently has been identified as an important ingredient in the production process (Thomas 1979) and, consequently, only recently has been incorporated in the analysis. Third, adequate databases were not available to give researchers the opportunity both to investigate the basic learning process and to analyze policy issues.

We have been able to overcome some of the difficulties that plagued past studies, particularly as they apply to evaluating the effects of collective bargaining. First, we have acquired a database with student-specific information, school- and district-level characteristics, and information on bargaining outcomes. With this comprehensive database, we can trace the effects of collective bargaining from the negotiating table to the classroom. Second, the use of process variables, such as the time teachers and adminis-

trators spend on various activities, better enables us to focus on the determinants that are brought to bear on student achievement and that are immediate consequences of collective bargaining. By observing school districts at work at all levels of operation, classroom, school building, and district, as well as the behavioral responses of teachers to different institutional arrangements one can examine the effects of teacher collective bargaining on student achievement.

The chapter is divided into two sections. The first section discusses the educational production-function literature and reviews findings from previous research on teacher effectiveness in an attempt to identify factors that are considered significant determinants of student achievement. The second section describes our own attempt at estimating an educational production using data from a national survey of schools. Our estimation differs from past studies by looking at variables on principal leadership and by entering teacher time explicitly into the achievement-gains equation. In addition, we are able to rank the importance of key educational inputs. Assessing the relative importance of the various inputs will aid in determining the effect of teacher collective bargaining on student achievement, as discussed in chapter 6.

Measuring the Effects of Collective Bargaining on Student Achievement

Teacher contracts are negotiated by the district; students are educated primarily in the classroom. To establish a link between collective-bargaining outcomes and student achievement, it must be shown that the consequences of negotiations are felt in the classroom. Bargaining outcomes enter the classroom primarily through their effects on teachers. As discussed in chapter 2, negotiations can affect class size; the time teachers spend on instruction and preparation; the amount of administrative and clerical duties required of teachers; teachers' attitudes; the age, experience, and educational composition of the teaching force; administrative leadership; and classroom organization. Unlike previous studies, which concentrate on these direct effects of collective bargaining, the present analysis goes one step further. We consider the link between teacher collective bargaining and student achievement. Once the relative importance of teacher, student, and organization characteristics has been identified through the use of an educational production function, the second step is to identify the direct effects of collective bargaining on the quantity and quality of these factors. Combining these two steps shows the paths through which collective bargaining can affect student achievement. The remainder of this chapter considers the first step—identification of the major determinants of student achievement.

Educational Production Functions

A large number of quantitative studies relating school resources to student achievement have appeared over the last twenty years.[3] Although these students are referred to by different names—as input-output studies or as studies of teacher effectiveness, school effectiveness, or educational production functions—they share a common methodology. Murnane (1981), in a critique of this literature, characterizes these studies as multivariate analyses of the variation in student outcomes explained by variations in school resources. Since the variation in resources is created by the operation of a school system, not by a controlled experiment, the analysis is a snapshot of the school system at work. The central figures in the snapshot are information on the school resources that children receive at a given time and one or more measures of student progress.

Research on educational production functions asks two basic questions. Do schools matter in explaining student achievement? And if so, what school resources are important in the educational process? First attempts at answering these questions produced results both surprising and unsettling to the education profession. The Coleman Report (1966) was perhaps the largest and most comprehensive, and definitely the most hotly debated study to emerge from the early attempts at estimating an educational production function. The study attempted to determine the school and nonschool factors related to the achievement of over 600,000 students across the country. The findings showed very little association between these inputs and student test scores—that is, schools do not matter.

The report has received close scrutiny and tremendous criticism, and the data has been reanalyzed numerous times since the study first appeared. Currently the general consensus of researchers in this area is that schools *do* matter. The change in opinion is due to a number of advances made in conceptualizing the educational process and in estimating the production function. First, researchers have learned the importance of using the individual child as the unit of observation, rather than using school or district aggregates. Utilizing student-specific information, and at the same time identifying the school resources that each student actually receives (rather than using average resources present in the school or district) provides a much stronger link between inputs and outputs. Second, measures of school resources and student achievement also have changed since the Coleman Report. The first studies focused on the physical capital of schools—for example, libraries, laboratories, and number of textbooks. Since then the definition of resources has expanded to include teacher characteristics, classroom organization variables, measures of teacher quality, and time on task. The use of time-on-task variables has proven especially significant since they measure the actual flow of services between teacher and student rather than the stock of potential services. Third, researchers also have

recognized the importance of considering gains in student achievement rather than the levels of achievement. This approach accomplishes two things. It permits the researcher to control for characteristics of students and teachers that do not change significantly over time but that affect the level of student achievement. In addition, by looking at achievement gains, the researcher can account for the effect of those resources that have influenced student achievement over a given school year, rather than capturing the cumulative effect of past years of schooling.

Although studies differ in their assessment of the relative importance of school resources in the educational production function, most agree that teachers are the critical resource in schools. This is not to say that researchers have been able to claim unequivocally that certain resources actually cause instructional effectiveness. Nor is it to say that the characteristics can be ranked according to importance (Edmonds 1982:4). From the perspective of assessing the impact of collective bargaining on student achievement, the second caveat is the more troublesome. Since collective bargaining affects numerous educational determinants, it is necessary to know the relative contribution of these determinants in order to derive an overall assessment of the influence of collective bargaining. However, it is not possible to rank the importance of school resources by comparing findings from different studies. Estimates obtained by using regression analysis are sensitive to the measurement of variables and the specification of the model. Since studies differ considerably on these two points, estimates are not comparable. It is possible, on the other hand, to rank the importance of variables within a specific study. We proceed, therefore, to specify an educational production function, to discuss the findings of a number of past studies, and then to use what we have learned from these to estimate an educational production function that uses the same database used in subsequent analyses of the effect of collective bargaining on teacher behavior and student outcomes.

Basic Models

Education is a service that takes a student, with whatever attributes that individual brings to the classroom, and transforms the student into someone with different qualities. Educational production functions relate differences in the quality of students to differences in school resources received by students. Because specifications of educational production functions differ among studies, it is impossible to capture with one specification all the features of all the models constructed to date. However, most studies share the features described by equation (3.1), which is borrowed from Hanushek (1979).

$$A_{it} = f(B_{it}, P_{it}, S_{it}, I_i), \tag{3.1}$$

where A_{it} = student outcomes of ith students at time t

B_{it} = vector of family background influences of ith student cumulative to time t

P_{it} = vector of influence of peers of ith student cumulative to time t

S_{it} = vector of school inputs of ith student cumulative to time t

I_i = vector of innate abilities of ith student

The model incorporates a number of essential aspects of the educational process. First, inputs are those that are relevant to the individual student. Second, the inputs are cumulative, which reflects the fact that schooling and other experiences in past years have a bearing on student outcomes in the present period. Third, school inputs include purchased (teachers) as well as nonpurchased inputs (peer groups). Fourth, the allocation of resources is predetermined from the perspective of the production function.

A somewhat popular variant of the model and one that requires substantially less data collection is the value-added model. Instead of considering the contribution of past inputs on student outcomes, this specification considers the changes in student outcomes between two time periods, usually the beginning and end of a certain school year. This formulation reduces the data requirements, since inputs are only collected over the same two-year period. The value-added model results from simply subtracting equation (3.1) for period t^* from (3.1) for period t.

$$A_{it} = f^*(B_i(t - t^*), \quad P_i(t - t^*), \quad S_i(t - t^*), \quad I_i, \quad A_{it}^*). \tag{3.2}$$

Student outcomes in the earlier period (A_{it}^*) may be reflected in scores from pretests taken by students at the beginning of the school year. These scores are then compared with scores of tests taken at the end of the school year. In this way the gains in student outcomes attributed to a flow of educational services within a given time period can be assessed.

Given the basic structure of the model, the next task is to describe the variables used to estimate the production function. We first consider the dependent variable and then proceed to discuss the independent variables used by various studies, including our own study, and to report the general findings associated with these variables.

In most of the studies considered under the rubric of educational production functions, standardized test scores of cognitive skills are used as the

measure of student outcome. Test scores obviously are not intended to measure all the attributes of education. School outcomes encompass, in addition to the acquisition of skills, conveyance of social norms, development of creative skills, and the provision of custodial services. A few studies have considered student attributes other than test scores as dependent variables. For example, Levin (1970), Michelson (1970), and Boardman and others (1973) considered student attitudes; Katzman (1971) looked at attendance rates; and Katzman (1971) and Burkhead and others (1967) used college continuation and dropout rates.

These are all sensible measures. The decision of the vast majority of studies to use cognitive test scores results from a combination of availability of such scores and a certain conceptualization of education. Most school districts administer some form of standardized tests. Even though there is considerable controversy over what these tests actually measure, educators tend to believe that they are important. Performance on tests is used to advance students through the educational system, evaluate programs, and even to allocate funds. Further, it appears given the recent concern over declining Scholastic Aptitude Test (SAT) scores, that interest in test scores is increasing.

Whether standardized tests reflect the value of education is still open to debate. A definition of education useful in discussing the merits of standardized tests is offered by Hanushek, who sees the value of education as relating to the "perceived importance of school in future capabilities" (1979:355). Future capabilities can include performance in the labor market, participation in the political system, and achievement in future educational endeavors. Considerable work has been done in linking educational achievement to these topics, particularly on the first one. Economists have analyzed the influence of education on earnings and labor market performance (see, for example, the reviews in Mincer 1970 and Rosen 1977). Other researchers have explored the effects of schooling on occupational choice, mobility, earnings, and the relationship between schooling and personal and family characteristics (see Hanushek 1979 for a fairly extensive bibliography of these studies). Although the direct links between formal education and earnings, occupational choice and other outcomes have yet to be unambiguously identified, it is agreed that education, at least in the basic skills, is important in the future performance of individuals.

Past Findings of Determinants of Student Achievement

It is difficult to compare results of past studies because of the many inconsistencies in the way the models are specified. Studies differ in the way the dependent is measured and in how it is entered in the regression analysis.

Although most studies use standardized test scores, the scores are not comparable in many cases, and a change in the score of one test is not equivalent to a change in another test. Also, some studies use achievement levels while others use achievement gains. Inconsistencies also appear in the types of explanatory variables included in the production function. Although it is implicitly assumed that educational models include all of the relevant variables and that they are measured accurately, this usually is not the case. Omitting important variables causes the estimates of the production function to be biased. Thus, even if the same database were used in all the studies, it would be highly probable that models that included different combinations of variables would yield different estimates for the same coefficients. Despite these problems with comparing the results across studies, a judicious interpretation of the findings is useful in understanding the nature of the educational process, that is, the robustness of results across all studies.

Murnane (1981), in critiquing the past literature on teacher effectiveness, has identified four groups of factors that have been shown to affect student test scores significantly: (1) student characteristics, (2) teacher characteristics, (3) time in instruction, and (4) curriculum and mode of instruction. Murnane cautions that these groups should not be treated in parallel fashion. Rather, teachers and students are the primary resources, whereas physical facilities, class size, and instructional strategies are secondary resources that affect student learning through their influence on the behavior of teachers and students. Furthermore, the relationship between primary inputs and student outcomes is sensitive to the incentives and constraints placed on teachers by the school district. Thus institutions, such as teacher unions, can have a major impact on the educational process by affecting the allocation of secondary resources and the motivation, attitudes, and quality of the primary resources. In reviewing the findings related to these four groups of determinants, it is important to keep in mind the possible connections between teachers' collective bargaining and these factors.

Teachers. Murnane reports that virtually every study of school effectiveness finds that some attribute of teachers is significantly related to student achievement. Studies have found that teachers with some experience are more effective than teachers with no experience. A teacher's performance on verbal ability tests or the quality of the college the teacher attended is positively related to student test scores. Teachers with high expectations for their students are effective in helping children acquire cognitive skills.

A somewhat surprising result uncovered by many studies is that teachers with master's degrees are no more effective, on average, than teachers with only bachelor's degrees. Murnane attributes these findings to a self-selection process. Before salary schedules were based on educational attain-

ment, only highly motivated teachers sought additional education. Now that a majority of teachers have advanced degrees either for the purpose of salary increases or to meet state certification requirements, the possession of a master's degree no longer signals a difference in motivation.

Mode of Instruction. We include under this category characteristics of the organization of the classroom that may affect student achievement. One of the most thoroughly researched factors in this groups is class size. Perhaps one of the reasons that class size has received so much attention is that, in addition to being a highly visible indicator of teacher-student interaction, it subsumes a number of complex and perhaps competing microeffects. For instance, class size can be considered a measure of the amount of time the teacher interacts with students. Larger class sizes introduce congestion and the teacher must spend either more time with the whole group or less time with individual students. Class size also may reflect the organization of the classroom. A recent study by Glass and Smith (1979) shows that the size of the instructional unit has a significant effect on the achievement levels of students. Using meta-analysis to synthesize the results of past studies, they show that as the size of the instructional unit increases from 0 to 20 students, the achievement levels of students dramatically decrease, falling by over 20 percentile rankings. For class sizes greater than 20, an increase in enrollment has very little effect on achievement.

The reasons behind the conclusions regarding class size are rooted in the dynamics of the interaction between student and teacher. One important measure of this interaction is the time spent in instruction. Recent attention to this determinant has produced encouraging results. Several studies report systematic relationships between time and student achievement (see Wiley and Harnishfeger 1974; Fisher and others 1980; Monk 1980; and Thomas 1979). Another dimension of class size is its effect on the instructional strategies that can be employed in the classroom. A teacher's ability to provide students with individualized instruction or to work in small groups depends upon the number of students for which the teacher is responsible. If the group is large and the teacher does not have the assistance of an aide, the possible kinds of instructional arrangements are reduced. In principle this interaction between class size and instructional strategy can be investigated, but due to the lack of reliable information on instructional strategy, the analysis has been limited to small samples.

Class size has a third possible effect. Except in individualized instruction, teachers interact simultaneously with most of the students in the classroom. In this sense the teacher's time is shared equally by all students. However, since students are characterized by different learning abilities and home environments, the common time the teacher spends with students influences each student differently. Thus the consequences of a large class

may not be borne proportionately by all students in the class. A comprehensive analysis of this effect would require interacting student characteristics with class size, but this is rarely done in the studies due to the large data requirements.

Peer Groups. Another aspect of classroom interaction as a shared service is the effect of classmates on a student's achievement. Henderson and others (1978) and Summers and Wolfe (1977) provide evidence that elementary school children with low initial skill levels who attend schools in which the average achievement level is relatively high make more progress than such children who attend schools in which the average achievement level is relatively low. Winkler (1975) shows that the same is true for students of different socioeconomic backgrounds. The issue of the effect of the composition of the student body on achievement levels received considerable attention when school desegregation and integration were hotly contested issues. From the standpoint of collective bargaining, however, peer groups have little importance, since teachers have little control over the types of students who enter their district.

Administration Leadership. Currently there is much debate about the potential of administrative leadership to increase student achievement. Although *instructional leadership* has been defined in a variety of ways, we will generally use this term to include activities such as program evaluation, supervision and support of teachers, and curriculum development and coordination. A number of studies have provided evidence that administrative leadership is indeed a promising area for research relating to school improvement. For example, Keeler and Andrews (1973) find that the leadership behavior of principals, as perceived by their staffs, was significantly related to the productivity of the schools (Miller 1976:337). More recently a number of other researchers have provided evidence to corroborate the hypothesis that school-principal involvement in instructional leadership is correlated with improved student outcomes (Edmonds 1979; Mann 1979; Brookover and others 1979; and Wellisch and others 1978).

While the studies noted support the notion that a principal's involvement in instructional leadership leads to school improvement, others have informed us that the principals who actively engage in such activities are indeed rare (Deal and others 1975; Lortie 1969; Corwin 1970; Cohen and Miller 1980). Moreover, even researchers who accept the notion that instructional leadership is linked to school improvement have asserted that it is not the principals themselves who are important but rather the critical support functions offered by principals. These support functions may be performed by a variety of school personnel other than the principal—curriculum specialists, department heads, and teachers (Gersten and Carnine

1981; Pitner 1980). Finally, still others caution that even where principals engage in the comprehensive set of tasks referred to as instructional leadership, the participation of teachers also must be considered as a critical ingredient (Wellisch and others 1978).

If administrative leadership is important to student achievement, what elements of administrative behavior are most important? Although an important role of the principal is to provide instructional leadership, very little of the principal's time is spent in any instructional interaction with students. The time the principal does spend with students is involved in some disciplinary matter or related to observing and evaluating teachers in the classroom. The effect of principals on student achievement primarily comes through various interactions with teachers. The potential effect of this interaction can be understood best by considering what the ideal role of a principal should be. Work previously cited by Edmonds, Cohen, Brookover, Gersten and Carnine, to mention a few, identify a number of ways in which the principal can improve educational programs. These elements include maintaining order, acting as an agent of change, setting clear objectives, conveying high expectations of student achievement, offering support and guidance to teachers, providing public rewards and incentives, and spending time in the classroom. These activities have not yet been entered in any systematic way into the educational production functions. We attempt to examine the effect of certain aspects of principals' leadership in our analysis reported in the next section.

From the characteristics of a successful administrator, it is clear that the effectiveness of administrative leadership is contingent on close cooperation and shared goals between teachers and principals. The net effect of teacher collective bargaining on the educational program through the effectiveness of principals is closely tied to the posture that teachers and principals take when forced to choose sides at the negotiating table. The positions taken by principals are unclear, as indicated in the different observations of a number of case studies. Griffin (1974) reports that some teachers' representatives see the principal as the person most knowledgable about the needs, abilities, desires, and effectiveness of the teachers in his school. The principal therefore makes an execllent ally. Griffin finds that on the other hand the fear of "administrative coercion" serves as a primary deterrent for not including the principal on the teachers' negotiating team. Perry and Wildman (1970) and Cooper (1982) find that building principals, by being squeezed between the very vocal demands of central administration and teacher unions, feel alienated from the decision-making process and may even opt for their own union.

The pertinent question regarding the effectiveness of building administrators is whether they have lost their role of instructional leader by losing the power to administer policy at the school level. A conclusive answer has

not been found. Randles (1975) expresses the views of some researchers who believe that contracts give principals more legitimacy in enforcing contractual provisions than they formerly enjoyed. Nicholson and Nasstrom (1974) note that principals who functioned under collective-bargaining contracts "tended to make more decisions exclusive of central office involvement." They attribute this to the fact that the formalized procedures outlined in contracts allows principals more freedom from central-office interference in decision-making.

Although contracts may give building principals certain freedom from the central office, principals also must stay within the bounds set out by the contract. Brandsletter (1970) and Nicholson and Nasstrom (1974) found that principals perceived negotiated contracts as having curtailed their supervisory authority in such areas as teacher transfer and evaluation, scheduling, and determining program level and subject matter. These same authors conclude, however, that "negotiations per se have not necessarily reduced authority, but instead have required a redefinition of the parameters of authority." Berg's study (1973) of 118 principals finds that "collective bargaining does not seem to have exerted the major impact on the principal which most have presumed and some have feared."

Analysis of the Determinants of Mathematical Skills

Much of the variation in the results found in the literature is due to different data sets used in the analyses. Thus, in order to analyze the effect of collective bargaining on achievement scores, the analysis must be based on the same data set. We use a database containing information that can accommodate both an estimation of an educational production function and an analysis of union effects. The database was developed by the Systems Development Corporation under contract with the U.S. Office of Education for the purpose of assessing the costs and benefits of compensatory education. Since no one has used the data to estimate an educational production function of the form to be presented in this chapter, we have undertaken that task and present the methodology and results in this section.

The basic model chosen for this study is the achievement growth model described in equation (3.2). An achievement-growth model explains the gains in student achievement due to changes in educational resources the student received over a given time. The model that we estimate is slightly different from the model presented previously. Because of our concern with the effects of collective bargaining, we focus primarily on those explanatory variables that possibly may be affected by collective bargaining. Of course certain variables, such as student characteristics, are included in the analysis in order to control for their effects on student achievement. Consistent with previous analyses, we ignore possible causal interactions among various

types of achievement (for example, between achievement in mathematics and in reading) and rely upon a linear functional form. We do, however, investigate nonlinearities by experimenting with quadratic and interaction terms.

Description of the Data

The database contains data on mathematics and reading programs for 328 elementary schools selected randomly nationwide. In this analysis, however, we consider only the mathematics scores of fourth graders. Since students receive less math than reading instruction at home, gains in math skills should be associated more directly with school activities. The sample contains observations on over 14,000 fourth graders enrolled during the late 1970s. Five general categories of variables were collected: (1) achievement growth in mathematics for each student; (2) measures of the individual student's background, (3) characteristics of the student's math classroom teacher for the year; (4) the amount of time the teacher spent in instruction, preparation, and administrative duties; and (5) characteristics of principals, including leadership activities and qualities. The achievement-growth measure was based on two tests. At the beginning of each school year, an at-level test was given to assess the student's mastery of certain mathematical skills acquired up to that time. At the end of the school year, a similar test, asking questions with the same level of difficulty as were asked at the beginning of the year, was administered to determine the gain in skills over the school year.[4] The achievement-growth measure then captures the increase in skills attributable to resources received during the school year.

The student-background measures include age, sex, race, early childhood educational experience, parental involvement, exact grade level, and economic status of the student. Teacher characteristics include the teaching experience, highest degree earned, college courses taken in mathematics in the last three years, hours of math inservice in the last three years, and the amount of time given to preparation for class.

Three categories of teacher time are included in the educational production function. Two categories, time spent in instruction and time spent in preparation, are expected to positively influence student achievement gains. The third category, time spent performing administrative and clerical duties, which includes attending staff meetings, is expected to have a negative effect. Although time spent in total instruction is not the same as time spent in math instruction, we find that the two activities are highly correlated, and thus total instruction is a good indication of the flow of teacher services received by the student. These time groups account for 90 percent of the time the average teacher spends in school-related activities.

Characteristics of principals—experience in teaching, experience as a

principal, and highest degree earned—were also included in the production function. Also available were measures of the level and quality of principal's instructional leadership. Two types of variables were considered. The first set of variables records the amount of time principals spend in activities related to math curriculum development and related to assessing needs, planning math programs, and evaluating these programs. The second set reflects teachers' and administrators' assessments of the effectiveness of certain leadership activities and how well the staff works together. Teachers and principals were asked if they strongly agree (value = 4), agree (value = 3), disagree (value = 2), or strongly disagree (value = 1) with the following statements:

School programs are well planned and clear.

Principal provides active leadership to math program.

Teachers in this school work well together.

Administrators keep teachers well informed.

Conflicts among individuals are identified and faced, and not allowed to fester.

By having the responses to these questions from both teachers and administrators, it is possible to check whether an individual's own assessment of his or her actions is more effective than someone's else assessment.

District-level variables measuring the ratio of staff to students also are included in the analysis. Class size, as approximated by the teacher/student ratio, has been used extensively to reflect the flow of teacher services. Although we have a direct measure of the flow of services in the instructional time variable, it is useful to include class size in order to reflect characteristics of the organization of the classroom. In like manner, the number of administrators per student is included to capture certain features of the organization of the district.

Results

The achievement-growth model, described in equation (3.2), is estimated using ordinary least squares. All the variables discussed in the previous section, however, are estimated simultaneously. For ease of discussion, the results are grouped by categories and displayed in tables 3-1 to 3-4. The estimates are encouraging on two counts: first, they are consistent in most regards with past studies; but second, they appear to uncover relationships between teacher time, principals' leadership characteristics, and student

Table 3-1
Effect of Student Background Measures and Pretest Scores on Fourth-Grade Mathematics Scores

Variable Description		Coefficient	Means
Sex (male = 1)		−.074	.5023
		(13.29)	
Race (white = 1)		.051	.7292
		(7.94)	
Childhood experience		.00002	1.0529
		(.004)	
Parental involvement		.016	1.8772
		(2.73)	
Economic status		.107	224.9576
		(16.32)	
Pretest	STD Beta	.665	
	Beta	.89	28.671
		(24.27)	
Pretest squared	STD Beta	−.014	915.914
	Beta	−.0003	
		(.05)	
N		14,882	
R^2		.55	
F		521.1	

Note: All variables included in tables 3-2 to 3-5 were estimated simultaneously. Coefficients are expressed as standardized betas; t-statistics in parentheses.

achievement not previously found. By reporting standardized betas instead of the parameter estimates, we are able to compare the relative importance of each input in explaining the gains in student achievement.[5]

Although we are primarily concerned with school-based variables that can be influenced by collective bargaining, a number of student background variables are included in order to control for the aptitude, motivation, and home experience students bring to the classroom. The coefficients of these three control variables are shown in table 3-1. Only parental involvement and the family's economic status are statistically significant. A comparison of the standardized betas associated with these two variables reveals that an increase of one standard deviation in the student's economic status contributes over six times more to student achievement gain than does an increase of one standard deviation in parental involvement. The sex and ethnic origin of students are significantly related to achievement gain. Although white students appear to have higher achievement growth than nonwhites, this may be due to the importance of omitted variables such as language barriers and family background, and we do not venture any interpretation

Table 3-2
Effect of Teacher Measures and Teacher Time Allocation on Fourth-Grade
Mathematics Scores

Variable Description	Coefficient	Means
Total years teaching	.013 (2.21)	11.987
Highest degree attained	−.031 (5.22)	2.465
Number of college-level courses related to teaching math taken in last three years	.004 (.74)	.607
Staff development/inservice training related to math instruction taken in last three years	−.019 (3.27)	7.363
Principal's leadership (composite index of extent principal makes policy decisions)	.002 (.35)	3.455
Principal encourages teachers to try new teaching methods	−.003 (5.10)	3.168
Time spent in instruction per day	.032 (5.41)	4.889
Time spent in class preparation per day	.017 (2.93)	1.405
Time spent performing administrative duties per day	−.009 (1.52)	.790

Note: Coefficients are standardized betas; t-statistics in parentheses.

of this variable. It is included only to control for student backgrounds that are difficult to quantify.

The pretest score, from a math test administered in the fall, is entered both linearly and as a squared term. The combination of the two variables allows for the possibility that the relationship between the pretest and posttest may be nonlinear. For example, nonlinearities could occur due to the fact that each test has a finite number of questions, and students who began the school year with a higher test score would be less likely to make significant gains than students who began the year with much lower pretest scores. Since the coefficient associated with the squared pretest score is insignificant, the relationship between pretest and posttest scores is linear. The magnitude of the regression parameter indicates that an increase of one point on the pretest increases the posttest score by about nine-tenths of a point when everything else is held constant.

Most studies have found that teacher experience and highest degree attained by teachers are significant determinants of student achievement. Our results reinforce this conclusion. Teachers with more experience are more effective in raising student achievement levels, whereas teachers with more formal education appear to be less effective. For the negative relation-

Table 3–3
Effect of Principal Measures and Staff Size on Fourth-Grade Student Scores

Variable Description	Coefficient	Means
Highest degree attained	− .022 (3.88)	2.997
Experience teaching	.024 (4.20)	10.188
Total experience as principal	.030 (5.23)	8.867
Time spent during school year in activities related to math curriculum development	− .015 (2.00)	9.760
Time devoted to needs assessment, program planning, and evaluation for math program	.036 (4.46)	11.876
Instructional leadership (composite index)	− .015 (1.77)	53.528
Administrators per district enrollment	− .019 (2.96)	.0039
Teachers per district enrollment	.024 (3.73)	.0545
Clerical staff and aides per district enrollment	− .015 (2.42)	.0188

Note: Coefficients are standardized betas; t-statistics in parentheses.

ship between education and achievement gain, Murnane (1981) offers the explanation that the motivation for additional college credit is less for self-improvement than for salary increases, which appears to be a counterproductive pursuit with respect to student achievement.

Also included as teacher characteristics are measures of teacher activities related to the mathematics program. Results show that college-level courses related to teaching math do not contribute significantly to achievement gains. Moreover, staff development and inservice training related to math instruction appear to decrease achievement gains. In the same way teachers who are encouraged by principals to try new teaching methods are less effective than teachers who do not receive such encouragement. It is difficult to explain these results. Some researchers in the instructional leadership field, however, find that when teachers receive only intermittent training or are not given the opportunity to follow up on new techniques or programs, very few positive results come from these activities (Gall 1983). A similar situation may be prevalent in the schools we studied. Another explanation may be that teacher involvement in inservice training is a distress signal, and the negative sign indicates that teachers taking these programs are initially below par.

Table 3-4
Effect of Attitudes of Principals and Teachers about Principal's Instructional Leadership on Fourth-Grade Mathematics Scores

Variable Description	Respondent	Coefficient	Means
School programs are well planned and clear.	P	−.013 (1.91)	3.249
	T	.005 (.73)	2.585
Principal provides active leadership to math program.	P	−.011 (1.61)	3.121
	T	.016 (2.35)	2.307
Teachers in this school work well together.	P	.012 (1.64)	3.432
	T	−.003 (.40)	2.994
Administrators keep teachers well-informed.	P	.001 (.09)	3.373
	T	−.009 (1.30)	2.330
Conflicts among individuals are identified and faced, and not allowed to fester.	P	.012 (1.73)	3.274
	T	.001 (.12)	2.279

Note: P designates principal's response to question; T designates teacher's response to question. Coefficients are standardized betas; t-statistics in parentheses.

As expected, the time teachers spend in instruction and in preparation is positively and significantly related to achievement gains. Moreover, results in table 3-2 show that time spent in instruction is almost twice as effective as time spent in preparation. Since time in instruction is an important indicator of the interaction between student and teacher, this result is important when assessing the way in which collective bargaining can enter the classroom.[6] As mentioned earlier, time spent in instruction includes instructional activities other than math programs. Variables reflecting the time students were engaged in math instruction also were available and were regressed against student achievement. Since these results did not differ significantly from the results reported in table 3-2, we chose to use total instruction as the time variable. This suggests what most educators already argue, that instruction has complementary effects on a number of areas.

The teacher/student ratio traditionally has been entered into educational production functions as a proxy for the amount of instruction received by students. Students in larger classes, even though they may spend the same amount of time with the teacher, may not receive the same level of

instruction as a student in a smaller class, since the teacher's time is divided among a greater number of students. The teacher/student ratio, as reported in table 3-3, is positively related to student-achievement gains. This finding concurs with previous studies as well as with our own work, which classified instructional time by the size of the instructional unit.

The characteristics of principals produced results very similar to those found for teachers. Estimates displayed in table 3-3 reveal that principals with more experience, either as teachers or as administrators, are found to be more effective. Principals with more education, on the other hand, are less effective. As was found for teachers, time spent by principals on activities related to math curriculum development is associated with lower achievement gains. This result is offset, however, by an increase in achievement gains when time is devoted to needs assessment, program planning, and evaluation of the math program. A composite index of teacher responses to questions concerning the principals' instructional leadership is negatively related to student achievement gains, but it is not statistically signigficant at a reasonable confidence level. A curious result is that students in districts with higher than average ratios of administrators to students have lower achievement gains than students in districts with lower than average ratios of administrators to students. The ratio of administrators to students could be a reflection of certain district characteristics that are not controlled for in the regression.

The final set of variables entered into the educational production function reflects the attitudes of principals and teachers about the principal's instructional leadership and the degree of cooperation among the staff. The interesting result emerging from the effects of these attitudes on student achievement gain is that in many cases self-assigned scores of teacher or administrator performance are inversely related to student achievement, whereas assessment by another party is related to student achievement in proper fashion. For example, both principals and teachers were asked to assess the principal's instructional leadership to the math program. When principals rate their leadership highly, student-achievement gains are lower than otherwise. When teachers rate the same principals highly, however, achievement gains are in fact higher than otherwise. The same relationship occurs for assessments of the ability of teachers to work well together. A high rating by the principal is associated with positive achievement gains, whereas a high rating by the teachers has no significant relationship with gains in test scores.

Our estimates of the educational production function are basically consistent with past studies. We find that class size and teacher experience are positively related to student achievement gains and that student background variables also are important determinants. Our results further reinforce the basic notion that the interaction between teacher and student, as measured

by instructional time, is an important determinant of student achievement. In addition, quality-related teacher characteristics remain significant even when explicit measures of services flows are introduced. Including principal characteristics and activities related to instructional development, on the other hand, produces some curious, if not counterintuitive, results. The experience of principals, for example, is positively related to achievement gains. With regard to instructional leadership, however, only the time principals spend evaluating and planning math programs is positively related to student achievement gains. The other variables are either negative or statistically insignificant.

Conclusions

We began this chapter with the premise that in order for teacher collective bargaining to influence student outcomes, the effect of collective bargaining must be experienced in the classroom. We explored the scope and trends of collective bargaining and identified aspects of bargaining agreements that could affect the educational process. We continued the investigation by determining which of the variables that are potentially influenced by collective bargaining are also significant determinants of student achievement. As one might suspect, a critique of past studies and our own analysis indicates that teachers and students are the primary actors in the educational process. The interaction of these two parties is affected by the allocation of resources and by the incentive mechanisms embodied in the institutional structure of school districts.

The findings point to a number of teacher- and principal-related factors that are important determinants of the educational process. Basing the importance of the educational determinants on the magnitude of the standardized beta coefficients reveals the ranking of inputs displayed in table 3–5. Among the factors that contribute positively to achievement gains, the time principals spend assessing and evaluating math programs ranks first, followed closely by the time teachers spend in instruction. The next highest ranked determinants are related to the experience of principals. The teacher/student ratio is next, followed by the time teachers spend in preparation. Finally, teacher experience ranks last among the teacher and principal characteristics with significant effects on student achievement.

Of those factors negatively related to achievement gains, the effects of the highest degree attained by teachers and principals rank first and second, respectively. The number of administrators per student ranks third.

We conclude, therefore, that if collective bargaining affects these factors, especially the highest ranked factors, in significant ways, then collective bargaining will affect student achievement, unless offsetting effects

Table 3-5
Ranking of Important Inputs into the Educational Production Function

Inputs that Positively Affect Student-Achievement Gains	
Time principals spend assessing and evaluating math program	(0.036)
Time teachers spend in instruction	(0.032)
Total experience of principals as administrators	(0.030)
Total experience of principals as teachers	(0.024)
Teacher/student ratio	(0.024)
Time teachers spend in preparation	(0.017)
Total experience of teachers	(0.013)

Inputs that Negatively Affect Student-Achievement Gains	
Highest degree attained by teacher	(-0.031)
Highest degree attained by principal	(-0.022)
Administrator/student ratio	(-0.019)

Note: Only school-related inputs were included in the rankings. Standardized betas in parentheses.

occur. The purpose of the next two chapters is to explore the link between collective bargaining and the two factors we find to be major determinants of student achievement—teachers and administrators.

Notes

1. A partial list of studies includes (1) for class size: Hall and Carroll (1973), Chambers (1975), and Cresswell and others (1978); (2) studies on provisions for salaries and fringes: Baird and Landon (1972), Lipsky and Drotning (1973), and Kasper (1970); (3) for teacher attitudes: Alluto and Belasco (1974), Herndon (1976) and Lortie (1977) (although the latter two do not address unionization directly); for teacher time: Eberts (forthcoming); and (4) for administrative leadership: Randles (1975) and Nicholson and Nasstrom (1974).

2. Cresswell, in a survey of the teacher's collective-bargaining literature, confirms our observation: "We found no studies which attempted to examine the question directly" (1980:60).

3. Cohn (1979), in his textbook *The Economics of Education,* lists no fewer than 65 specific production function studies. Undoubtedly, there are more. Four somewhat representative studies are Coleman (1966), Hanushek (1970), Murnane (1975), and A. Summers and Wolfe (1977).

4. The tests that were administered were the "Comprehensive Tests of Basic Skills" published by CTB/McGraw-Hill. Scores from tests covering both mathematics concepts and computations were used.

5. A standardized parameter estimate is a parameter estimate multiplied by the standard deviation of the associated regressor and divided by the standard deviation of the variable regressed. It can be interpreted as the increase in student achievement attributed to an increase of one standard deviation of the associated input. Since the magnitude of all coefficients are in essence standardized by a uniform unit of change (one standard deviation) the magnitudes of the coefficients can be compared.

6. We report in chapter 4 that teachers covered by collective bargaining devote less time to instruction but more time to preparation than teachers not covered. If these were the only variables altered by collective bargaining we would conclude that collective bargaining decreases student achievement. Many other variables come into play, however, and we will take these into account in chapter 6.

# 4

Teachers and Collective Bargaining

Some researchers have argued that collective bargaining has no systematic effects for teachers, that the consequences of bargaining exhibit no consistent patterns in salaries, fringe benefits, working conditions, the operation of schools, or educational policy.[1] In this view each district and teacher union is an isolated chapter in the mystery of collective bargaining. To accept this view, we must perceive the explosion of collective bargaining in public schools as an act of self-delusion or compulsion on the part of teachers, something akin to a hula hoop craze or a lemming run. We reject this view—if collective bargaining were generally unpredictable and ineffective, surely the sham would have been discovered by now. Instead we argue that collective bargaining is what it appears to be—a means of focusing the collective power of teachers to resolve issues that concern them in systematic, predictable ways.

Accordingly this chapter examines collective bargaining as it relates to teachers. The first section evaluates and tests alternative models of labor contracts and examines the issue of trade-offs among salaries, fringe benefits, and working conditions. The next section presents estimates and possible explanations of trends in the union-nonunion salary differential, as well as evidence on the strength of teacher unions compared to private-sector unions. The third section explores the intangible, but important, relationship between collective bargaining and teachers' attitudes. Next, a more general assessment of teacher labor markets is provided by examining teachers' mobility and wage equilibration and the influence of district policies and contract provisions. A final section briefly summarizes our major conclusions.

Labor Contracts, Compensation, and Working Conditions

In the industrial relations literature two fundamentally different models of collective bargaining have been offered as explanations for labor-contract outcomes. The *demand-constraint model* sets the employers' demand curve for labor as the constraint facing a union seeking to maximize both compensation and employment (e.g., Dertouzos and Pencavel 1981). Since the

demand curve is downward-sloping, higher compensation, for example, means lower potential employment, everything else the same. Thus the union assumes the relatively passive role of simply selecting the preferred point on the employers' demand curve.

Alternatively the *contract-curve model* suggests that unions are able, through the use of increasingly effective employment-security provisions, to move beyond the employers' demand curve and outward along a contract curve defined by points of tangency between the firm's isoprofit curves and the union's isoutility curves (e.g., McDonald and Solow 1981). Thus the union faces a greater range of alternatives than in the demand-constraint model. An isoprofit curve is a locus of points representing the same level of profit (or an equivalent measure for public-sector activities). By definition, profit remains the same along any one isoprofit curve. Under standard assumptions isoprofit curves are shaped like an inverted U, as illustrated in figure 4–1. Isoprofit curves closer to the horizontal (employment) axis rep-

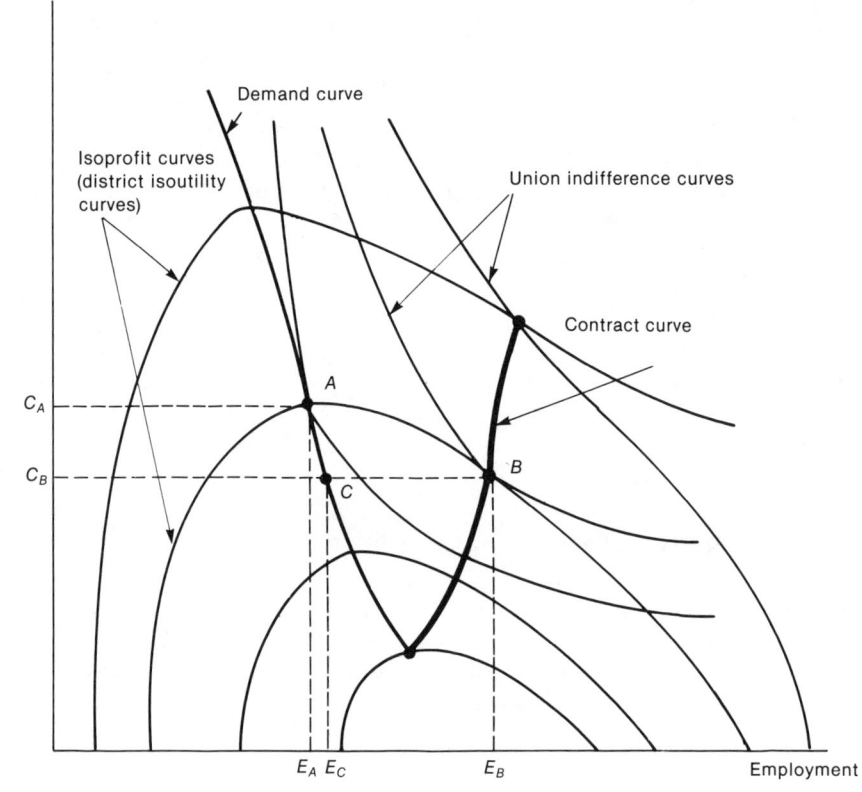

Figure 4–1. Diagram of Contract-Curve Model

resent higher levels of profit. The ridge of these curves (the locus of the highest points) is the standard demand curve for labor. A union's isoutility curve is a locus of points representing various combinations that yield the same level of satisfaction or utility—that is, combinations to which the union is indifferent. Under standard assumptions, unions' isoutility curves have negative slopes and are bowed toward the origin, as illustrated in figure 4–1. Isoutility curves farther away from the origin represent higher levels of utility.

The highest indifference curve the union can reach in the demand-constraint model is the one just tangent to the demand curve (see point A in figure 4–1). However, contracts that make one party better off as compared to point A and leave the other party at least as well off are possible in the shaded lens area to the southeast of point A. At point B, for example, the union is clearly better off (since it has reached a higher isoutility curve) and the employer is no worse off (since profit is the same at points A and B). Points such as B, where the isoprofit curve is tangent to a union indifference curve, are referred to as *efficient* because one party cannot be made better off without making the other party worse off. The locus of such points is called the *contract curve*.

In the demand-constraint model, point A can be reached by bargaining only over the level of compensation, since the employer will voluntarily set employment at E_A if compensation is set by the contract at C_A. Point B, however, cannot be reached in this fashion. If the contract only sets the compensation level C_B, the employer will voluntarily set employment only at E_B, rather than at E_C, since profit is higher at the lower level of employment. Hence various restrictions on employment (employment-security provisions) are required to reach efficient bargains such as point B because employment is excessive from the employer's perspective at every point on the contract curve beyond the demand curve.

Despite the widespread application of the demand-constraint model and the significant, but less widespread, interest in the contract-curve model, no empirical tests have been performed (for public school districts or for labor relations in general) to discriminate between the two models. In addition, the models have not been extended to account for multidimensional compensation, including salary, fringe benefits, working conditions, and employment-security provisions. In the remainder of this section we describe the contract-curve model in the context of school district contracts, extend the model to account for multidimensional compensation, and derive predictions from the model that discriminate it from the demand-constraint model. Next we present estimates of the model that enable us both to test it against the demand-constraint model and to address the issue of possible trade-offs among salary, fringe benefits, working conditions, and employment-security provisions. Finally we discuss a few of the limitations to our analysis.

Model of Efficient District Contracts

We choose to test the nature of district labor contracts within the contract-curve framework since it appears to best describe the institutional structure of public schools. Two features of internal labor markets of public schools may help to promote efficient bargains. The first of these is the universal adoption of a tenure system that constrains the district's employment decisions. Under ordinary enrollment changes, natural attrition of the workforce tends to insulate tenured teachers against layoff. The second is the presence in many collective-bargaining agreements of employment-related provisions such as reduction-in-force procedures and class-size limitation measures. These provisions deal primarily with the contingencies associated with extraordinary enrollment changes. If employment-related provisions do indeed promote efficient bargains, as MacDonald and Solow suggest for the contract-curve model, three effects should occur: the presence of the tenure system should place all districts on or near the contract curve; the adoption by some districts of a reduction-in-force or class-size provision should, all else the same, move the bargaining position in favor of the union; and the presence of favorable job characteristics should be offset by compensating variations in other elements of the job package. On the other hand, if employment-related provisions do not promote efficient bargains, but are simply job characteristics, which have implicit prices in negotiations, such provisions will be offset by compensating variations. This result would support the demand-constraint model.

Our model of efficient bargains is derived in four major steps (the formal mathematical derivation is presented in the appendix to this chapter). First, we derive the contract curve for local public school districts. Although taxpayers do not hire teachers directly, we assume that district administrators act as agents for taxpayers in providing them with educational services. Thus employment decisions regarding teachers are ultimately determined by the preferences of taxpayers and the constraints they face. By assuming that taxpayers as a group make decisions commensurate with the preferences of the median voter, the derivation of the taxpayers' utility function can focus on a single taxpayer. We assume that a taxpayer maximizes utility based on educational services and a composite private consumption good subject to his share of the total district education costs and wealth. Educational services are a positive function of the teacher/student ratio and other inputs. By taking the educational process (or technology) as predetermined by the district administrators, taxpayers choose the level of educational services and private consumption by implicitly choosing (through the district administrator) the teacher/student ratio and the level of other inputs.

In this framework, the cost-minimizing labor-demand curve is the locus

of points of tangency between the district isoutility curve and the horizontal wage lines—that is, the ridge of the district isoutility curves. The union's isoutility curves are downward-sloping and bowed toward the origin, as in figure 4-1. The contract curve for efficient bargains is derived by setting the slopes of the isoutility curves for the employer and the union equal for common values of compensation and employment.

Second, to identify the distribution of consumer/producer surplus between the taxpayers and union members, we specify the determinants of bargaining strength. Under the assumption that the contract curve is upward sloping, the total wage bill relative to the (hypothetical) competitive wage bill is a measure of a union's bargaining strength. This relation is only an identity, however, not a theory or explanation of bargaining strength. For an explanation we turn to a fundamental prediction of the contract-curve model—that increasingly effective employment-security provisions are required to move negotiated contracts outward along the contract curve, improving the relative position of the union. Hence we specify the index of bargaining strength as a function of various employment-security provisions and other factors likely to be associated with bargaining strength (enrollment trends, total expenditures per student, and proportion of total budget devoted to personnel costs).

Third, to account for multidimensional job and teacher attributes, we introduce a hedonic wage equation. The observed salary of teachers is not the full measure of compensation from employment. Total compensation is not directly measurable and consists of teacher salary, fringe benefits, and numerous other job attributes. In addition the productive attributes of teachers are also heterogeneous. To deal with all these problems, we appeal to the hedonic wage literature (e.g., Antos and Rosen 1975). In the hedonic approach the exchange value placed by employees and employers on attributes of the job package depends upon the preferences of employees and the associated direct and indirect costs to the employer. The exchange value of teacher attributes depends upon the costs to employees of acquiring the attributes and the benefits to the employer associated with the attributes.

The coefficients of the hedonic wage equation represent the implicit exchange value of a particular element of the job package in terms of salary. Under perfect competition, each coefficient is simply the price established by competitive market equilibration. In a bargaining context, the trade-offs are established by negotiations within each district, with partial insulation from external market forces. Since both preferences and costs tend to vary across districts, the hedonic coefficients are more properly interpreted for a cross-section of districts as the average of the implicit prices established in each district, rather than as a single market price.

Finally, we derive the reduced-form equation for salary. If the primary effect of employment-security provisions is to move the bargaining position

along the contract curve in favor of the union, then these provisions will be positively related to salary, consistent with our hedonic version of the contract-curve model. A hedonic version of the demand-constraint model, however, leads to an inverse relationship between employment-security provisions and salary, since in this model the provisions are simply job characteristics that have implicit prices in negotiations and have no role in establishing efficient bargains.

We rely upon a reduced-form equation rather than a set of structural equations (the underlying district and union utility functions, the bargaining strength equation, and the hedonic wage function) because the central issue here is movement along the contract curve rather than identification of the full structure. Identification of the structure is unlikely in any case. A wage equation is used, rather than an employment equation, since wages are specific to individuals, hence offer the detail required to account for individual teacher attributes. The level of employment on the other hand is purely district-specific and does not permit accurate analysis of individual teacher characteristics. Although measures of the average teacher characteristics in a district could be included in an employment equation, there are no theoretical predictions for the effects of such aggregated variables (the full joint distribution is also required).

Empirical Test

Our analysis is based upon data obtained from the New York State Department of Education for the school years 1972–73 and 1976–77. From the population of all elementary and secondary classroom teachers, we drew a random sample of those who were employed full time in the same district in both 1972–73 and 1976–77.[2] The two years of matched data permit the use of a fixed-effects model to account for unobserved, but fixed, individual-specific (hence also district-specific) variables. In addition, these data permit a more detailed specification of hedonic salary equations than is usually possible.

We specify the hedonic salary equation in traditional semilogarithmic form—all monetary values are expressed as logarithms and remaining variables are generally expressed in level or dummy-variable form. Since we rely upon a fixed-effects model, all variables are measured as the difference between the 1972–73 and 1976–77 values. Variable names, definitions, and sample means are presented in table 4–1. The independent variables are grouped into four categories: bargaining strength, teacher attributes, job attributes, and other (primarily district-related) variables.

The feature that distinguishes the contract-curve model from the demand-constraint model lies not in the variables included in the two

Table 4–1
Estimates of Hedonic Wage Equation

Variable	Definition	Mean	Coefficient
Independent variables			
Bargaining strength			
GCSIZE	Gained class-size provision	.032	.012 (2.20)
LCSIZE	Lost class-size provision	.101	− .005 (− 1.28)
ACSIZE	Always had class-size provision	.635	.013 (5.35)
GRIF	Gained RIF provision	.388	.007 (2.83)
LFRIF	Lost RIF provision	.038	− .008 (− 1.40)
ARIF	Always had RIF provision	.135	.021 (6.38)
I*GCSIZE	(Increasing enrollment) × (Gained class size)	.012	− .016 (− 1.40)
I*LCSIZE	(Increasing enrollment) × (Lost class size)	.019	.033 (4.28)
I*ACSIZE	(Increasing enrollment) × (Always had class size)	.156	− .006 (− 1.38)
I*GRIF	(Increasing enrollment) × (Gained RIF)	.089	− .004 (− .89)
I*LRIF	(Increasing enrollment) × (Lost RIF)	.005	.016 (1.14)
I*ARIF	(Increasing enrollment) × (Always had RIF)	.033	− .0004 (− .06)
Δ SHARE	Change in share of total budget going to personnel	− .039	.284 (19.66)
Teacher attributes			
Δ ED	Change in educational attainment of teachers	.416	.024 (14.92)
Δ EDSQ	(Education 1976)^2 − (Education 1972)^2	.965	.006 (10.44)
ED72	Educational attainment 1972	1.14	− .009 (− 9.43)
Δ EXPSQ	(Within-district EXP 1976)^2 − (Within-district EXP 1972)^2	83.23	− .001 (− 32.28)
LEFT	Value = 1 if teacher left district between 1972 and 1976	.071	− .014 (− 4.00)
Job attributes			
Δ TENURE	Value = 1 if teacher gained tenure between 1972 and 1976	.264	.024 (9.70)
Δ LEAVE	(Leave provisions 1976) − (Leave provisions 1972)	.156	− .002 (− 2.45)

Table 4–1 continued

Variable	Definition	Mean	Coefficient
Δ HEALTH	Log($ health benefits 1976) – Log($ health benefits 1972)	.682	–.036 (–8.28)
Δ OTHER	Log($ other benefits 1976) – Log($ other benefits 1972)	.465	–.002 (–2.41)
Δ T/E	Change in teacher/student ratio	.002	–3.61 (–12.21)
Other			
Δ LOGENR	Change in log of student enrollments	–.057	.308 (3.23)
Δ LOGESQ	$(\text{Log(ENR 1976)}^2) - (\text{Log(ENR 1972)}^2)$	–.979	–.010 (–1.79)
Δ LOGBUD	Change in log of total operating expenditures per student	.342	.382 (22.35)
Δ BLACK	Change in percentage of black teachers in district	.001	.773 (4.87)
Δ DROP	Change in dropout rate	.043	.007 (2.95)
Intercept		—	.299 (47.50)
Dependent variable			
LOGS	Change in the log of annual salary	.343	
R^2			.437
Number of observations			7,396

Note: t-statistics in parentheses below coefficients. Data provided by the New York State Department of Education. All changes not otherwise specified are between 1972 and 1976. See text for additional explanation of each variable.

models, but in the qualitative predictions for the employment-related contract provisions. For our data these include contract provisions that limit class size (GCSIZE for gaining the provision, LCSIZE for losing the provision, and ACSIZE for always having the provision) or that establish reduction-in-force (RIF) procedures (GRIF for gaining the provision, LRIF for losing the provision, and ARIF for always having the provision). Because of the enrollment-contingent nature of these contract provisions, they are interacted with a dummy variable for increasing district enrollments. Also included is the change in the proportion of the district budget devoted to personnel costs (Δ SHARE), which is related both to bargaining strength and to the price and level of other productive inputs. The contract-curve model predicts significantly *positive* coefficients for the employment-related provision.[3] The demand-constraint model, on the other hand, pre-

dicts that these variables will induce compensating differentials, yielding significantly *negative* coefficients.

Both models predict that other teacher and job attribute coefficients will indicate compensating differentials. Thus the power of our test of the two models lies in obtaining estimates of the signs of the coefficients for the employment-related (bargaining strength) variables, which will discriminate the two models, while concurrently obtaining estimates of the signs of the coefficients for teacher and job attributes (not hypothesized to be related to bargaining strength) consistent with the compensating differentials predicted by hedonic versions of both models.

Our measures of teacher attributes are change in level of education (ΔED-with less than a bachelor's degree equal to zero, bachelor's degree equal to one, master's degree (or thirty graduate hours) equal to two, and master's degree plus thirty hours (or Ph.D.) equal to three); change in education squared (ΔEDSQ); initial education (ED—included due to significant change in the coefficient for education between 1972–73 and 1976–77); the change in the squared term for experience (ΔEXPSQ); and a binary variable indicating if the teacher left the district temporarily during the period (ΔLEFT). Change in experience is the same for everyone, hence omitted from the regression.

The job-attribute variables available and included in the regression are change in tenure (ΔTENURE—the criteria are set by state policy), change in paid leave days (ΔLEAVE), change in the (log) of the cost of health coverage (ΔHEALTH), change in the (log) of the cost of other personnel-related expenditures (ΔOTHER), and the change in the teacher/student ratio (ΔT/E). The common inflationary trend in the nominal monetary values of these variables will be captured by the intercept.

Finally an assortment of other district-related variables are also included. These are the change in the (log) of enrollment (ΔLOGENR), change in the square of the log of enrollment (ΔLOGESQ); change in the log of the total budget (ΔLOGBUD); change in the proportion of black teachers (ΔBLACK); and change in the dropout rate (ΔDROP).[4]

The coefficient estimates presented in table 4–1 support the predictions of the contract-curve model: the coefficients for GCSIZE, ACSIZE, GRIF, and ARIF are significantly positive (at the 5 percent level or better). The LCSIZE and LRIF coefficients are insignificant, and the coefficient for the change in the proportion of the budget devoted to personnel cost is significantly positive.[5] All but one of the coefficients for the interacted variables are insignificant (the exception is I*LCSIZE). Consistent with the predictions of both the contract-curve and demand-constraint models, coefficients for the teacher-attribute variables are all significant with the expected sign (where expectations are present), and coefficients for the job-attribute variables indicate hedonic compensating differentials for ΔLEAVE,

Δ HEALTH, Δ OTHER, and Δ T/E.[6] The significantly positive coefficient for change in tenure (Δ TENURE) reflects the premium associated with having tenure (or the discount associated with not having tenure). Finally, although the results for the other district-related variables appear consistent with what one might expect, we do not attempt to interpret their reduced-form effects.

To summarize, first, the employment-related contract provisions enter the regression with signs supporting the bargaining-strength predictions of the contract-curve model rather than the compensating-differential predictions of the demand-constraint model. Second, the teacher- and job-attribute variables all enter the regression with signs consistent with the compensating differentials predicted by both models. The second set of results reinforces the validity of the first set as a discriminating test of the two models and provides estimates of compensating differentials not commonly found in similar studies.[7] The strong showing for compensating differentials is probably due to the fact that we focus on a single occupation and to the availability of both worker- and employer-specific data, which permit the use of a fixed-effects model.

Limitations

One limitation to the general applicability of our results is the argument offered by Hall and Lillien (1979) that unions can move beyond the employer's demand curve without the aid of explicit employment-related contract provisions (or at least without provisions contingent upon market conditions facing the firm). This would be true, for example, if employees who form the union constituency are nearly indifferent between employment and (temporary) unemployment. As Hall and Lillien point out, public and private unemployment compensation may play a role in establishing this indifference for some private-sector industries. The degree to which efficient labor contracts require explicit employment-related provisions depends in part on the market conditions facing the firm. Standard seniority and tenure restrictions (even implicit ones), for example, may be sufficient to establish bargains on the contract curve if the natural attrition rate of the workforce and product-market conditions virtually guarantee continued employment for workers forming the union constituency. In declining sectors, however, more restrictive employment-related provisions may be required. Results in table 4-1 can be interpreted as providing some evidence, albeit weak, to support the Hall-Lillien argument—the employment-related contract provisions appear to play a less significant role as bargaining-strength variables in increasing enrollment districts. Thus in

districts with strong and persistent increases in enrollment, the evidence for the Hall-Lillien arguments might be stronger.

A second possible limitation is the intractable issue of simultaneity. Although many teacher and job attributes can be considered strictly predetermined, some cannot. Our rationale for specifying salary as the dependent variable in the estimated reduced-form equation is that, in periods of relatively strong inflation (such as the mid-1970s), salary is probably the most flexible, hence least predetermined, variable in the system. Even so, our coefficient estimates should be interpreted qualitatively, based on sign, rather than as unbiased point estimates.

The Union-Nonunion Salary Differential

In the previous section we investigated the nature of district contracts, the importance of employment-security provisions, and the various trade-offs among salary, fringe benefits, and working conditions. In this section we attempt both to measure and to explain the degree to which teacher unions are able to raise compensation for their members above that for comparable nonunion teachers. Proponents of the weak-union view of teacher unions argue that wage demands by teachers are severely constrained by the tax-revolt spirit of public opinion. Equally important to this view, however, is the argument that teachers have a nonunion mindset, in which union membership and activity are seen as inappropriate and incompatible with professionalism. An alternative, strong-union view of teacher unions suggests that such unions play a key role in the political process, threatening to make an end run around normal collective-bargaining procedures by making wages and other benefits issues in their support for candidates and public officials. Politicians and public administrators are presumed to be more responsive to the highly focused benefit demands of an organized minority than to the broader concerns of the public at large, in part because the costs of conceding to union demands are diffused over time and over many taxpayers, while the costs to the public of enduring a strike are intensive and immediate. In addition the demand for education services is typically a legal monopoly or near-monopoly.[8]

Virtually all the empirical research conducted thus far indicates that teacher unions increase relative wages only marginally.[9] Perry (1979), for example, recently concluded in a study of nine diverse school districts that the impact of collective bargaining on "average teacher salary, overall budget size, and percent of budget devoted to teacher salaries has not yet been substantial in aggregate terms." In this section we present new evidence that indicates a significant increase in the union premium during the 1970s, evidence that tends to dispel the weak-union paradigm of teacher unions.[10]

Measuring the Union-Nonunion Differential

We employ two different techniques for measuring the impact unionism has on relative wages. The first is a traditional method based upon cross-section wage regressions of the type:

$$\text{LnWAGE}_t = X_t\,\beta_t + U_t\,\gamma_t + \epsilon_t, \tag{4.1}$$

where LnWAGE is the natural logarithm of the wage per hour, X is a vector of personal and job-related characteristics, β is a vector of corresponding coefficients, U is a binary variable indicating union membership for each teacher, γ is the union membership coefficient, and ϵ is the error term in time period t.[11] The equation is specified in the traditional semilog form, and estimates of γ approximate the proportionate impact of unionism on relative wages.

Unfortunately, not all relevant personal characteristics are observed for each teacher. In national samples, usually only race, sex, experience, education, and grade range taught (or specialty) are known. If a union wage premium does exist, then employers of union workers are likely to hire more selectively than otherwise, increasing the quality of their workforce. Moreover, if employers have more information about teacher applicants than is contained in the data sets available to researchers, unmeasured personal characteristics embedded in the error term will be correlated with U, biasing the estimate of γ upward.

We can minimize this source of bias by employing a method suggested by Mellow (1981) that is based upon wage changes rather than wage levels. Here we use this method to measure the wage change associated with becoming a union member. If one begins with a sample of nonunion teachers in one period and observes the same teachers in a subsequent time period $(t + 1)$, the following equation can be identified:

$$\text{LnWAGE}_{t+1} = X_{t+1}\,\beta_{t+1} + U_{t+1}\,\gamma_{t+1} + \epsilon_{t+1}. \tag{4.2}$$

Subtracting equation (4.1) from equation (4.2) and regrouping terms yields the following difference equation:

$$
\begin{aligned}
\text{LnWAGE}_{t+1} - LnWAGE_t = {} & (X_{t+1} - X_t)\beta_{t+1} + X_t(\beta_{t+1} - \beta_t) \\
& + (U_{t+1} - U_t)\gamma_{t+1} \\
& + U_t(\gamma_{t+1} - \gamma_t) + \phi,
\end{aligned}
\tag{4.3}
$$

where ϕ equals ϵ_{t+1} minus ϵ_t. In this formulation the effects are decomposed into those resulting from changes in the variables and those resulting from changes in the coefficients. Unmeasured personal characteristics com-

mon to both ϵ_{t+1} and ϵ_t and affecting wages similarly in both periods are netted out of ϕ, the wage-change error term. Thus the correlation between U and ϵ induced by these unmeasured personal characteristics (and the resulting upward bias in estimates of γ) is eliminated. Hence we also obtain estimates of the union premium based upon the wage change associated with becoming a union member.

These two alternatives approaches (wage-level regressions versus wage-change regressions) differ in other respects. Wage-level regressions provide estimates of the union wage premium for the average member. Wage-change regressions, however, provide estimates more akin to the marginal premium, since a change in union membership (in our case, becoming a union member) is used to estimate the premium.[12] The average premium is likely to exceed the marginal, since mobility and competition between union and nonunion sectors is usually strongest for entry positions. Moreover, since union membership expanded during the period we examine, some of the new union members are members of new unions not yet well-established. Hence the union premium may still be quite small for these teachers. On these grounds we would expect the wage-change approach to provide a lower estimate of the impact of unionism on relative wages.

Estimates of the Differential

The data used to estimate equations (4.1) and (4.3) are taken from the Current Population Survey (CPS). The CPS is a stratified random sample of about 56,000 households taken monthly by the U.S. Bureau of Census. In the past, the May survey has contained information on the wages and union membership of household members. Because the CPS also has some limited longitudinal or panel properties, it is possible to match respondents in May surveys a year apart. This property enables us to estimate equation (4.3), the wage-change equation, based upon those teachers employed in both years. The years 1974 and 1977 are used for the wage-level regressions, and the years 1974–75 and 1977–78 for the wage change regressions. The CPS includes union-membership status in all years, but coverage by a collective-bargaining contract only in 1977.[13] Estimates for 1977 based on coverage, however, are also discussed (but not presented). Job-specific information is limited in the CPS to occupation (grade range taught or specialty) and geographic location (state/region, large metropolitan city).

Variables used in the wage-level regressions for kindergarten through secondary teachers in 1974 and 1977 are listed along with their definitions and sample means in table 4–2.[14] Twenty-six state/region binary variables are not listed, but those that are significant at the 5 percent level are included in the final regressions. Table 4–2 also presents the results of the

Table 4–2
Wage-Level Regressions for 1974 and 1977

Independent Variable	Definition	Mean		Coefficient	
		1974	1977	1974	1977
Intercept	——	——	——	.01 (.05)	.51*** (3.98)
RACE	One if nonwhite, zero	.07	.08	.05 (.97)	.05 (1.10)
EXP	Years of experience (proxied by age minus education minus 6)	16.14	13.75	.03*** (3.68)	.02*** (3.49)
EXPSQ	EXP squared	407.15	313.20	−.0005** (−2.37)	−.0003* (−1.61)
SEX	One if female, zero otherwise	.72	.70	.01 (.18)	−.11** (−1.97)
FEXP	(EXP) × (SEX)	12.42	9.98	−.01* (−1.48)	−.001 (−.09)
FEXPSQ	FEXP squared	329.28	234.71	.0003 (1.18)	−.0001 (−.69)
EDUC	Years of education completed	16.39	16.27	.08*** (7.01)	.06*** (9.00)
LSMSA	One if in one of 44 largest SMSAs; zero otherwise	.67	.35	.12*** (3.56)	.10*** (3.95)
UNION	One if member of union (or association similar to a union) at primary job; zero otherwise	.30	.45	.07** (1.89)	.21*** (8.79)
SEC	One if secondary teacher; zero otherwise	.40	.41	−.10** (−2.01)	−.14*** (−3.53)
ELEM	One if elementary teacher; zero otherwise	.45	.40	−.13*** (−2.67)	−.14*** (−3.45)
KIND	One if kindergarten teacher; zero otherwise	.05	.09	−.22*** (−2.69)	−.26*** (−4.81)
R^2				.34	.35
Number of observations				617	1037

Note: t-values in parentheses. The dependent variable is the natural logarithm of the hourly wage; mean is 1.57 in 1974 and 1.69 in 1977. Coefficients are ordinary-least-squares estimates. The omitted dummy variable for the SEC, ELEM, and KIND variables is OTHER (special education teachers, adult education teachers, and librarians). Dummy variables for twenty-six states/regions are not reported here, but those significant at the 0.05 level are included in the regressions. Thus New York, New Jersey, and Illinois are included in both years; Michigan, North Carolina, and California only in 1974; and Massachusetts, Ohio, and the northwest region only in 1977. Data are from the Current Population Survey.

*Significant at the 0.10 level, one- or two-tail test, as appropriate.

**Significant at the 0.05 level, one- or two-tail test, as appropriate.

***Significant at the 0.01 level, one- or two-tail test, as appropriate.

wage-level regressions for teachers for the years 1974 and 1977. The signs, magnitudes, and significance levels of most of the coefficients for the traditional wage-determining variables are generally as expected and are not discussed here. For 1974 the estimated union wage premium is about 7 percent (significant at the 5 percent level, one-tail test). For 1977, however, the estimated premium is 21 percent (significant at the 1 percent level, one-tail test). The estimated premium in 1977 based upon coverage by a collective-bargaining agreement is 22 percent, consistent with the 21 percent union membership estimate.[15] Based upon the union-membership regression equations, the teacher/union premium rose by 14 percentage points from 1974 to 1977 (a change significant at the 1 percent level, two-tail test).[16] The 1974 estimate of the union premium is generally consistent with earlier studies, but the 1977 estimate indicates a dramatic increase in the premium.

Estimates of the wage-change equation, (4.3), confirm the increase in the union premium suggested by the wage-level regressions. Beginning with a sample of nonunion teachers, we estimate the wage premium associated with their being union members one year later. These estimates and the means of the variables for the matched years 1974–75 and 1977–78 are presented in table 4–3. As expected, these estimated premiums are lower than those from the wage-level regressions. The estimated premium for a union joiner in 1974–75 is 4 percent (but insignificant), while in 1977–78 the estimated premium is 12 percent (significant at the 1 percent level, one-tail test). Hence the estimated change in the premium from 1974–75 to 1977–78 is 8 percentage points, but not statistically significant.[17] Most of the other coefficients in both wage-change regressions are insignificant, because they are estimates of the change from one year to the next in the corresponding coefficient in the wage-level equations.

Some Potential Limitations

Three potential limitations of our methodology remain to be discussed. First is the issue of simultaneity bias. A number of researchers have suggested that union membership and wages are simultaneously determined.[18] Hence simple regression estimates of the impact of unions on wages may be biased. To test for simultaneity bias we also obtained instrumental-variable estimates of the impact of unions on wages, employing a two-stage procedure to obtain consistent estimates. Using the logit procedure, we estimated a reduced-form equation predicting the probability of union membership (or of joining a union for the wage-change approach); then using the estimated probabilities from the first stage as instrumental variables, we estimated the wage (and wage-change) equations. The identifying variables are those detailed state/region binary variables not included in the relevant wage equation, but included in the union logit equation.[19] The union impact estimated in this way is 0.09 (t-statistic equals 0.88) for 1974 and 0.26 (t-sta-

Table 4-3
Wage-Change Regressions for 1974–75 and 1977–78

Independent Variables	Mean		Coefficient	
	1974–75	1977–78	1974–75	1977–78
Intercept	——	——	.10 (.35)	.19 (.71)
RACE	.08	.08	.09 (1.17)	−.07 (−.90
EXP	16.41	15.12	.00 (.01)	.02 (.99)
EXPSQ	408.70	353.37	−.0001 (−.18)	−.0005 (−1.23)
SEX	.73	.76	.04 (.41)	.07 (.56)
FEXP	12.81	11.43	−.01 (−.68)	−.02 (−.99)
FEXPSQ	331.79	266.25	.0003 (.80)	.0006* (1.36)
EDUC	16.42	16.22	−.003 (−.17)	−.02 (−1.18)
Δ EDUC	.18	.06	−.00 (−.13)	.00 (.02)
LSMSA	.59	.26	.02 (.54)	−.00 (−.10)
Union joiner	.14	.29	.04 (.60)	.12*** (2.54)
SEC	.42	.36	.05 (.62)	.00 (.06)
ELEM	.44	.48	.05 (.57)	.06 (.78)
KIND	.05	.06	−.10 (−.80)	.03 (.28)
R^2			.02	.06
Number of observations			318	233

Note: t-values in parentheses. The dependent variable is the natural logarithm of the ratio of the 1974 (1977) hourly wage to the 1975 (1978) hourly wage. Coefficients are ordinary-least-squares estimates, and the sample consists of teachers not union members in 1974 (1977).

*Significant at the 0.10 level, one- or two-tail test, as appropriate.

**Significant at the 0.05 level, one- or two-tail test, as appropriate.

***Significant at the 0.01 level, one- or two-tail test, as appropriate.

tistic equals 2.19) for 1977 for the wage-level regressions, and −0.14 (t-statistic equals −0.68) for 1974–75 and 0.31 (t-statistic equals 1.76) for 1977–78 for the wage-change regressions. None of these estimates are statis-

tically different from the corresponding ordinary-least-squares (OLS) estimates, suggesting that simultaneity bias may not be important for teachers.

A second potential limitation of our methodology is that we have not considered possible spillover benefits: those benefits that may accrue to unorganized teachers because of the bargaining efforts of others. Previous research suggests that these benefits increase with the proportion of teachers organized, which is directly associated with large urban areas and particular geographic regions.[20] Consequently failure to control for these effects should bias the estimates of the union-nonunion wage differential upward in the wage-level regressions, since the union-membership variable is directly correlated with union density. This problem is less likely to apply to the wage-change estimates, however, since spillover effects that are the same in the two adjacent years are eliminated. On these grounds the wage-level estimates should be closer to the sum of the union-nonunion differential and the spillover effect, and the wage-change estimates closer to the simple union-nonunion wage differential.

A final potential limitation is that the CPS data contain only salaries and usual hours worked, not the full benefit package provided teachers. For union members in the economy at large, fringe benefits are larger than for nonunion members, and there is some evidence that this is also true for teachers.[21] Omission of fringe benefits is likely to exert a downward influence on the estimates. Thus accounting for the total benefit package would likely strengthen the results, leaving our basic conclution intact.

Possible Explanations

Our results clearly suggest that the impact of unions on wages has increased dramatically. Moreover, the union premium for teachers appears at least as large as the union premium in the general economy.[22] At least three explanations for the increase seems plausible. First, during the period studied, existing unions may have matured and consolidated the power to negotiate increasingly favorable contracts. By 1974 many bargaining units were still relatively new, had negotiated only a few contracts, and may not have realized their full potential. By 1977-78, however, additional bargaining experience had been accumulated, and teachers, administrators, and the public were all at least more familiar with collective bargaining in education (if not more inclined to accept it). In fact the growth of unionism continued throughout the 1970s.

A second complementary explanation lies in the growth of state-level legislation favorable to teacher collective bargaining. As discussed earlier in chapter 2, the number of states with such legislation increased rapidly in the late 1960s and early 1970s and continued to increase during the period

studied. By 1973 twenty-four states had legislation clearly permitting teacher collective bargaining over terms and conditions of employment and going beyond mere meet-and-confer laws; fifteen states assigned significant roles in this regard to state public-employee-relations boards; and five states explicitly allowed teachers some rights to strike (U.S. Department of Labor 1972). By 1978 an additional seven states had legislation permitting explicit bargaining; an additional seven states had assigned roles to public-employee-relations boards; and one more state permitted strikes by teachers (Ross 1978). Thus by 1978, 61 percent of classroom teachers resided in states permitting formal collective bargaining in education (U.S. Department of Education 1980). One would expect these legislative changes to facilitate the collective-bargaining process for teachers and to contribute to the strength of contracts negotiated.

To explore this issue the union-membership variable in the wage-level equations for 1974 and 1977 (4.1) can be interacted with a binary variable for the presence of a favorable state-level collective-bargaining law for teachers.[23] The regression results (not presented here) indicate that in 1974 *all* of the union-nonunion wage differential is due to the joint effect of union membership coefficient is now significant and approximately equal to the interaction effect. Thus the union premium did not grow more rapidly in those states with existing legislation, and a significant premium emerged by 1977 even in states without legislation. Hence the expansion of such legislation provides a significant, but partial, explanation for the increase in the union wage premium. Of course, higher wages might be associated with favorable collective-bargaining legislation simply because both are possible consequences of strong unions.

A third explanation may lie in the familiar observation that the union-nonunion wage differential in the economy at large tends to increase during periods of labor excess supply and decrease during periods of excess demand (Lewis 1963; Rees 1977; Moore and Raisian 1981). The labor market for teachers during the 1970s was generally characterized by persistent excess supply. Moreover, the inflation rate for the 1973–74 school year was 9.7 percent, more than twice the rate for the previous school year, and high rates of inflation continued throughout the 1970s (NEA 1980:7). Thus market forces placed strong downward pressure on real wages without putting comparable pressure on nominal wages. Under these circumstances, union objectives logially include maintenance of real wages for their members, and the union-nonunion wage differential could increase substantially without having either large real-wage increases for union members or nominal-wage decreases for nonunion members. Between the 1974–75 and 1977–78 school years the average teacher salary increased by approximately 22 percent, while the Consumer Price Index (CPI) increased by approximately 21 percent (NEA 1980:7). Since the union wage premium also increased during

this period, it is clear that the real wages of unionized teachers *increased* on average, while those of nonunionized teachers *declined*. Thus we suggest that inflationary pressures, excess teacher supply, growth in legislation favorable to collective bargaining, and maturation of teacher unions combined to yield a significant increase in the union-nonunion wage differential during the 1970s.

Teacher Attitudes, District Policies, and Collective Bargaining

Our discussion thus far in this chapter has been primarily in terms of economics, narrowly defined—as compensation, working conditions, and job security. The impact of collective bargaining, however, is more than this. Collective bargaining provides teachers both the opportunity to voice their opionions on a wide range of district and school issues and some degree of power to make their opinions count. Indeed it is the unions' function as a voice for their members that specialists in industrial relations typically highlight as the most fundamental contribution of collective organization (e.g., Hirschman 1970). The same point has been made explicitly for teachers (e.g., Moskow and others 1970). In fact industrial democracy, the process of providing workers with the opportunity for participating in both making and interpreting the rules under which they work, is one of the reasons most often cited for the growth of collective bargaining among teachers. As the president of one union local put it: "I think the increased ability to be heard is the most important thing to come out of bargaining" (Duckworth and DeBevoise 1982:21).

Why this is true seems obvious. Teachers have always derived much of their compensation in implicit, nonpecuniary ways. Many researchers (Herndon 1976, Lortie 1977, Duke and others 1979, and Alluto and Belasco 1974) have confirmed that teachers derive much psychological value from pedagogical and professional activities. Relationships between teacher and student, organization of the classroom, selection of curriculum and materials, nonteaching responsibilities, relationships between teacher and administrator, and the perceptions and pressures of parents and community are all important to teachers. Hence, as the whirlwind issues and problems swept through education during the last two decades, it is not surprising that teachers became increasingly dissatisfied with their profession. The degree of dissatisfaction has been documented by Donley (1976), Steele (1976), and McDonnell and Pascal (1979).

In this section we attempt both to measure and to explain differences in perceptions of the workplace between teachers covered by collective bargaining and those not covered. In a national survey more than 2000

teachers in over 200 schools were asked to respond to a number of questions concerning attitudes about their working environment (Systems Development Corporation 1978). The questions address two specific aspects: attitudes about the decisions and behavior of administrators and attitudes about the effectiveness of the school. The first category covers typical workplace issues, as well as issues of educational policy and practice; the second, however, stresses only the latter.

Two questions fall under the first category dealing with administration:

1. How satisfied are you with the way most decisions are made in your school? Teachers responded as follows: very satisfied (31 percent); somewhat satisfied (57 percent); and not satisfied (12 percent).
2. Which phrase best describes your principal's (or other members of the administrative staff) support of your work as a teacher? The responses were as follows: very supportive (59 percent); somewhat supportive (25 percent); neutral (9 percent); somewhat unsupportive (5 percent); and very unsupportive (3 percent).

Questions related to the second category, dealing with school effectiveness, as teachers to indicate their general feelings (i.e., strongly agree, agree, disagree, or strongly disagree) about the following statements.

1. Teachers in this school conduct effective instruction (26 percent, 65 percent, 2 percent, and 7 percent, respectively).
2. Teachers in this school work well together (28 percent, 55 percent, 2 percent, and 13 percent, respectively).
3. The school is a satisfying place in which to work (30 percent, 53 percent, 3 percent, 11 percent, respectively).
4. The programs are successful in meeting students' needs (23 percent, 53 percent, 6 percent, 14 percent, respectively).

The means of the responses to these questions are displayed in table 4-4 by union affiliation. In all cases except the question related to effective instruction, teachers covered by collective-bargaining agreements were significantly less enthusiastic about their schools than teachers not covered. (The difference in responses to the question on effectiveness instruction is not statistically significant.) For example when asked about their satisfaction with administrative decisions, the average response of teachers covered by collective bargaining was 2.15 (with a range of 1 to 3 for "not satisfied at all' to "very satisfied"), whereas the average response for nonunion teachers was 2.26. The difference between the means is statistically significant at the 0.01 level.

The obvious question raised by these findings is whether the difference in attitudes is the *result* or the *cause* of collective organization. We lean

Table 4–4

Difference in Means of Response of Union and Nonunion Teachers

	Union	Nonunion	t-Statistic
Satisfaction with decisions	2.15	2.26	− 4.01
Administrative support	4.26	4.43	− 4.25
Successful programs	2.42	2.66	− 5.68
Effective instruction	3.07	3.09	− .57
Work well together	2.92	3.00	− 2.04
Satisfying place	2.89	3.07	− 4.53

Note: t-statistics were computed assuming equal variances.

toward the view that the difference in attitudes is more likely to be a cause of organization. Farber and Saks (1980), for example, found that an individual's vote in local certification elections is affected both by the preunion level of satisfaction with workplace issues and by expectations about the effect organization is likely to have on these issues. For example, individuals currently dissatisfied, who expect organization to improve areas of concern, are obviously more likely to vote for collective bargaining than individuals currently satisfied, who expect organization to make things worse. Our position, however, does not mean that collective bargaining has not improved the satisfaction of organized teachers. It means that although organized teachers remain less satisfied than teachers in unorganized districts, they may be more satisfied than they were before they organized.

To pursue the issue of whether or not collective bargaining alters the structure of district policies or the attitudes of teachers about the way the district is run, we divide teachers covered by bargaining agreements into two groups, those covered by staffing and class-size provisions and those not covered. Next we test for significant differences in the responses of the two groups to the questions listed above. In only two cases, administrative support and ability to work well together, do the responses differ significantly. Teachers covered by staffing and class-size provisions felt that administrators were more supportive than teachers not covered. Teachers covered by the provisions, on the other hand, felt less able to work well with their colleagues.

The teachers listed a number of factors as explanations for their attitudes toward administrators and working conditions. To evaluate these factors, we employ regression analysis, which permits us to determine the direction and level of significance of their relationship between these factors and teacher attitudes. Again, we examine teachers covered by collective bargaining and those not covered separately. The results are displayed in table 4–5.

Table 4–5
Regression Analysis of Determinants of Selected Teacher Attitudes, by Union
Affiliation vs. Nonaffiliation

	Satisfaction with Decisions		Satisfying Place	
	Union	Nonunion	Union	Nonunion
Importance of teacher participation (I)	−	−	−	−
Teacher participation (D)				
D*I		+		
Hired to specific school		(+)		+
Hired by system/given choice		+	−	
Both school need and choice		+		
Teacher/school staff	+			
Parents/students			+	
Choose school	+	+	+	+
Class size	−		−	
Number of grades		+	+	
Exp/Pupil	(−)	−		−
Srace[a]				
Secon[b]				
Mrace[a]	+		+	
Mecon[b]			+	+
Mval[c]	(+)			
Sval[c]				+
R^2	.14	.10	.14	.08

Note: Plus or minus sign in parentheses indicates that the coefficient is significant at 0.10 level; otherwise significant at 0.05 level.

[a]The variables Mrace and Srace are the means and standard deviations, respectively, of the distribution of white students in the classroom.

[b]The variables Mecon and Secon are the means and standard deviations, respectively, of the distribution

Union and nonunion teachers placed the same weight on teacher participation. Also the ability to choose their assignment improved teachers' attitudes about decisions and administrative support. Personnel policies have
partly affected the attitudes of nonunion teachers about administrative
decisions and support, but not those of union teachers. Union teachers, on
the other hand, were more concerned with racial composition of schools,
with attitudes improving as the percentage of nonminority students increased. Union and nonunion teachers also differed about the ingredients
that make their school a satisfying place in which to work. Union teachers
were concerned about class size, whereas nonunion teachers were not. Both
groups of teachers were positively swayed by the economic status of the

Administrators' Support		Programs Successful		Effective Instruction		Work Well Together	
Union	Nonunion	Union	Nonunion	Union	Nonunion	Union	Nonunion
−	−	−	−	−	−	−	−
					−		
	+		+	+		+	
	(+)			(−)			
(−)	+					−	(−)
						+	
	+		(−)		−	+	
+	+						+
−		−	−		(−)		
			+		+		+
	−			+		+	−
			+		+	+	+
+			+	+		+	
		(+)	+		+		+
			+			−	(+)
.08	.07	.10	.09	.06	.07	.10	.08

of Orshansky Poverty index associated with students in each classroom. Lower value of index is associated with greater poverty.

[c]The variables Mval and Sval are the means and standard deviations, respectively, of the difference between post- and pretest scores of students in each classroom.

students. As before, teachers who felt strongly about participating in decisions were less satisfied with their working environment than teachers who gave participation a lower priority.

The results in table 4–5 suggest that the union status of teachers affects how they assess their working conditions. Teachers covered by collective bargaining appear to be less concerned with the personnel policies of the district than their nonunion colleagues. Perhaps this lack of interest is due to a greater reliance on the union to take care of personnel matters, as well as to more structured personnel practices in union districts. Union teachers, on the other hand, appear more sensitive to class size and the racial composition of the students than nonunion teachers. Concerns about class size

probably result from a conscious attempt on the part of the unions to educate teachers to be sensitive to this issue, since it is often a focal point in contract negotiations.

Teacher Labor Markets

The principal factors governing teacher labor markets have changed dramatically over the last three decades. During the 1950s and 1960s, teachers were in short supply, and personal and economic factors dominated the mobility of teachers. The abundance of teaching positions, along with general increases in real teacher salaries, gave teachers the opportunity to move into positions with more favorable salaries and working conditions. The late 1960s and early 1970s saw a reversal of these earlier trends. As enrollment growth turned to enrollment decline, personal and economic factors were sometimes displaced by district personnel policies and collective-bargaining provisions governing layoffs and transfers as the determinants of teacher turnover.

Thus to understand the possible consequences of collective bargaining for teachers, we must understand more about both the economic and institutional forces at work in teacher labor markets, as well as more about the relationship between these forces and collective bargaining. In this section, we provide a simple theoretical framework for the role of both market and institutional forces in teacher labor markets; we review the results of previous empirical studies; we present evidence on the role of market forces in teacher labor markets—the labor-market behavior of teachers and the wage-equilibration process; and finally we present evidence on the role of institutional forces in teacher labor markets—the separate and interactive roles of district policies and contract provisions. Both the market and institutional forces are examined under a variety of enrollment trends.

Theoretical Framework

The purpose of this brief theoretical discussion is to chart a simple theory of teacher labor markets that incorporates elements of both market and institutional forces. Three market considerations are particularly important—market equilibration, human capital, and internal labor markets. Market equilibration occurs in two complementary ways. Increases (decreases) in wage differentials between teaching and other occupations should increase (decrease) the probability that teachers will leave the profession, and similar changes in wage differentials among school districts should affect the probability that teachers will leave one district for employment in another. In

turn these movements of teachers, by easing excess demand in one area and excess supply in another, tend to restore earnings equilibrium. The change in wage differentials might only be an expected one—a projected change based on enrollment trends, other economic forces, district funding trends, and the like.

Explanations of teacher mobility to, from, and within school districts are also enhanced by human capital considerations. In the human-capital approach (e.g., Becker 1964), each individual is embodied with a valuable economic resource, human capital, that yields a stream of returns over his or her lifetime. Human capital can be partitioned into general and specific components. General human capital encompasses all those investments in education and training (formal and informal) that bring similar returns in different occupations. Specific human capital displays very different returns in different occupations, since the acquired knowledge is more germane to one occupation than another. The concept of specific human capital is relative. Knowledge of the idiosyncracies of a particular school principal, for example, is a form of human capital specific to a school. In education a master's degree is human capital that is specific to education, but not necessarily specific to different jobs within education.

The barriers to mobility created by the acquisition of specific human capital, as well as institutional and personal factors, tend to partition the educational labor market into partially autonomous submarkets or internal labor markets (see Kerr 1954). Within the education sector, for example, four internal labor markets are discernible. The first encompasses the primary and secondary teaching sector and is separate from all other occupations, including college-level teaching. The second is the teacher labor market delineated by the certification requirements of a particular state. The third consists of individual school districts—specific knowledge of district policies and procedures, salary schedules heavily weighted toward district tenure (which may or may not reflect district-specific human capital)—and vesting provisions of district retirement systems, all tending to impede movement across districts. The fourth internal labor market for teachers is the school; some nonpecuniary benefits from teaching, for example, might be school or even class-specific.

Institutional forces—that is, district policies and contract provisions established through collective bargaining—also play a dominant role in teacher labor markets. This is especially true as opportunities decline for voluntary movements between and within districts. The ability of teachers to move voluntarily within teaching is enhanced when teachers are in short supply. At that time there are more positions than teachers, hence greater opportunity for teachers to find assignments that match their preferences. When a shortage of teachers is replaced by a surplus, there are fewer opportunities to move to more desirable assignments, and in some cases teachers

are transferred or dismissed involuntarily. Districts that are forced to lay off teachers or transfer them involuntarily have instituted rules and procedures to perform these functions. In most states these rules reflect a combination of state labor law and collective-bargaining agreements.

Teacher mobility patterns will be influenced in different ways depending upon whether decisions to move are made voluntarily or involuntarily. For example, under conditions of increasing enrollment and an abundance of attractive alternative assignments, one would expect greater mobility at all levels of experience. Under declining enrollments, the reduction in the number of alternative positions reduces the probability that teachers can find an assignment that they find more attractive. Based on institutional forces (district policy and contract provisions), one would predict that teachers with low seniority would have a high transfer or dismissal rate under strong enrollment declines. This prediction follows from the bumping process that results from a reduction in teaching positions. Most locally negotiated reduction-in-force procedures call for staff layoffs inversely related to seniority. Seniority is also followed for granting assignments to teachers. Teachers with greater seniority are given the first opportunity of refusal whenever a position is vacated. In the case of declining enrollments and a low natural attrition rate of teachers, less-desirable positions are likely to be vacated before more-preferred assignments become available, since much of the turnover comes from the less senior teachers. We are concerned here with the ways in which various district policies influence teacher turnover (quits, transfers, and dismissals), the ways in which contract provisions established by collective bargaining (class-size and reduction-in-force provisions) influence turnover, and the interaction between district policies and contract provisions.

Previous Studies

In the past twenty years, a number of studies have emerged on teacher turnover. The more widely cited studies have been based on six databases: (1) a survey conducted by the U.S. Office of Education; (2) periodic surveys conducted by the National Education Association; (3) work by the Rand Corporation on the 1 percent sample of workers covered by Social Security in primary and secondary education; (4) an in-depth study of the San Diego School District also conducted by Rand; (5) an in-depth study of an anonymous school district by Murnane; and (6) a study of teacher turnover in Michigan by Greenberg and McCall.

The Office of Education studies were based on a survey of a stratified sample of over 2,000 school districts in 1957 and 1959. This study found the

rate of termination (or quits) to be about 8 percent between fall 1959 and fall 1960. The rate of transfers was around 5 percent for the same period. The study also showed that the termination and transfer rates were not greatly related to economic factors such as salaries and teacher/student ratios. They noted that the rate of termination was greater for small districts presumably because internal transfers are not as available in the smaller districts.

The NEA studies were based on questionnaires mailed periodically from 1955 to 1965 to a stratified sample of 2,000 teachers. The quit rate in these surveys varied from 7 percent to 11 percent and the transfer rates centered on 6 percent. The survey asked teachers why they decided to terminate. Over 70 percent of the teachers sampled cited personal reasons for their decisions to quit, while the remainder indicated they quit for economic reasons.

A 1 percent sample of wage earners in primary and secondary education covered by Social Security was constructed by the Rand Corporation for the years 1962–1966. Seven to 8 percent of the teachers in the sample were shown to terminate per year. It was also found that demographic factors were important in explaining terminations.

The Rand Corporation also conducted a study of teacher turnover in the San Diego school district between 1970 and 1972. In return for sacrificing the generality of their findings, this study was able to take a close look at the movements of teachers and the reasons for these changes. The analysis recorded far fewer teachers terminating (a 5 percent rate), but it confirmed earlier findings that personal characteristics of the teacher tend to be better indicators of terminations than economic conditions.

Murnane attempted to replicate the findings for San Diego by conducting an extensive survey of another large school district from 1965 to 1974. He found the rate of termination to be around 11 percent throughout the period. Transfer rates were 5 percent in 1965–1967 and increased to 7 percent in 1971–1974.

The Rand Corporation also conducted a study of teacher turnover in Michigan schools. Terminations averaged close to 10 percent a year from 1968 to 1971. Personal characteristics—females under 30, and male and females over 53—were found to be important.

Table 4-6 provides a comparison of the various rates of quits and transfers found by the first five of the six studies. The results are roughly consistent across the various studies, with the quit/termination rate averaging about 8 percent and the transfer rate about 6 percent. A major objective in the remainder of this section is to move beyond tabulations of turnover by education, experience, sex, etc., and attempt to explain various types of turnover first by market forces, then by institutional forces such as district policy and contract provisions.

Table 4-6

Comparison of Rates of Teacher Quits and Transfers from Selected Studies (%)

	Office of Education[a]	NEA[b]					Social Security Sample[c]	San Diego[d]		Murnane[e]		
	1957-59	1955	1957	1959	1964	1965	1962-66	1965-67	1971-74	1965-67	1968-70	1971-74
Quits	8	7	11	8	9	7	10	4.2	7.5	3.6	12.5	11.8
Transfers	5	6	6	5	7	6		5	7	5	6.2	6.9

Sources: [a]See Lindenfeld (1963).
[b]See NEA (1957, 1972).
[c]See Carroll (1973).
[d]See Greenberg and McCall (1973).
[e]See Murnane (1981).

Market Forces

The belief that educators are not responsive to wage differentials between teaching and other occupations or to differentials between districts within teaching is widespread. This belief, combined with apparently rigid wage structures within districts, leads to the related perception that wages for teachers are also unresponsive to these wage differentials, hence that existing differentials tend not to be eroded over time.

In this subsection we examine the wage determination process for educators and test four specific propositions.[24] The first two deal with interoccupational mobility and wage equilibration: (1) we test the degree to which educators are responsive to wage differentials between their teaching jobs and alternative occupations in deciding whether to leave teaching for other employment; and (2) we test if educators paid above (below) the wage they could expect in the economy at large experience less (greater) than average wage growth from one year to the next—that is, whether the existing premiums and discounts tend to be eroded. The second two propositions deal with interdistrict mobility and wage equilibration: (3) we test if educators are responsive to wage differentials within teaching in deciding whether to leave one school district for employment in another; and (4) we test if educators paid above (below) the average wage for educators with the same qualifications experience less (greater) than average wage growth from one school year to the next—that is, whether existing premiums and discounts *within* teaching also tend to be eroded. For all these tests, we deal exclusively with nonadministrative instructional personnel for kindergarten through the twelfth grade. Finally, we explore the relationship between interdistrict mobility and district enrollment trends.

Interoccupation Mobility and Wage Equilibration

Our empirical analysis of interoccupation mobility and wage equilibration is based upon the monthly Current Population Survey CPS taken by the U.S. Bureau of the Census. The CPS is a stratified random sample containing about 56,000 households. In the past the May survey has contained information on the wages and other related employment characteristics of household members. Because the CPS also has some limited longitudinal, or panel, properties, it is possible to match some respondents in May surveys a year apart. This property enables us to estimate wage-change equations based upon those teachers employed in adjacent years. The years 1974 and 1977 are used for wage-level regressions, and the years 1974–75 and 1977–78 for the occupational-mobility and wage-change analysis. Unfortunately, job-specific information for educators is limited to occupation

(grade range taught) and geographic location (state/region, large metropolitan city).

To obtain market wage differentials (the logarithmic difference between an educator's wage in teaching and the wage he or she could expect in the labor market at large), we estimate a standard cross-section wage equation of the form

$$Ln\ W = X\beta + \epsilon, \tag{4.4}$$

where Ln W is the natural logarithm of the individual's wage; X is a vector of personal and geographic characteristics, β is a corresponding vector of coefficients, and ϵ is the error term. (See for example Hanoch (1967) and Mincer (1974).) Table 4-7 presents estimates of equation (4.4) for nonagricultural wage and salary workers for the years 1974 and 1977. Variable names, definitions, and means are also presented. Twenty-six binary state/region variables are included in the regressions but omitted from the table for brevity. The results are entirely as expected given previous research using CPS data—wages are lower for nonwhite and female workers, higher for workers in large cities and union members, and increase with education and (at a decreasing rate) with experience. The experience variables interact with the binary variable for female workers for two reasons: first, years of experience (EXP) is proxied by age minus education minus 6, a more accurate proxy for men than women; and second, the true coefficients may also differ (women are typically found to have different wage-experience profiles). The results for FEXP and FEXPQ support these two factors jointly but cannot distinguish them.

If we assume that on average market differentials are zero, the wage predicted by the regression estimates of equation (4.1) is an individual worker's potential (or expected) wage in the labor market at large. Hence the residual (the logarithmic difference between the actual and predicted wage) from the regression equations in table 4-7 can be viewed as the worker's market differential (DIFF). Since we have embedded race, sex, union, and regional wage differentials in DIFF, our analysis assumes that these differentials are approximately the same over one-year intervals. DIFF contains a number of potential components, including worker-specific differences in job-search efficiency, compensating variations for training and working conditions, measurement error in the actual wage, and even a residual potential wage component if the wage determination process is incompletely specified (for example, if some abilities are not observed).[25] Knowledge of the components is important in interpreting results based upon DIFF in the analysis below.

As indicated earlier, the CPS has limited longitudinal properties. Hence it allows one to follow some of the respondents in one May survey to the

Table 4–7
Wage-Level Regressions, All Occupations (CPS Data)

		1974		1977	
Variable	Definition	Mean	Coefficient	Mean	Coefficient
Independent variables					
Intercept	——	——	.041	——	.325
			(1.77)		(21.78)
NWHITE	One if nonwhite; zero otherwise	.09	−.086	.11	−.092
			(−6.94)		(−10.58)
FEMALE	One if female; zero otherwise	.42	−.167	.44	−.145
			(−10.79)		(−13.69)
EXP	Years of experience (age − EDUC − 6).	20.65	.042	17.62	.043
			(42.27)		(54.91)
EXPSQ	EXP squared.	645.20	−.0007	519.48	−.0007
			(−32.89)		(−41.46)
FEXP	EXP × FEMALE.	8.62	−.023	7.60	−.020
			(−14.66)		(−17.41)
FEXPSQ	FEXP squared	269.66	.0004	224.03	.0003
			(11.13)		(11.55)
EDUC	Years of education completed	11.91	.071	12.25	.069
			(53.48)		(68.58)
LSMSA	One if in 44 largest SMSAs; zero otherwise	.71	.105	.38	.069
			(12.83)		(14.64)
UNION	One if union member; zero otherwise	.25	.182	.23	.238
			(21.4))		(36.48)
Dependent variable					
LnW	Natural logarithm of the wage per hour	1.33		1.50	
R^2			.457		.441
Number of observations			13,667		23,890

Notes: The t-statistics are in parentheses below the ordinary-least-squares coefficients. Twenty-six binary state/region variables are included in the regressions but are omitted here for brevity. Data are from the Current Population Survey, U.S. Bureau of the Census (see text for details). The sample consists of nonagricultural wage and salary workers.

May survey a year later. This enables us to observe educators who remain in teaching, as well as those who leave teaching. However, the data do not permit us to distinguish whether educators left teaching voluntarily or were discharged. For this reason, we view our turnover equation (the probability of leaving teaching) as a reduced-form representation of the equation explaining quit behavior for individuals and the equation explaining the discharge behavior for school districts. Our equation for the probability of leaving teaching for alternative employment takes the form

$$P(\text{OCCHG}) = f(\text{NDIFF}, \text{PDIFF}, X), \qquad (4.5)$$

where $P(\text{OCCHG})$ is the probability of changing occupations (leaving teaching); NDIFF (PDIFF) equals DIFF if DIFF is negative (positive) and X represents a vector of other relevant personal, job-related, and general economic characteristics. We expect workers to be less likely to quit the larger their actual wage relative to their predicted wage (the larger the value of NDIFF or PDIFF). Alternatively employers may be responsive to wage differentials in making layoff decisions. That is, they may attempt within the constraints imposed by tenure obligations to lay off workers with positive values of PDIFF. Consequently we expect the estimated coefficient for NDIFF to identify the quit response of individuals but the estimate for PDIFF to be a combination of the quit response of individuals and the layoff response of employers, if the latter exists to a significant degree. In fact however, there is little empirical evidence that wage differentials play an important role in employer layoff decisions (see for example Antos and Mellow 1979); this appears to be especially true for school districts that face tenure constraints on layoff decisions.

The occupational-mobility model is estimated using the multivariate logit technique. Ordinary-least-squares estimates are not efficient when the dependent variable takes on qualitative values (e.g., the zero-one values for OCCHG). The logit technique is used to account for the qualitatie nature of OCCHG. The probability that individual j leaves a teaching job in one year for a nonteaching job in the subsequent year is assumed to be expressed by

$$P_j(\text{OCCHG}) = e^{b'X_j} / (1 + e^{b'X_j}), \qquad (4.6)$$

where $b'(X)$ is a vector of coefficients (explanatory variables).

Maximum-likelihood estimates of the logistic empirical specification of the occupational-mobility model, equation 4.5, are presented in table 4–8 along with the sample means. The estimated coefficients are the percentage change in the odds of one event relative to the other for a unit change in an explanatory variable. The t-statistic for each coefficient follows in parenthesis. Below the t-statistic is the derivative, evaluated at the sample means. The derivatives express the absolute change in the probability of leaving teaching given a unit change in the independent variable. (See Nerlove and Press 1973).

The coefficient for NDIFF is significantly negative (0.05 level, one-tail test) in both equations, indicating that educators do respond to market wage differentials in deciding to leave teaching. For educators with an actual wage below their potential wage a 1 percent increase in the actual wage relative to the predicted wage decreased the probability that an educator would leave teaching by 0.11 in 1974–75 and by 0.14 in 1977–78.

Table 4–8
Determinants of Occupation Change for Educators (CPS Data)

Independent Variable	1974–75		1977–78	
	Mean	Coefficient	Mean	Coefficient
Intercept	——	4.408	——	8.223
		(2.35)		(5.17)
NDIFF	−.12	−1.482	−.15	−1.215
		(−1.88)		(−1.71)
		−.112		−.138
PDIFF	.18	−.167	.13	.543
		(−.23)		(.82)
		−.013		.062
NWHITE	.08	.304	.08	.227
		(.43)		(.38)
		.023		.026
FEMALE	.70	−.250	.71	−.828
		(−.40)		(−1.43)
		−.019		−.094
EXP	15.65	−.015	14.86	−.057
		(−.57)		(−1.93)
		−.001		−.006
FEXP	11.75	−.034	10.93	.034
		(−1.04)		(1.00)
		−.003		.004
EDUC	16.43	−.295	16.37	−.517
		(−2.75)		(−5.99)
		−.022		−.039
LSMSA	.67	−.016	.35	1.156
		(−.04)		(3.53)
		−.001		.132
UNION	.31	−.723	.50	−1.433
		(−1.58)		(−3.61)
		−.054		−.163
SEC	.41	−2.171	.41	−1.397
		(−4.03)		(−2.99)
		−.165		−.159
ELEM	.44	−1.502	.42	−2.025
		(−3.08)		(−4.16)
		−.114		−.231
KIND	.05	−.273	.08	−1.600
		(−.40)		(−2.55)
		−.021		−.182
F		(12,502) 3.306		(12,559) 6.190
Number of observations		513		570

Note: The dependent variable is (binary) occupation change from the first to the second year (mean is 0.08 for 1974–75, 0.11 for 1977–78). Coefficients are maximum-likelihood estimates of a logistic model obtained from the Predict procedure of the Statistical Analysis System. The asymptotic t-statistic is in parentheses below each coefficient, followed by the derivative evaluated at the mean. The omitted group for SEC(ondary), ELEM(entary), and KIND(ergarten) is OTHER (special-education teachers, librarians, et al.). See table 4–7 and text for explanations of the other variables.

Significantly, the larger coefficient is obtained in the period with the tighter labor market (1977–78). Auxiliary estimates for equation (4.5) for workers in the economy at large (not reported here) suggest that educators are at least as responsive to wage differentials in deciding whether to change occupations as other workers in general. Thus these results support our first proposition that educators are responsive to market wage differentials in deciding whether to leave teaching. The coefficient for PDIFF is insignificant in both regressions, suggesting that school districts are not responsive to PDIFF in discharging employees (or alternatively that the quit response for individuals cancels the employer response). This result is not surprising given the presence of tenure constraints on layoff decisions.

The remaining variables are of secondary but important interest. Experience (EXP), years of education (EDUC), being in a large city (SMSA), being a union member (UNION), and being a secondary (SEC), elementary (ELEM), or kindergarten (KIND) classroom teacher are linked (significantly in at least one regression) with being less likely to leave teaching. These results could be due to the presence of enclave rents associated with the characteristic (salary scales with undue compensation for experience or education, for example), with skills specific to the occupation, or with other fixities associated with occupational mobility.

To test our second proposition that the market wage differentials from equation (4.4) are a significant factor in determining individual patterns of wage change for educators, we estimate logarithmic wage-change equations using the same explanatory variables as in the occupation-mobility equations above. Here, however, we expect a priori that both PDIFF and NDIFF will have negative signs. This prediction arises from the hypothesis that market forces tend to erode noncompensating wage differentials. That is, the higher (lower) the initial wage relative to the potential or predicted wage, the lower (higher) the rate of wage growth. Our analysis of wage-change specifically for educators, therefore, resembles in varying degrees that of Taubman (1975), Ehrenberg and Oaxaca (1976), Mellow (1978), and Antos and Mellow (1979) in more general contexts.[26]

Estimates of the wage-change equation for 1974–75 and 1977–78 are presented in table 4–9. Again the dependent variable is the logarithmic difference between the wage in one year and the wage in the previous year. As predicted, the coefficients for NDIFF and PDIFF are significantly negative (0.01 level, one-tail test) in both regressions.[27] The coefficient for PDIFF, however, is significantly larger (0.01 level, two-tail test) than the coefficient for NDIFF in both regressions, suggesting that (within the span of a year) positive market differentials for educators are more readily liquidated than negative ones. This would tend to occur if the labor market at large were relatively slack or if the educator labor market were slack relative to the larger market. The periods examined generally exhibit both these charac-

Table 4-9
Wage-Change Regressions for Educators (CPS Data)

Independent Variable	1974–75 Coefficient	1977–78 Coefficient
Intercept	−.015	.176
	(−.08)	(1.23)
NDIFF	−.309	−.283
	(−4.27)	(−4.81)
PDIFF	−.763	−.674
	(13.65)	(12.47)
NWHITE	.132	.134
	(2.51)	(3.03)
FEMALE	.113	.024
	(2.22)	(.53)
EXP	−.004	−.006
	(−1.64)	(−2.67)
FEXP	.004	.003
	(1.52)	(1.18)
EDUC	.005	−.001
	(.48)	(−.08)
LSMSA	.048	−.009
	(1.60)	(−.36)
SEC	.024	−.076
	(.48)	(−1.65)
ELEM	−.026	−.039
	(−.55)	(−.93)
KIND	−.079	−.076
	(−.98)	(−1.22)
R^2	.372	.341
Number of observations	513	570

Note: The dependent variable in both regressions in the logarithm of the ratio of the wage per hour in the first year to the wage per hour in the second year (an approximate percentage change in wages). Coefficients are followed by t-statistics in parentheses. The omitted group for the SEC, ELEM, and KIND variables is OTHER (special-education teachers, librarians, et al.). See table 4-7 and text for explanations for remaining variables and table 4-8 for the sample means. Variables included in the regressions but omitted here for brevity are four regional binary variables and binary variables indicating transition among SEC, ELEM, KIND, and the omitted OTHER from the first to the second year.

teristics, although the national unemployment rate fell from 7.0 to 6.0 percent in 1977–78, compared to a rise from 5.6 to 8.5 percent in 1974–75. Thus the results in table 4–9 provide support for our second proposition that market wage differentials are a significant factor in determining individual patterns of wage change for educators—that is, the differentials tend to be eroded over time.

The effects of the other variables in table 4-9 have a number of competing explanations. They could represent general market equilibration, erosion of specific enclave rents associated with the characteristic, or compensation for changes in productive characteristics that are linked with initial characteristics (e.g., the level of experience in a wage change equation is clearly related to the quadratic term for experience in a wage level equation), or other factors. In any case, being nonwhite or female is associated with higher rates of wage growth in both periods (except for females in 1977-78), and experience is associated with lower rates of growth. The coefficients for the remaining variables are generally insignificant.

Interdistrict Mobility and Wage Equilibrium. Our empirical analysis of interdistrict mobility and wage equilibrium is based upon data from the Annual Report on Certificated Personnel maintained by the Oregon Department of Education. This is an annual census of all certificated teaching personnel in the state of Oregon, as of October 1 each school year. Thus we are able to observe employed educators from year to year within Oregon even if they move from one district to another. To maintain comparability with the estimates based upon the CPS in the previous section, we use the 1973-74 and 1976-77 school years for the wage-level regressions, and school years 1973-74 to 1974-75 and 1976-77 to 1977-78 for the interdistrict-mobility and wage-change analysis.

To obtain noncompensating wage differentials within the labor market for educators in Oregon (the logarithmic difference between an educator's actual wage and wage he or she could expect in the educator labor market), we estimate the standard cross-sectional wage equation, (4.4), based upon data for educators in Oregon. An individual's predicted or potential wage in education (in logarithmic form) can then be calculated by applying the estimated β coefficients to that individual's vector of personnel and job-specific characteristics.

Table 4-10 presents estimates of equation (4.4) for full-time Oregon educators for the school years 1973-75 and 1976-77. Sample means for the variables are also presented. The dependent variable is the logarithm of the total salary per contract day. The estimates provide no surprises (except perhaps for the coefficients associated with female educators). Wages increase significantly (at a decreasing rate) with years of actual experience in education (EXP) and increase significantly with levels of education acquired (EDUC1, EDUC2, and EDUC3). Higher wages are also associated (significantly) with teaching at the secondary level (SEC); not being a regular classroom teacher (OTHER); being responsible for a secondary teaching assignment (SECOND); performing work for extra pay (EXTRA); and being employed in the two most urbanized counties (LANE and MULT). The binary

Table 4–10
Wage-Level Regressions for Educators (Oregon Data)

Variable	Definition	1973–74		1976–77	
		Mean	Coefficient	Mean	Coefficient
Independent variables					
Intercept	——	——	3.692 (1034.84)	——	3.928 (1375.82)
FEMALE	One if female; zero otherwise	.57	−.018 (−4.50)	.56	−.015 (−4.59)
EXP	Total years teaching experience	9.39	.040 (64.27)	9.65	.038 (80.27)
EXPSQ	EXP squared	147.14	−.0009 (−40.27)	148.15	−.0009 (−50.38)
FEXP	EXP × FEMALE	5.46	−.004 (−5.82)	5.26	−.004 (−6.11)
FEXPSQ	FEXP squared	90.59	.0002 (5.81)	81.44	.0001 (6.45)
EDUC1	Bachelor's degree plus additional hours	.23	.050 (20.63)	.29	.068 (35.94)
EDUC2	Master's degree	.35	.117 (51.00)	.40	.124 (67.11)
EDUC3	Doctorate	.002	.227 (12.40)	.003	.218 (17.35)
KIND	One if kindergarten worker	.01	−.004 (−.44)	.01	−.004 (−.76)
SEC	One if secondary worker	.42	.020 (9.90)	.42	.021 (13.86)
OTHER	One if not regular classroom teacher	.07	.010 (2.81)	.07	.008 (2.89)
SECOND	One if responsible for secondary area	.16	.055 (22.54)	.17	.014 (7.80)
EXTRA	One if performing work for extra pay	.36	.018 (8.77)	.41	.028 (17.92)
LANE	One if working in Lane County	.11	.017 (5.68)	.10	.035 (15.63)
MULT	One if working in Multnomah County	.22	.140 (61.61)	.19	.046 (25.65)
Dependent variable					
LWAGE	Natural logarithm of the total salary per contract day	4.02		4.26	
R^2			.615		.700
Number of observations			23,335		24,264

Note: The t-statistics are in parentheses below the regression coefficients. Elementary workers are the omitted group for KIND and SEC. Data are described in the text.

variable for females (FEMALE) suggests that women educators are paid significantly less (about 2 percent less) than male educators with identical values for the explanatory variables included in the regression equations. Similarly, the experience variables interacted with the FEMALE variable (FEXP and FEXPSQ) indicate that over relevant periods of experience the wage-experience profile for female educators lies below that for males. These wage differentials by sex are unrelated to differential access to formal administrative positions; administrative workers (principals, super-intendents) are excluded from the analysis.[28]

Following a procedure similar to that for interoccupation mobility and wage equilibrium, we obtain wage differentials within the educator labor market in Oregon from the residuals of the regression equations in table 4-10. The caveats regarding the interpretation of the interoccupation wage differentials are also relevant here, although the more elaborate specifica-tion of the equations in table 4-10 may diminish their importance.

Using data for educators employed full time in adjacent school years (i.e., the school years 1973-74 to 1974-75 and 1976-77 to 1977-78), we are able to estimate an equation predicting interdistrict mobility. Again, we interpret this equation as a reduced-form representation of both the quit behavior of individuals and the layoff behavior of employers. Thus the pre-dictions for PDIFF and NDIFF are the same as those in the first section. Maximum-likelihood estimates of the logistic empirical specification of the determinants of interdistrict mobility are presented in table 4-11, along with the sample means. The estimated coefficients represent the percentage change in the probability of leaving one district for employment in another district within Oregon, relative to the odds of staying in the same district, given a unit change in an explanatory variable. The t-statistic for each coef-ficient follows in parentheses. Derivatives are below the t-statistic and ex-press the marginal effect of a unit change in the independent variables on the relative probability of leaving one school district for employment in another. Derivatives are evaluated at the sample means.

The coefficient for NDIFF is significantly negative (0.01 level, one-tail test) in both equations, indicating that educators paid below their potential wage respond to the differential in deciding to change districts. For these educators, a 1 percent increase in the actual wage relative to their potential wage decreased the probability of changing districts by 0.08 in 1973-74 to 1974-75 and by 0.09 in 1976-77 to 1977-78. The coefficient for PDIFF is also significantly negative in both equations, suggesting that districts are not sensitive to wage differentials, but that individuals are. For educators paid above their potential wage a 1 percent increase in their actual wage relative to the predicted wage decreased the probability they would change districts by 0.10 in 1973-74 to 1974-75 and by 0.13 in 1976-77 to 1977-78. The coefficient for PDIFF is larger in absolute value than the coefficient

Table 4–11
Determinants of Interdistrict Mobility of Educators (Oregon Data)

Independent Variable	1973–74 to 1974–75		1976–77 to 1977–78	
	Mean	Coefficient	Mean	Coefficient
Intercept	——	−2.470 (−12.33) −.055	——	−2.573 (−15.29) −0.64
NDIFF	−.05	−3.580 (−4.01) −.079	−.04	−3.510 (−4.62) −.087
PDIFF	.03	−4.499 (−2.83) −.099	.03	−5.394 (−4.08) −.133
FEMALE	.56	.018 (.81) .004	.55	−.390 (−1.92) −.010
EXP	10.42	−.198 (−4.47) −.004	10.63	−.226 (−6.74) −.006
EXPSQ	165.27	.003 (1.57) .0001	165.84	.004 (3.28) .0001
FEXP	5.90	−.036 (−.66) −.001	5.65	.067 (1.42) .002
FEXPSQ	98.17	.001 (.39) .0000	88.22	−.003 (−1.38) −.0001
EDUC1	.23	−.240 (−1.76) −.005	.29	−.218 (−1.95) −.005
EDUC2	.36	−.158 (−1.29) −.004	.40	−.301 (−2.71) −.007
EDUC3	.002	−4.105 (−.86) −.091	.003	−4.012 (−1.07) −.099
KIND	.01	.130 (.25) .003	.01	−.798 (−1.36) −.020
SEC	.42	.256 (2.49) .006	.42	.581 (6.41) .014
OTHER	.07	.590 (3.55) .013	.08	.352 (2.34) .009
SECOND	.16	.484 (2.49) .011	.17	−.025 (−.21) −.001
SECOND2	.17	−.551 (−2.75) −.012	.13	−.037 (−.29) −.001

Table 4–11 continued

Independent Variable	1973–74 to 1974–75		1976–77 to 1977–78	
	Mean	Coefficient	Mean	Coefficient
EXTRA	.37	1.635	.42	.481
		(9.08)		(5.14)
		.036		.012
EXTRA2	.39	−1.643	.04	.275
		(−9.02)		(1.51)
		−.036		.007
LANE	.11	−.297	.11	−.358
		(−1.84)		(−2.20)
		−.007		−.009
MULT	.21	−1.144	.18	.670
		(−7.11)		(6.50)
		−.025		.017
F		(19,19992) 22.448		(19,20783) 24.608
Number of observations		20,801		20,010

Note: The dependent variable is a binary variable indicating a change in school district from the first to the second year (mean is 0.02 for 1973–74 to 1974–75, 0.03 for 1976–77 to 1977–78). Coefficients are maximum-likelihood estimates of a logistic model obtained from the Predict procedure of the Statistical Analysis System. The asymptotic t-statistic is in parentheses below each coefficient, followed by the derivative evaluated at the men. The omitted group for KIND(ergarten) and SEC(ondary) is ELEM(entary); the omitted group for OTHER is CLASS(room) teacher. Variables followed by a "2" are values for the second year). See table 4–10 and text for explanations of the data and other variables. Coding error in EXTRA2 prohibits an accurate interpretation of EXTRA and EXTRA2 in the 1976–77 to 1977–78 regression.

for NDIFF in both regressions, significantly so in the later period. Two speculative explanations for the larger coefficient for PDIFF are (1) that a 1 percent increase in DIFF decreases the number of potential job openings with even higher wages proportionately more for those paid above their predicted wage than for those below their predicted wage, and (2) that educators with positive wage differentials exhibit unexplained characteristics relevant to wage determination (e.g., low job-search cost or extraordinary personal pressures for higher earnings). In any case these estimates provide support for the proposition that educators are responsive to wage differentials within the teaching profession in deciding whether to change districts.

The remaining variables do not generally have direct, unambiguous interpretations. The EXP, FEXP, and EDUC variables may reflect job-specific skills (or enclave rents associated with the variables) that tend to tie workers to a particular district. The variables for secondary teaching assignments (SECOND and SECOND2) and for extra-pay assignments

(EXTRA and EXTRA2) suggest that some educators are pushed and others pulled across district lines (or, alternatively, some educators are held by districts) by the presence of these assignment opportunities or responsibilities. Thus individual educators tend to sort themselves according to their preferences regarding secondary subject area and extra-pay assignments and regarding the wage premiums attached to the assignments.

To test our final proposition that the wage differentials within the educator labor market are a significant factor in determining individual patterns of wage change for educators, we estimate logarithmic wage-change equations using the same explanatory variables as in the interdistrict-mobility equations. As in the interoccupation wage-change analysis, we expect both PDIFF and NDIFF to have negative coefficients. Estimates of the wage-change equations for school year 1973–74 to 1974–75 and 1976–77 to 1977–78 are presented in table 4–12. The dependent variable is the logarithmic difference between the wage in one year and the wage in the previous year.

As predicted, the coefficients for NDIFF and PDIFF are significantly negative (0.01 level, one-tail test) in both regressions. The coefficient for NDIFF is substantially below that for PDIFF (in absolute value) for 1973–74 to 1974–75, but approximately the same in 1976–77 to 1977–78. That is, positive differentials are more readily liquidated than negative differentials in the earlier period. This is exactly the result one would expect given the substantial excess supply of teachers in Oregon during this period (relative to the later period of 1976–77 to 1977–78). Thus these estimates tend to affirm our final proposition that existing wage differentials within education are a significant factor in determining individual patterns of wage change from one school year to the next—that is, existing wage differentials within teaching are eroded (at a modest rate) over time.

The results for the remaining variables are generally similar to those in the earlier wage change equations for interoccupation differentials. However, significant differences between the responses of wage changes to changes in the level of experience for males and females are present in the Oregon estimates. Moreover, the relationship between wage changes and experience is clearly nonlinear.[29]

Is the equilibration process for noncompensating wage differentials within education at least partly the results of realignments *within* district salary structures, or is it entirely the result of relative movements among overall district salary schedules? To answer this question we also considered wage-change equations for individual teachers in a cross-section of twenty-four individual school districts. The results (not presented here for brevity) provide substantial evidence that significant wage equilibration occurs even within districts. Although only a one-year period is considered, about one-half of the school districts exhibit significant wage equilibration within the

Table 4–12
Wage-Change Regressions for Educators (Oregon Data)

Independent Variable	1973–74 to 1974–75 Coefficient	1976–77 to 1977–78 Coefficient
Intercept	.140 (81.90)	.107 (75.88)
NDIFF	−.088 (−13.33)	−.147 (−25.32)
PDIFF	−.298 (−41.19)	−.153 (−22.26)
FEMALE	−.005 (−2.37)	−.003 (−1.76)
EXP	−.004 (−15.74)	−.003 (−16.75)
EXPSQ	.0001 (9.32)	.0001 (8.73)
FEXP	.0007 (2.28)	.0006 (2.19)
FEXPSQ	−.00002 (−1.36)	−.00002 (−1.87)
EDUC1	.002 (2.13)	.002 (2.62)
EDUC2	.000 (.15)	−.001 (−1.05)
EDUC3	−.002 (−.19)	−.011 (−2.10)
EDOT	.021 (7.64)	.008 (5.77)
KIND	.005 (1.20)	.002 (.83)
SEC	.004 (4.32)	.002 (3.32)
OTHER	.002 (1.18)	.002 (1.49)
SECOND	−.030 (−16.79)	−.006 (−6.30)
SECOND2	.012 (7.15)	.003 (3.42)
EXTRA	−.019 (−12.45)	−.005 (−7.76)
EXTRA2	.024 (16.02)	.012 (7.62)
LANE	.009 (1.29)	−.005 (−.98)
LANE2	.004 (.61)	.004 (.84)

Table 4–12 continued

Independent Variable	1973–74 to 1974–75 Coefficient	1976–77 to 1977–78 Coefficient
MULT	−.054 (−9.45)	−.030 (−5.73)
MULT2	.035 (6.17)	.016 (3.07)
R^2	.241	.192
Number of observations	20,010	20,801

Note: The dependent variable in both regressions is the logarithm of the ratio of the total salary per contract day in the first year to that in the second year (an approximate percentage change in salary per day). Coefficients are followed by t-statistics in parentheses. See table 4–11 for means and explanations of variables. Coding error in EXTRA2 prohibits an accurate interpretation of EXTRA and EXTRA2 in the 1976–77 to 1977–78 regression.

district salary schedule. This occurs primarily by realigning the premium (or discount) associated with various teacher attributes or job assignments to match more closely the premium (or discount) prevalent in the market as a whole.

Interdistrict Mobility and Enrollment Trends. To explore the importance of enrollment trends in interdistrict mobility we present in table 4–13 separate estimates for decreasing and increasing enrollment districts. The results for NDIFF and PDIFF are striking. In decreasing enrollment districts, NDIFF is significant at the 1 percent level (one-tail test), but PDIFF is not significant at any standard confidence level. Thus only the underpaid teachers in such districts are sensitive to wage differentials in deciding to change districts. This is consistent with simple market expectations: underpaid teachers in districts with declining enrollments know that current and future wage increases are likely to be well below the market average, so they are particularly likely to quit for employment elsewhere. Overpaid teachers presumably have similar wage-trend expectations, and the negative effect PDIFF might otherwise have is apparently erased by expectations of a below-average wage trend in the district. Thus such expectations appear to interact with the responses to the wage differentials NDIFF and PDIFF.

In increasing enrollment districts, just the reverse pattern holds. PDIFF is significant at the 10 percent level (one-tail test), but NDIFF is insignificant. This pattern is also consistent with market expectations: overpaid teachers in districts with increasing enrollments know that current and future wage increases are likely to be well above the market average, so they

Table 4–13
Interdistrict Mobility by Enrollment Trend

Independent Variables	Definition	Decreasing-Enrollment Districts		Increasing-Enrollment Districts	
		Mean	Coefficient	Mean	Coefficient
Intercept	——	——	−2.543 (−6.29)	——	−2.184 (−5.98)
NDIFF	Logarithm of ratio of total salary per contract day to predicted salary if negative; zero if positive	−.04	−7.331 (−3.45) −.135	−.04	2.301 (.85) .068
PDIFF	Logarithm of ratio of total salary per contract day to predicted salary if positive; zero if negative	.03	.636 (.19) .012	.02	−5.807 (−1.56) −.170
FNDIFF	NDIFF interacted with a female binary variable	−.02	4.882 (1.34) .090	−.02	−7.452 (−1.96) −.218
FPDIFF	PDIFF interacted with a female binary variable	.02	−6.202 (−1.05) −.114	.01	3.518 (.63) .103
FEM	One if female; zero zero otherwise	.54	.051 (.10) .001	.54	−.594 (−1.23) −.017
EXP	Total years teaching experience	11.07	−.251 (−3.41) −.004	10.07	−.244 (−3.27) −.007
EXPSQ	EXP squared	177.65	.005 (1.64) .0001	151.75	.005 (1.58) .0001
FEXP	EXP interacted with FEM	5.83	.022 (.21) .001	5.37	.017 (.16) .001
FEXPSQ	EXPSQ interacted with FEM	93.49	−.001 (−.13) −.0000	81.10	−.002 (−.44) −.0001
ED1	Bachelor's degree plus additional hours	.30	−.105 (−.41) −.002	.31	−.165 (−.70) −.005
ED2	Master's degree	.40	−.076 (−.29) −.001	.35	−.363 (−1.45) −.011

Table 4–13 continued

Independent Variables	Definition	Decreasing-Enrollment Districts		Increasing-Enrollment Districts	
		Mean	Coefficient	Mean	Coefficient
ED3	Doctorate	.002	-2.627	.002	-2.469
			$(-.39)$		$(-.39)$
			$-.048$		$-.072$
F		(21,5802)	5.454	(21,4515)	5.232
Number of observations			5,822		4,535

Note: The dependent variable is a binary variable indicating a change in school district from the 1976–77 to the 1977–78 school year (the mean is 0.02 for the declining districts and 0.03 for the increasing districts). Coefficients are maximum-likelihood estimates of a logistic model obtained from the Predict procedure of the Statistical Analysis System. The asymptotic *t*-statistic is in parentheses below each coefficient, followed by the derivative evaluated at the sample mean. Variables for teaching level, extra-pay assignments, secondary teaching assignments, the two most urban counties are included in the equations but omitted here for brevity. See text for explanation of data source and definition of increasing and decreasing-enrollment districts.

are particularly *unlikely* to quit for employment elsewhere. For underpaid teachers, however, the expected negative effect of NDIFF is apparently erased by the decreased likelihood of quitting that results from expectations of an above average wage trend in the district. Thus the effects of NDIFF and PDIFF interact with district enrollment trends (and expectations of district wage trends) to produce distinctive patterns of interdistrict mobility.

To summarize, our evidence for Oregon suggests that in decreasing enrollment districts only underpaid teachers are sensitive to wage differentials within teaching in deciding whether or not to change districts, whereas in increasing enrollment districts only overpaid teachers are sensitive to such wage differentials.

Institutional Forces

As we discussed earlier in this section, district personnel policies and contract provisions established by collective bargaining play a more important role in governing terminations and transfers under conditions of strong enrollment decline. Our purpose in this subsection is to explore this role, to

explore the impact of district personnel policies and contract provisions, as well as the interaction between the two. Our analysis is based primarily on data from a national survey of over 2,000 elementary teachers in more than 200 districts (the same data used in the preceding section). This data set is an improvement over data used by previous researchers, since it provides information about teacher attitudes, district policy, and contract provisions. Measures of teacher attitudes include responses to questions about administrative decisions, the support they receive from administratiors, the effectiveness of the instructional program, and satisfaction with their workplace. Measures of district policy include who makes hirign and firing decisions and the level of participation of teachers in the decision-making process. Contract information includes the presence or absence of a contract, as well as the presence or absence of class-size limitations and reduction-in-force procedures. One drawback of the data is that transfers cannot be separated from terminations. Therefore we supplement the analysis with evidence based upon data for New York, in which transfers and terminations can be distinguished.

District Personnel Policy and Teacher Hiring Decisions. Before exploring the effects of district personnel policy on teacher turnover, it is necessary to describe the decision-making process of the districts included in the national study. Basically three levels of decision-making are represented. The decision to hire or fire teachers is made by district administrators, building administrators, or building staff and individual teachers. Table 4–14 shows the percentage of districts and teachers corresponding to each of the three levels of decision-making. When principals were asked to indicate which parties were included in the hiring and firing decisions, 80 percent responded that district administrators were the principal authority. Seventeen percent of the principals reported that building administrators (principals) were responsible for this decision. Since the individual teacher is the unit of analysis when considering teacher turnover, the distribution of teachers across districts distinguished by varying administrative procedures is important. Results show that the distribution of teachers across districts coincides almost exactly with the distribution of districts across various policies.

The nature of the decision-making process may affect the freedom of teachers in moving between schools within districts. Teachers were asked how they happened to be assigned to their current school. Three responses were recorded: Forty-three percent of the teachers reported, "I chose to work in this school." Fifty-five percent replied, "I was placed in this school." The remaining teachers said, "This is the only school in the district in which I am qualified to teach."

The first two responses are good indicators of the individual discretion given to teachers in determining their own assignments. One would expect,

Table 4–14

Distribution of Principal and Teacher Responses to Questions about Teacher Personnel Decisions

Parties Making Hiring and Firing Decisions	Principal Responses		Teacher Responses	
	Number	Percentages	Number	Percentages
Individual teachers	0	0	0	0
School staff	2	1	18	1
Principal	30	17	398	16
District staff	141	80	2,023	81
Parents	2	1	32	1
Students	1	0	26	1
Total	177	100	2,497	100

therefore, to find a greater percentage of teachers who gave the first response to be from district that decentralize the hiring and firing decisions by placing it in the hands of school principals. Districts that centralize the hiring and firing decisions on the other hand would be expected to exercise greater control over teacher assignments. Table 4–15 compares the assignment procedure of teachers with the district personnel procedures. The hypothesis that teachers who chose their assignment came from districts with a decentralized personnel policy can be casually examined by comparing the percentage of teachers in such districts who chose their assignment with the total percentage of teachers in the district. For example, given the distribution of teachers among the three types of personnel policies, one would expect 16 percent of the teachers who chose their own assignments to be in districts in which principals have the hiring and firing authority. Table 4–15 shows, however, that 20 percent of the teachers were found in this type of district. For districts in which district administrators handle personnel matters, only 76 percent of the teachers who chose their assignment were in these districts, compared with an expected 81 percent. Thus there appears to be a positive relationship between decentralized decision-making and individual freedom to chose teaching assignments.

The level of teacher participation in decisions at the school level may also be important in determining individual choice in personnel matters. Teachers were asked to indicate their level of participation in deciding on teaching assignment in schools. Five responses were recorded, with the corresponding percentages.

1. "Administrators decide with no input from teachers." (47 percent)

Table 4–15

Distribution of Teacher Responses to Questions Concerning Teacher Assignment and Personnel Decisions

Teacher Assignment	School Staff	Principal	District Staff	Parents	Students	Row Percentage
Teacher chose school.	12	221	825	16	6	44
	1.11	20.46	76.39	1.48	.56	
	66.6	59.1	41.0	50.0	23.08	
Teacher was placed in school.	6	153	1187	16	20	56
	.43	11.07	85.89	1.16	1.45	
	33.3	40.9	59.0	50.0	76.92	
Column percentage	.73	15.19	81.72	1.30	1.06	

Note: First entry in each cell is the number of respondents; second is the row percentage; third is the column percentage.

2. "Administrators decide after informal suggestions from teachers." (26 percent)
3. "Administrators decide after systematically getting input from teachers." (12 percent)
4. "Administrators and teachers jointly decide." (13 percent)
5. "Teachers decide with no input from administrators." (1 percent)

Table 4–16 compares responses to these five levels of participation with the way teachers assignments were made. Tabulations show that a lower-than-expected percentage of teachers who chose their own school assignment came from schools in which principals made the decision with no teacher input. As teachers gained input into the decision process, a greater than expected percentage of teachers who chose their own assignment were represented.

Casual observation therefore suggests that the freedom of teachers to determine their own assignments is fostered, as one might expect, by decentralized decision-making and teacher participation. To formalize this notion, a logit analysis is performed to determine the factors associated with individual freedom in choosing assignments. The dependent variable in the equation is the odds of a teacher choosing his or her own assignment. To capture the type of decision-making in the district, a variable (HF) is included that equals one if principals have hiring and firing authority and zero if district administrators deal with this matter. The level of teacher participation (DECISION) is measured by the relative amount of teacher input into decisions made at the school level. Unionization may also affect the manner in which personnel decisions are determined and administered.

Table 4-16

Distribution of Teacher Responses to Questions Concerning Teacher Assignment

	Degree of Teacher Participation in Decision Process					
	(1)	*(2)*	*(3)*	*(4)*	*(5)*	*Row Percentage*
Teacher chose	426	302	156	185	11	43.3
school.	39.4	28.0	14.4	17.1	1.0	
	36.2	45.8	51.2	56.6	37.9	
Teacher was placed	735	348	143	138	18	55.4
in school.	53.2	25.2	10.4	10.0	2.3	
	62.5	52.8	46.9	42.2	62.1	
Only school in	16	9	6	4	0	1.4
the teacher was	45.7	25.7	17.1	11.4	0	
qualified to	1.4	1.4	2.0	1.22	0	
teach.						
Column percentage	47.14	26.4	12.2	13.1	1.16	

Note: First entry in each cell is number of respondents; second entry is row percentage; third entry is column percentage.

Coding for teacher participation:

1. Administrators decide with no teacher input.
2. Administrators decide after informal suggestions from teacher.
3. Administrators decide after systematically getting input from teacher.
4. Administrators and teachers jointly decide.
5. Teachers decide with no input from administrators.

Thus both HF and DECISION are interacted with the union variable (which equals one if teachers are covered by a collective-bargaining agreement and zero if not). The teacher's level of seniority may also be important in the degree of freedom the teacher enjoys in changing assignments. As found in Murnane (1981), the most senior teachers have the first refusal of a vacated position, if they desire to transfer. Given this pecking order of transfers, one would expect that senior teachers will be more likely to choose their present assignment than junior teachers. The experience level of teachers (EXP) is included for this reason. District size (SIZE) and unionization (UNION) are also included to account for other differences in district policies and behavior of teachers.

The results (shown in table 4-17) support the hypothesis that decentralized decision-making and teacher participation promote the freedom of teachers to choose their own assignment. The coefficient on HF and DECISION is positive and statistically significant at the 0.01 level, which indicates that the odds of a teacher choosing his own position is higher when principals make the hiring and firing decisions and when teachers increase

Table 4–17
Logit Estimation of the Odds That an Individual Teacher Chose to Work in Present Assignment

Variable	Definition	Mean	Coefficient
Constant			−1.15 (5.52)
Size	District enrollment	64,438	2.2 E-7 (.63)
HF	Equals one if principal has hiring authority; zero if district administrators have authority	.72	.31 (2.51)
U*HF	Union × HF	.26	−.027 (.13)
Decision	Teacher participation in decision process	1.95	.26 (5.62)
U*Decision	Union × Decision	.68	.03 (.31)
Union	Equals one if teacher represented by bargaining unit	.64	.22 (.66)
EXP	Experience level of teacher	11.26	.03 (4.85)

$F = 9.02$ (7,2471)

their level of participation in the decision process. Unionization, on the other hand, has no direct effect on choice in assignments (the coefficient on UNION is statistically insignificant) and has no indirect effects either, through district policy or school-based decision-making (the interacted variables are insignificant). The experience of teachers is the only other variable whose coefficient is statistically significant. Consequently, the structure of the decision-making in the district is important in determining teacher freedom in assignment choices.

District Policy, Contract Provisions, and Turnover. The effect of district personnel policy, collective bargaining, and teacher attitudes on teacher turnover can be explored by explaining terminations and transfers with a subset of the variables discussed previously. The odds that a teacher will either transfer between schools within a district or leave the district (CHANGE) takes the implicit form

$$P(\text{CHANGE}) = f(X), \tag{4.7}$$

where P(CHANGE) is the probability that a teacher changes positions and X represents a vector of variables recording teacher attitudes and attributes, and district personnel policy. First, teacher mobility is determined by personal preferences. The principal factor considered here is the teacher's satisfaction with his or her present position. One would expect that teachers who are more satisfied with their present position are less apt to move. Three areas of satisfaction are included: satisfaction with decisions (SATDEC), success of instructional programs (SUCCESS), and overall satisfaction (SATALL). Because of human-capital considerations and seniority rules (Greenberg and McCall 1973; Murnane 1981; or Eberts 1982), teacher mobility should be inversely related to the experience level of teachers. Three categorized experience variables are included in the analysis (EXP1—one year or less; EXP23—2 or 3 years; EXP45—4 or 5 years; with 6 years or greater included in the intercept). District policy is accounted for with two variables, HF and DECISION (defined earlier). District size (SIZE) is also included to account for employment opportunities related to district size and also size-related differences in administrative policies.

To examine the effect of teacher unions on teacher turnover in detail, the sample of elementary teachers was separated into those covered by a master contract negotiated with a recognized bargaining unit and those not covered. Maximum-likelihood estimates of the logistic specification of the determinants of CHANGE are presented in table 4–18 for both groups. Since the dependent variable is the logarithm of the odds that a particular choice will be made, the estimated coefficients can be interpreted as the effect of the respective variables on the odds of changing positions. The effect of unions can be estimated by calculating the difference in coefficients between the two samples.

As expected, experience and overall satisfaction about current position (SATALL) are positively and significantly related to CHANGE. Teachers who are satisfied with their present position are less likely to move, and if they do, the more junior teachers are more likely to leave than more senior ones. None of the other coefficients in the analysis are statistically significant. The coefficients on HF and DECISION are in the anticipated direction for union teachers but not significant at reasonable confidence levels.

When the coefficients associated with union teachers are compared with those for nonunion teachers, the difference between the two sets of coefficients is not statistically significant. (The t-statistics of the difference in coefficients are not shown in table 4–18 since all are insignificant at any reasonable confidence level.) Thus the findings indicate that the mobility behavior or union and nonunion teachers are the same.

Even if mobility behavior is the same, however, specific contract provisions established by collective bargaining (such as class-size-limitation provisions and reduction-in-force provisions) may significantly affect teacher

Table 4–18

Logit Analysis of Teacher Turnover, by Union Affiliation vs. Nonaffiliation

Variable	Definition	Mean		Coefficient	
		Union	Nonunion	Union	Nonunion
Constant				−1.25 (4.35)	−.83 (2.05)
Size	District enrollment (X1000)	67.4	59.08	.0003 (.467)	−.0005 (.68)
HF	One if principal has hiring authority; zero otherwise	.71	.74	−.29 (1.76)	−.10 (.56)
Decision	Teacher participation in teacher assignment	1.96	1.92	.072 (1.22)	−.066 (.81)
EXP1	Teacher has one year's experience	.12	.18	1.16 (6.24)	1.00 (4.37)
EXP23	Teacher has two or three years' experience	.10	.12	.84 (4.16)	.89 (3.40)
EXP45	Teacher has four or five years' experience	.26	.25	.40 (2.54)	.57 (2.60)
SATDEC	Satisfaction with administrative decisions	2.15	2.26	−.058 (.48)	−.12 (.73)
Success	Successful programs	2.42	2.67	.087 (1.20)	.097 (1.00)
SATALL	Satisfying place to work	2.89	3.07	−.202 (2.81)	−.243 (2.38)

$F(9,1588) = 6.89$ $F(9,875) = 3.56$

Dependent variable: Odds of quitting or transferring

Note: Asymptotic t-statistics in parentheses.

turnover in unionized districts. We explore this possibility first by estimating the coefficients for teachers covered and not covered by staffing and class-size provisions. The results are displayed in table 4–19. Compared with the coefficients obtained from the union-nonunion dichotomy, the differences between coefficients are striking. Control of hiring and firing decisions (HF) by principals reduces the likelihood of a change in position for teachers covered by staffing or class-size provisions but has *no* significant effect on teachers not covered. Only first-year teachers are more likely to transfer than teachers with six years or greater experience when not covered by staffing or class-size provisions, whereas teachers with one to five years' experience are more likely to change positions when covered by the provisions. These differences in coefficients are statistically significant at the 0.05 level.

Table 4-19
Logit Analysis of Teacher Turnover, By Class Size and Staffing Provision

Variable	Definition	Mean		Coefficient		t-statistic of Difference in Coefficients
		Provision	No Provision	Provision	No Provision	
Constant				-1.14 (2.88)	-1.57 (3.24)	.68
Size	District enrollment (× 1,000)	61.28	74.11	-.0012 (.87)	.0016 (2.02)	1.76
HF	One if principal has hiring authority; zero otherwise	.67	.76	-.52 (2.58)	.25 (.77)	2.02
Decision	Teacher participation in teacher assignment	2.07	1.84	.042 (.54)	.103 (1.12)	.51
EXP1	Teacher has one year's experience	.13	.11	1.22 (4.78)	1.09 (3.89)	.34
EXP23	Teacher has two or three year's experience	.08	.13	1.44 (5.08)	.28 (.92)	2.79
EXP45	Teacher has four or five year's experience	.24	.29	.72 (3.28)	.083 (.35)	1.97
SATDEC	Satisfaction with administrative decisions	2.18	2.12	.024 (.15)	-.163 (.88)	.76
Success	Successful programs	2.43	2.41	.083 (.85)	.062 (.57)	.14
SATALL	Satisfying place to work	2.90	2.87	-.22 (2.12)	-.174 (1.63)	.31
F				5.02	3.53	

Dependent Variable: Odds of quitting .21 or transferring .18.

Note: Asymptotic t-statistics in parentheses. Provision refers to the presence of class-size and staffing concerns in contract; "No provision" refers to the absence of such provisions.

To explore the role of contract provisions even further, we turn to data for New York that permit us to distinguish between terminations and transfers and to account for varying enrollment trends. During the period to which our data pertain (1972–1977), public education in New York experienced an overall decline in enrollments. This was not the case, however, in all school districts. The effect of class-size provisions in a district contract depends upon enrollment trends within the district. For transfers between schools, a class-size provisions would be expected to increase the number of transfers within the district under either increasing or decreasing enrollments. In both cases, a change in enrollment forces the administration to move teachers within the district to maintain the specified teacher/student ratio. For terminations teachers covered by a class-size provision in increasing enrollment districts are less likely to be dismissed than teachers not covered. On the other hand teachers covered by a class-size provision in declining enrollment districts are more likely to be dismissed than teachers not covered.

The effect of a reduction-in-force provision also depends upon enrollment trends. When enrollment declines are severe enough to warrant the dismissal of teachers, the decision must be made as to which teachers will be dismissed first. Districts that have negotiated a reduction-in-force provision will in most cases have a preplanned procedure for determining the sequence of layoffs, usually based upon seniority in the district. With such a provision, the least senior teachers are released first, followed by teachers with slightly more seniority. Thus by interacting a reduction-in-force provision with a variable measuring the experience of a teacher within a district, one should find the reduction-in-force provision to have the greatest effect for those with the least seniority, and the least effect for those with the greatest seniority. Reduction-in-force provisions may also affect the transfer of teachers through a bumping process initiated by terminations. Teachers in increasing enrollment districts who are covered by a seniority clause should be unaffected by the provision since there is no reason to implement the procedure if layoffs are unnecessary. The relationship between the class-size provision and the reduction-in-force provision is also interesting. If the presence of a class-size provision promotes the dismissal of teachers in districts with declining enrollments, then the reduction-in-force provision will be invoked more often with the class-size provision than without it.

Maximum-likelihood estimates of a logistic specification of the determinants of transfers are presented in table 4–20 for 1972–1976. Since the dependent variable is the logarithm of the odds that a particular event will occur, the estimated coefficients can be interpreted as the effect of the respective variables on odds of transferring (or terminating employment). By comparing the estimated coefficients across the three categories of en-

Table 4-20
Estimates of the Odds of Transferring

Variable	Definition	Mean			Coefficient		
		Increasing	Slightly Declining	Rapidly Declining	Increasing	Slightly Declining	Rapidly Declining
Constant					-2.33 (13.9)	-3.07 (8.6)	-2.81 (22.8)
EXP1	Value = 1 if one year's experience	.085	.068	.048	.52 (2.39)	.82 (4.17)	.93 (5.10)
EXP23	Value = 1 if two or three years' experience	.237	.192	.159	.38 (2.48)	.48 (3.34)	.55 (4.36)
EXP45	Value = 1 if four or five years' experience	.196	.162	.165	.31 (1.88)	.22 (1.38)	.37 (2.88)
MALE	Value = 1 if male teacher	.450	.450	.460	.10 (.85)	-.14 (-1.31)	-.31 (-3.32)
SIZE	District enrollment per 1,000	7.400	7.636	13.344	-.006 (-.56)	.024 (4.96)	.010 (3.52)
CLASSIZE	Value = 1 if class-size provision in contract	.768	.796	.732	.31 (2.13)	.31 (1.96)	.34 (2.89)
MINT72	Percentage black teachers in district	.007	.023	.025	-10.3 (-2.12)	1.60 (1.31)	.60 (.60)
MINS72	Percentage black students in district	.019	.070	.077	-1.47 (-.76)	.59 (1.18)	.91 (2.60)
SENIORITY	Value = 1 if seniority provision in contract	.184	.154	.142	-.12 (-.48)	-.025 (-.12)	-.04 (-.19)
S*EXP1	Seniority × EXP1	.020	.010	.006	-.86 (-1.46)	-.12 (-.23)	.24 (.46)
S*EXP23	Seniority × EXP23	.049	.028	.019	.16 (.44)	.09 (.24)	.17 (.47)
S*EXP45	Seniority × EXP45	.034	.024	.022	-.35 (-.78)	-.04 (-.09)	.61 (1.86)
F					2.15	11.4	14.6

rollment trends, a number of interesting patterns emerge. One of the most striking results is the regularity with which transfers follow the hierarchy of seniority. In all three subsamples the odds that a teacher with one year of experience within the district will transfer is greater than the odds that a teacher with greater experience will transfer. The magnitudes of the coefficients associated with one year and two or three years of experience increase for teachers in districts facing larger enrollment declines. These results are due presumably to the bumping process initiated by terminations. Furthermore, as opportunities to move to preferred positions are reduced by declining enrollments, more senior teachers are less likely to move voluntarily.

Class-size and RIF provisions are entered both independently and interactively with the experience measures. When entered independently, the coefficient on class size is statistically significant, but the RIF provision is not. The presence of a class-size provision increases the odds that a teacher will transfer. This result is consistent across all categories of enrollment trends, with roughly the same magnitude found in each group. It appears, however, that reduction-in-force provisions have no effect on the odds that a teacher within a given experience category will transfer.

Variables similar to those used to explain transfers are used to determine the odds that a teacher will leave (quit or be dismissed from) a district. The results of the logit analysis are shown in table 4–21. The experience levels of teachers were entered to explain the order of priority given to layoffs. Since some teachers may leave for personal reasons, the possibility that a teacher may retire is accounted for by including a dummy variable to denote teachers who were at retirement age in 1972. The results for the effect of seniority on terminations follow the same general pattern found for transfers, with larger coefficients (in absolute value) for teachers in decreasing enrollment districts.

The contract provisions appear to affect terminations primarily in districts characterized by declining enrollment. For teachers in districts with slightly declining enrollment, for example, the presence of a reduction-in-force provision based on seniority reduces the likelihood of terminations for teachers as a group. The seniority provision, on the other hand, increases the odds of termination for a teacher with less than six years' experience (with respect to teachers with more than six years' experience). These results are consistent with the presumed intent of such provisions—to protect the jobs of the most senior teachers, even at the expense of junior teachers. For teachers facing more severe enrollment declines, the seniority provision increases termination rates. The seniority provision, in this case, may serve as a signal of actual layoffs or conditions that cause teachers to search actively elsewhere for better job prospects. Thus the provision tends to distinguish those districts in distress within each enrollment category. In addition the fact that the percentage of teachers covered by seniority provisions

Table 4-21
Estimates of the Odds of Terminating Employment

Variable	Definition	Mean			Coefficient		
		Increasing	Slightly Declining	Rapidly Declining	Increasing	Slightly Declining	Rapidly Declining
Constant					-.82 (7.73)	-1.44 (16.21)	-1.66 (21.4)
EXP13	Value = 1 if one to three years' experience	.33	.31	.25	.94 (9.78)	1.35 (16.88)	1.59 (21.16)
EXP45	Value = 1 if four or five years' experience	.18	.15	.16	.30 (2.36)	.60 (5.78)	.88 (9.78)
AGE55	Value = if over age 55	.08	.09	.09	2.96 (8.36)	2.39 (21.4)	2.28 (22.95)
MALE	Value = 1 if male teacher	.38	.40	.41	-.88 (10.16)	-.71 (10.34)	-.69 (11.03)
SIZE	District enrollment per 1,000	7.149	7.289	12.875	-.04 (4.56)	.007 (1.88)	-.002 (.89)
CLASSIZE	Value = 1 if class-size provision in contract	.76	.78	.72	-.019 (.20)	-.14 (1.80)	.022 (.32)
MINT72	Percentage black teachers in district	.007	.02	.03	1.07 (.38)	-2.46 (2.39)	-.01 (.01)
MINS72	Percentage black students in district	.02	.07	.08	-3.51 (2.72)	.91 (2.49)	.90 (3.23)
SENIORITY	Value = 1 if seniority provision in contract	.18	.16	.14	-.12 (.67)	-.25 (1.77)	.29 (2.49)
S*EXP13	Seniority × EXP13	.08	.05	.03	.025 (.11)	.44 (2.24)	-.21 (1.13)
S*EXP45	Seniority × EXP45	.03	.03	.02	.004 (.01)	.50 (2.02)	-.26 (1.12)
Percentage	terminations	.28	.29	.28			
F					27.32	48.46	65.48

Note: *t*-statistics in parentheses.

falls as enrollment declines may indicate that administrators are sometimes able to avoid the restrictions of a seniority provision by keeping it out of the contract if they feel that layoffs are imminent. Evidence of such behavior is found in Eberts (1982a).

Class-size limitation provisions also significantly reduce terminations in districts with slightly declining enrollment. If these provisions place a floor (as well as a ceiling) on class size, then one would expect declines in enrollment to cause more teachers to be laid off as the district seeks to maintain a specified teacher/student ratio. Our findings show the opposite to take place, however. Since enrollment declines are not severe in the declining-enrollment category, there may be sufficient slack in the class-size restrictions to allow more teachers to stay with the district than otherwise would be the case.

To summarize briefly, the mere presence of collective bargaining has little discernible effect on teacher turnover. No statistically significant difference between the estimated coefficients of teachers covered by collective bargaining and those not covered could be found. These results should not be interpreted, however, to indicate that collective bargaining has no effect. Indeed the presence of staffing and class-size provisions in contracts does appear to affect mobility among teachers covered by a collective-bargaining contract, a result supported both by our national data and by the more detailed data for New York. Class-size provisions increase the probability of transfers and reduce the probability of terminations, whereas seniority-based reduction-in-force provisions only affect the termination rates of teachers in districts with rapidly declining enrollment. Thus the specific provisions present in a contract appear to have a greater effect than the simple existence of a contract and whatever implicit effects one might associate with collective bargaining.

Conclusions

We began this chapter by arguing that collective bargaining is what it appears to be—a means of focusing the collective power of teachers to resolve issues that concern them in systematic, predictable ways. The remainder of the chapter pursued this point by exploring the fundamental nature of labor contracts, trade-offs among various elements of job packages, the strength of teacher unions and the union-nonunion wage differential, attitudinal differences between union and nonunion teachers and among union teachers covered by different sorts of contracts, as well as the behavioral characteristics with collective bargaining.

In the first section we investigated the range of possible wage-employment outcomes to bargaining by addressing the question: Do labor con-

tracts push wage-employment outcomes beyond the employer demand curve, as predicted by the contract-curve model, or do labor contracts confine wage-employment outcomes to the employer-demand curve, as predicted by the demand-constraint model? After modifying the contract-curve model to incorporate multidimensional (hedonic) contracts for public-sector activities, we tested the contract-curve model against the more traditional demand-constraint model using data for public school teachers in New York State. Our estimates of an hedonic salary equation and the differing predictions of the models for the effects of employment-related contract provisions indicate that such provisions enable teacher unions and school districts to reach settlements on the contract curve, a rejection of the demand-constraint model. In addition, we found strong evidence for compensating differentials among other teacher and job-related attributes—an uncommon result among hedonic wage studies. Of particular importance is the teacher/student ratio, which carries a large implicit price in the estimates. This result tends to confirm the traditional emphasis on the teacher/student ratio as a key element in labor contracts (whether implicit or explicit).

We turned our attention to the union-nonunion salary differential for teachers and the strength of teacher unions relative to private-sector unions. The evidence we presented is based on two complementary research designs—cross-section wage-level and wage-change regressions—and national samples of teachers for 1974–75 and 1977–78. Our results confirm the previous studies that found relatively small union gains during the early 1970s but show that union gains increased substantially by the late 1970s, reaching a level comparable to the average union wage-premium in the private sector. This result, combined with evidence on inflationary trends and average teacher salaries, suggests that, on average, the real wages of unionized teachers increased slightly during the period studied, while those of nonunionized teachers declined. Our explanation of the increase in the union premium for teachers involves inflationary pressures combined with excess teacher supply, growth in legislation favorable to teachers collective bargaining, and the maturation of relatively new teacher unions.

In the third section we explored the intangible issue of differences in attitudes between union and nonunion teachers. Union teachers, for example, were less concerned about personnel policy than nonunion teachers but more concerned about class size. The concern with class size is consistent with the large implicit price on the teacher/student ratio found in the first section. In addition, union teachers appeared to be less satisfied in general about their workplace than nonunion teachers. Although these differences in attitudes and perceptions were significant, the differences did not appear to be large enough to register any significant influence on turnover behavior of union and nonunion teachers. Among organized teachers, those covered

by staffing and class-size provisions felt that administrators were more supportive than did those teachers not covered. On the other hand teachers covered by the provisions felt less able to work well with the colleagues.

Finally, we turned to a wide range of issues related to teacher labor markets. We began by testing four propositions related to the labor-market behavior of individual teachers and the process of wage equilibration. First, we tested whether teachers are sensitive to wage differentials between their teaching jobs and alternative occupations in deciding whether to leave teaching for other employment. Our empirical results suggest that teachers are at least as responsive to wage differentials as other workers. One implication of this finding is that the monopsonistic power of local school districts is not significantly greater than that of employers in general. Second, we tested whether these wage differentials between teaching jobs and alternative occupations are significant factors in determining individual patterns of wage change from one year to the next—that is, whether the differentials tend to be eroded over time. Our empirical analysis suggests that within the span of one year positive market-wage differentials, premiums above the predicted wage, tend to be liquidated more readily than negative ones. This would tend to occur if the labor market at large were relatively slack or if the teacher labor market were slack relative to the larger market. The 1970s generally exhibited both characteristics.

The third and fourth propositions deal with interdistrict behavior. We tested whether teachers are responsive to wage differentials within teaching in deciding whether to leave one school district for employment in another. We found that teachers are responsive to wage differentials for teaching jobs but not as strongly responsive as to wage differentials between teaching and other occupations. Moreover, responsibilities for secondary subject areas and extra-pay assignments tend to pull some teachers and push others across district lines. The final of the four propositions we tested regarding teacher labor-market behavior is whether wage differentials within teaching are a significant determinant of individual patterns of wage change from one school year to the next—that is, whether these wage differentials also tend to be eroded over time. Our results indicate that both negative and positive wage differentials tend to be eroded but that positive differentials are more readily liquidated than negative ones when the relevant teacher labor market has excess supply.

By looking at individual districts under varying enrollment trends, we also found that (1) a substantial part of the erosion of wage differentials occurs through adjustments *within* district salary schedules (e.g., by altering the premium associated with different levels of education), not just by relative movements of entire schedules among districts, and (2) in declining enrollment districts only underpaid teachers are sensitive to wage differentials in deciding to leave, whereas in increasing enrollment districts only

overpaid teachers are sensitive to wage differentials. The second set of results provides evidence that teachers base labor-market decisions both on current conditions and on conditions expected to prevail into the foreseeable future.

Our last topic was the role of institutional forces in teacher labor markets. We presented evidence on the separate and interactive roles of district policies and contract provisions under a variety of enrollment trends. To summarize our results briefly, we found no effect for the mere presence of collective bargaining—there is no statistically significant difference between the labor-market behavior of teachers covered by agreements and those not. This result does not indicate, however, that collective bargaining has no effect on teacher mobility—on transfers, quits, or dismissals. In fact our evidence clearly indicates that staffing and class-size provisions included in contracts *do* affect mobility. Class-size provisions increase the probability of transfers and reduce the probability of terminations, whereas seniority-based reduction-in-force provisions only affect termination rates for teachers in districts with rapidly declining enrollments. Thus the contents of a contract appear to make a difference, but not the mere presence of a contract (or whatever related effects one might implicitly associate with collective bargaining).

Notes

1. See for example S.M. Johnson in Duckworth and DeBevoise (1982:143–42).

2. Our sample is a one-in-four random sample excluding teachers in public-school districts in New York City (slightly over 7,000 teachers are in our sample). Virtually all public-school districts in New York State are covered by collective-bargaining agreements in both years.

3. The relative effect of losing a provision (compared to never having the provision) is unclear, and we have no theoretical predictions for this effect.

4. Other important variables implied by theory are assumed to be either uniform across districts, different across districts but fixed (hence eliminated by the fixed-effects specification), or controlled by other included variables not central to our test.

5. Because it is possible that ΔLOGBUD, ΔT/E, and ΔSHARE are endogenous, we also obtained estimates with each of these variables deleted from the equation and found that their absence does not significantly alter the coefficients of the remaining variables.

6. Teachers in New York public-school districts are covered by a statewide retirement system in which the local school districts and the state

contribute a uniform percentage of the teacher's salary (see Schmid 1971). As one would expect under the circumstances, change in pension cost has no significant effect when entered in the regression because it exhibits no systematic variation across districts.

7. C. Brown (1980) provides both an example and a survey of previous examples of empirical rejection of compensating differentials.

8. For an introduction to these issues, see Ehrenberg (1973), Shapiro (1978), and Burton (1979).

9. For a comprehensive review of this research, see Lipsky (1982).

10. A more detailed presentation and discussion of these results can be found in Baugh and Stone (1982a).

11. For applications of this methodological approach, see Ashenfelter (1972), Oaxaca (1975), and Kalachek and Raines (1976). The slope coefficients for the X vector might also vary between the union and nonunion sectors, but auxiliary empirical estimates suggest that such variations are insubstantial for teachers.

12. To measure the impact on relative wages, one could use observations on both those who leave and those who join unions. However, few teachers in our sample left unions, and the measure for those who left appeared to be very cyclically sensitive (the measured premium was very large during economic downturns and even negative for upturns).

13. In 1974 the union membership status question was "Does . . . belong to a labor union?" In 1975 "on this (the primary) job" was added to the end. In 1977 and 1978 the question was "On this (the primary) job, is . . . a member of a union or an employee association similar to a union?" The mean values for union membership in the CPS data are lower than those published elsewhere. This appears to be due primarily to the fact that most sources count *all* members of the National Education Association as union members, even including those in states that ban collective bargaining by teachers, whereas such teachers are not automatically counted as members by the CPS. Burton, "The Extent of Collective Bargaining in the Public Sector," p. 30, for example, estimates the organized proportion of full-time teachers at about 75 percent in 1976, while the CPS figure for full-time teachers is 52 percent in 1977.

14. One set of variables requires further explanation. Women teachers are permitted different coefficients for EXP and EXPSQ (see FEXP and FEXPSQ). This is done because EXP is proxied by age minus education minus six, a more accurate proxy for men than women, and because the true coefficients may also differ (women have different wage-experience profiles).

15. Coverage by a collective-bargaining agreement is only available for 1977. In this year 45.3 percent of teachers indicate coverage by a collective-bargaining agreement, with an additional 11.5 percent unsure. Hence between 45 and 57 percent appear to be covered in 1977.

16. If usual weekly earnings are used in place of wage per hour as the dependent variable, the estimated union premium for full-time teachers is about 5 percent in 1974 and about 17 percent in 1977, significant at the 5 and 1 percent levels, respectively. While these estimates are slightly lower than those based on hourly wage, the difference is not statistically significant even at the 10 percent level.

17. As in the study by Mellow (1982), the R^2s for the wage-change regressions are quite low. The mover-stayer problem common to most mobility studies is not likely to be serious in the CPS data, since those teachers we observed changing union membership status did not change residence.

18. For arguments that unionism and wages are simultaneously determined see Ashenfelter and Johnson (1972), Lee (1978), and Duncan and Leigh (1980). In particular Lee's finding that probability of union membership is positively related to the difference between the alternative union wage and the available nonunion wage suggests that within teaching any simultaneity bias in estimates of the effects of unionism on wages is likely to be negative.

19. The difference in the functional specification of the wage and union logit equations also provides some identification. The maximum-likelihood PROC PREDICT procedure of the Statistical Analysis System (SAS) was used to obtain the logit estimates. For more detailed information regarding logit procedures, see Nerlove and Press (1973).

20. For evidence on density of unionism and spillover effects, see Chambers (1977).

21. For evidence in the economy at large, see Freeman (1981). For evidence regarding teachers see Garms and others (1978).

22. Mellow (1981), for example, found union premiums in 1977–78 of 21 percent in wage-level regressions for the economy at large and 5 to 8 percent in wage-change regressions.

23. Unfortunately, not all states can be identified separately in the CPS data, since some smaller states are grouped by region. Grouped states were classified according to the majority classification in the region.

24. A more detailed presentation and discussion of these tests can be found in Baugh and Stone (1982b).

25. Antos and Mellow (1979:69) provide a discussion of these issues, and Lillard (1977) presents results suggesting that more than half of the residual variance in general cross-section wage regressions is due to the omission of worker-specific factors.

26. As in most of these studies, we must explicitly assume that the initial wage is measured without error; otherwise spurious correlation arises between the dependent variable (wage change) and NDIFF and PDIFF. Experimentation with an auxiliary specification not subject to the possibility of this spurious correlation suggests that the problem is insubstantial.

Alternative estimates for both the CPS and Oregon data based upon the subsequent wage rather than wage change as the dependent variable and upon separate coefficients for the predicted and initial wages as explanatory variables are strongly consistent with the estimates reported here, suggesting that the reported estimates for NDIFF and PDIFF in the wage-change equations are not subject to serious measurement bias.

27. Turnover is clearly an intermediating variable in the wage-determination process. However, alternative regression equations including turnover as an explanatory variable yield similar estimates for PDIFF and NDIFF, suggesting that their effects are primarily direct for the group as a whole.

28. Unfortunately, there is no race information in the Oregon data, hence a race variable could not be introduced into our equations for Oregon. Most of the black population, however, is concentrated in Multnomah County, the most urban county, which is included as a binary variable.

29. Quadratic terms for experience in the wage-change equations for the CPS (not presented here) are not significant at the 5 percent level. This may be due to a combination of factors: the imputation of EXP from age and education; the small numerical magnitude of the effect; and the smaller sample size for the CPS estimates.

Appendix 4A:
Formal Derivation of
Contract-Curve Model

Assume that the objective function of the teacher union is to maximize the wage bill, as Dunlop (1944) suggested for private-sector unions. To avoid the unsatisfactory possibility that the union would be willing to lower its wage indefinitely to increase employment, a variation of the wage bill hypothesis, used by McDonald and Solow, is adopted. Suppose that the local teacher union has N identical teachers, T of whom are employed. If each member has probability T/N of holding a teaching job, the expected utility of the union member is

$$EU(w,T) = (R/N)[U(w) - D] + (1 - T/N)[U(w_n)]. \quad (A4.1)$$

Thus the utility of a member holding a teaching job is a function of the wage rate less the fixed additive disutility of holding the teaching job (D), and the utility associated with not holding a teaching job is equal to the wage of the next best alternative (w_n). Equation (A4.1) can be simplified by assuming that w_n and N are treated parametrically by the union. In this case D plus $U(w_n)$ can be set equal to $\bar{U}$, and we respecify (A4.1) as

$$EU(W,T) = T[U(w) - \bar{U}]. \quad (A4.1')$$

The utility function is assumed to be strictly concave with respect to its arguments, yielding downward-sloping convex indifference curves in the (w,T) plane.

Although taxpayers do not hire teachers directly, we assume that district administrators act as agents for taxpayers in providing them with educational services. Thus the employment decisions regarding teachers are ultimately determined by the preferences of taxpayers and the constraints they face. If taxpayers as a group make decisions that are commensurate with the median voter's, the derivation of the taxpayers' utility function can focus on a single taxpayer. We assume that such taxpayers maximize utility based on educational services (z) and a composite private consumption good (x) subject to their share of the total district education costs (c) and wealth (x_o). Educational services are a positive function of the teacher/student, or teacher/enrollment, ratio (T/E) and other inputs (A/E). The taxpayers' optimization problem is

$$\text{MAX } V(z,x), \tag{A4.2}$$

$$\text{s.t. } z = z(T/E, A/E), \tag{A4.3}$$

$$x_o = x + c \cdot (wT + aA), \tag{A4.4}$$

where a is the price of alternative inputs A. By taking the educational production function as predetermined by the district administrators, taxpayers choose z and x by choosing T, A, and x.

The isoutility curve for the taxpayer (employer) in the (w,T) plane can be derived by substituting the production function and budget equation for z and x, respectively, in the taxpayers' utility function.

$$V[z(T/E, A/E), x - c \cdot (wT + aA). \tag{A4.5}$$

Taking the total derivative of $V[\cdot]$ and solving for the slope of the isoutility curve in the (w,T) plane, one obtains

$$dw/dT = [(1/E)(V_z z_T)/V_x cT] - w/T. \tag{A4.6}$$

The contract curve for efficient bargains is derived by setting the slopes of the union and taxpayer isoutility curves equal for common values of w and T:

$$(U - \bar{U})/U_w = w - (1/E)(V_z z_t/E) V_x c. \tag{A4.7}$$

Except at the competitive point, the union member's utility is greater than $\bar{U}$, and the marginal cost of hiring an additional teacher exceeds the marginal benefit.

The total derivative of equation (A4.7) reveals the contract curve to be upward sloping from the competitive position if the composite private good (x) encompasses a sufficient quantity and variety of private goods such that an additional unit of x or z does not affect the marginal utility of x, (i.e., $V_{xx} = V_{xz} = 0$). This requires the assumption that the taxpayers' utility function exhibit constant marginal utility for x and be separable in z and x.

Our index of bargaining strength (K) is

$$K = Tw/w_n T_n \tag{A4.8}$$

where T_n is the hypothetical competitive level of employment. In turn we specify K as a function of various employment security provisions (a vector P) and other factors (a vector R) likely to be associated with bargaining strength. Thus we have

$$K = k(P,R).$$ (A4.9)

Since total compensation (w) is not observed, we specify the following hedonic equation.

$$w = h(S,B,Q),$$ (A4.10)

where S is the explicit salary, B a vector of money-valued benefits, and Q a vector of qualitative job and teacher attributes. The partial derivatives of these arguments represent the implicit exchange value in terms of w.

Substituting bargaining strength, equations (A4.8) and (A4.9), for T in the contract-curve equation (A4.7), and substituting the hedonic salary equation, (A4.10), for w in the contract-curve equation yields the following reduced-form equation for observed salary:

$$S = s(x_o,E,c,a,A,w_n,T_n,D,P,R',B,Q')$$ (A4.11)

Where R' is the vector R excluding x_o and E, and Q' is the vector Q excluding P. Equation (A4.11) is the reduced-form salary equation mentioned in the first section of the chapter.

5

Administrators and Collective Bargaining

In this chapter we investigate the effects of collective bargaining on two broad areas of administrative behavior and discretion—resource allocation and educational policy and practice. Unions for public school teachers have aggressively negotiated contract provisions that address such topics as class size, workloads and assignments, reduction-in-force procedures, grievances, arbitration and impasse procedures, evaluations of teachers, promotions, and the distribution of salary increases. As Freeman and Medoff (1979) suggest, some of these provisions have the potential to benefit both sides of the bargaining table. In this view teachers gain through increased participation in the decision-making process by altering working conditions to match more closely the preferences of the teaching staff. In addition management gains through the increased productivity associated with lower turnover, improved cooperation among teachers and administrators, and the like.

The negotiation of these provisions is not without costs, however. Numerous authors, including Moskow (1966), Summers (1976), Kochan and Block (1977), and Perry (1979) argue that the establishment and administration of negotiated work rules place constraints upon both the administrative discretion and the educational policy prerogatives of principals, superintendents, and school boards. In addition the public at large appears to be increasingly sensitive to the possibility that teacher unions cause district administrators to reallocate educational expenditures and to alter both educational policy and practice.

The decision and behavior of administrators in education can be influenced by collective bargaining in a variety of ways. A negotiated increase in compensation, for example, will implicitly shift resources away from some categories of expenditures when educational output is held constant, and the educational process itself can be directly altered through negotiated changes in the workplace. However, the influence of collective bargaining on managerial behavior and discretion arises not just from the individual effects of particular provisions, but also from the interactive effect of all the provisions in the contract. That is, the way in which a particular contract provision constrains or alters the decisions or behavior of administrators depends in large measure on other provisions in the contract. The effects of

131

a particular kind of reduction-in-force provision, for example, vary with the nature of class-size provisions that might also be in the contract, as demonstrated in chapter 4.

The effect of this web of rules was first discussed by Kerr and Siegel (1955) and Dunlop (1958) and has been largely ignored in empirical research. The explanation for the paucity of empirical research is simple: data on specific contract provisions for a variety of contracts are difficult to obtain, especially in conjunction with other information about both the employers and employees. To avoid this problem, most empirical studies use a 0 − 1 dummy variable for the presence or absence of a collective-bargaining contract. This appears to be too simplistic—negotiated labor contracts vary extensively, and the use of a dummy variable constrains all contracts to be the same. Indeed we argue that part of the answer to how collective bargaining affects administrative decisions and behavior is found in the complexity of the contract itself.

We also argue that one must look at more than simply what the contract says, since the presence of a particular contract provision will not necessarily alter management decisions or behavior. There are at least three reasons why a contract provision might be impotent in practice: (1) some provisions apply only when certain contingencies occur, such as declining enrollments; (2) administrators may act in accordance with the provision even in its absence; and (3) in practice administrators may be able to work around or even ignore the provision. Hence the effect of collective bargaining on administrative decisions and behavior is an empirical question that depends not only on the content of a contract but also on its context.

In this chapter we investigate the separate and interactive effects of contract provisions in two broad areas of administrative behavior and discretion—resource allocation and educational policy and practice. We present first a simple model of the allocation of educational expenditures, explore some of the major nonunion determinants of district expenditures, evaluate alternative measures of the structure of district contracts, and investigate the effects of teacher contracts on both the allocation and level of district expenditures. We then go beyond budgetary issues to look at the relationship between teacher contracts and various dimensions of educational policy and practice—mode of instruction, the interaction between principal and teacher, and the extent of teacher participation in various administrative decisions.

Resource Allocation and Teachers' Contracts

Our primary purpose in this section is to examine the impact of individual contract provisions on the allocation of educational resources in New York

State public school districts for the 1976–77 school year. Despite the wide-spread belief that unions affect budgetary and management decisions as well as salaries, most of the empirical evidence to date supports only salary increases.[1] The handful of studies that have considered the effects of collective bargaining on resource allocation find little significant impact. Chambers (1977) reports very few significant effects, even after accounting for spillover effects between union and nonunion districts, and Gallagher (1979) suggests that increases in teachers' compensation are gained largely through budget expansion rather than through significant internal reallocation. However, unlike the present analysis, previous studies were not able to explore the impact of individual contract provisions on administrative decisions and behavior. We present a model of district resource allocation, examine nonunion determinants of district expenditures, discuss various measures of the structure of teacher contracts, and finally, investigate the relationship between contracts and both the allocation and level of district expenditures.

Model of Resource Allocation

Before we can address the effects of collective bargaining on the allocation of district resources we need at least a simple model of district expenditures. Since teacher collective-bargaining contracts are negotiated at the district level, the model we derive describes the behavior of individual school districts. District budget decisions are made by district administrators who (1) maximize an objective function of educational outcomes, representing the preferences of the school board, subject to production, input, and budgetary constraints; (2) have full knowledge of the set of educational objectives they wish to pursue and of the inputs required to attain these objectives; and (3) know the possibilities for substituting among objectives when they are faced with a change in resources or other constraints.

Many arguments have been made against the use of utility maximization to describe decision-making in public schools. Problems arise due to the uncertainty of the educational process, the lack of adequate and generally accepted measures of output, and the absence of incentives to minimize costs. However, since the primary reason for constructing a model of district decision-making is to derive budgetary expenditure equations, it is sufficient to recognize that even though administrators may not have perfect knowledge of the relationship between inputs and outputs, they do have preconceived notions about the effects of their resource decisions that are based upon their own experience, intuition, and ideologies.

Basic Model. Our basic model can be formulized by the following four equations first set forth by Brown and Saks (1975):

$$\text{Max } W(S_1, \ldots, S_N; Z_1); \tag{5.1}$$

$$S_j = f_f(x_{1j}, \ldots, x_{Mj}; Z_2) \qquad j = 1, \ldots, N; \tag{5.2}$$

$$x_{kM} = g_k(x_{k1}, \ldots, x_{kN}) \qquad k = 1, \ldots, M; \tag{5.3}$$

$$R = \sum_{i=1} P_k x_k. \tag{5.4}$$

The district welfare function $W(\cdot)$ is a function of the student test scores (S) and community characteristics (Z_1). Student outcomes are the result of the interaction of M educational inputs (x_{k1}) shared by the N students in the district who have different abilities and endowments (Z_x). The school administrator employs inputs, primarily teachers with different education and experience levels, subject to the prices of factor inputs and the budget. The budget (R) is predetermined by a prior community decision to allocate resources between educational services and other goods..[2]

Collective bargaining affects the allocation of resources by placing additional constraints on administrators and by altering the administration's decision set. Administrators face additional constraints through the establishment of negotiated work rules. Many contracts contain articles describing specific procedures that must be followed in carrying out certain management directives. Contracts also contain items placing limits on the amount of certain resources that can be employed, such as teacher aides and the size of classes. Collective bargaining expands the administrator's decision set by representing the preferences of the inframarginal teacher. By shifting the administrator's attention away from the marginal teacher (the teacher closest to indifference between leaving or remaining in a district) to the desires of the median teacher, collective bargaining should be able to cause administrators to make decisions they would not ordinarily make.

District Expenditure Equations. Equations (5.1–5.4) yield district expenditures (E) equations for the M inputs of the general form

$$E_1 = E(Z_1, Z_2, D, R, a, Q_1, \ldots, Q) \qquad i = 1, \ldots, M. \tag{5.5}$$

The internal allocation of the district budget depends upon the following factors:

1. Community preferences for teacher attributes as related to educational outcomes and the attractiveness of the community to teachers (Z_1)
2. The parameters of the educational production process as described by school officials (a), which in the present case cannot be measured directly

3. The endowments, innate abilities, and nonschool inputs of students (Z_2)
4. Working conditions of teachers (D)
5. The district budget (R)
6. The contract items (Q)[3]

Wages are considered to be endogenous and thus do not appear as explanatory variables.[4]

Nonunion Determinants of District Expenditures

Before examining the effect of teacher contracts, we look first at some of the major nonunion determinants of district expenditures. For this analysis, we divide the district budgets for New York into four categories: instructional expenditures per pupil; administrative expenditures per pupil; employee benefits per pupil; and total teachers' salaries per pupil. Estimates of equations with the teacher/student ratio and average teacher salary as dependent variables are also obtained to aid in the interpretation of the expenditure equations.

Figure 5-1 shows the various accounting identities of the budget and their relationships. Total operating expenditures per pupil are divided between instructional, administration, employee benefits, and a residual category labeled "other." Instructional expenditures per pupil are allocated primarily to teachers' salaries, and an incremental increase in salaries can go either to raise the average salary of teachers or to increase the teacher/student ratio.

$$\frac{\text{Total operating budget}}{\text{Pupils}} = \frac{\text{Instructional expenditures}}{\text{Pupils}} + \frac{\text{Administration}}{\text{Pupils}}$$

$$+ \frac{\text{Employee benefits}}{\text{Pupils}} + \frac{\text{"Other"}}{\text{Pupils.}}$$

$$\frac{\text{Instructional}}{\text{Pupils}} = \frac{\text{Total teaching salaries}}{\text{Pupils}} + \frac{\text{Materials}}{\text{Pupils}}.$$

$$\frac{\text{Total teacher salaries}}{\text{Pupils}} = \frac{\text{(Teachers)}}{\text{Pupils}} \times \text{(Average salary)}.$$

Figure 5-1. Definitions of District Financial Categories

Several factors contribute to school administrators' perceptions of quality and, consequently, to the allocation of educational resources. The first factor is the composition and size of the student body. Districts with a relatively large percentage of students from low-income families or students having little motivation (proxied by a high dropout rate) may require different educational services than districts with more affluent and motivated students. Another factor is the attributes and preferences of the community. Districts with a larger-than-average proportion of parents who have attended college and thus place a relatively high value on education will place greater emphasis on instructional expenditures.

The expenditure equations are estimated using data from public schools in the state of New York for the 1976–77 school year. District, student, and teacher statistics are obtained from unpublished records collected by the New York State Department of Education. The New York City school district is excluded from the analysis because of its unusual size and other unique characteristics.

The estimates of the educational-input demand equations are displayed in table 5–1. Results show that a higher-than-average total operating budget per pupil increases all categories of inputs. Manipulation of the estimates reveals that for every $1 of total budget per pupil, $0.48 is allocated for instructional purposes, $0.03 for administrative purposes, $0.13 for employee benefits, and the remaining $0.36 for other functions. Of the $0.48 that goes to instructional expenses, roughly 60 percent or $0.20 is spent on salaries and the remainder on textbooks and materials. Furthermore, it appears that very little of the $0.29 allocated to salaries is used to increase the teacher/student ratio, going rather to increase the average salaries of teachers. Estimates of the influence of community and student characteristics on the various budget categories are also presented in table 5–1. The signs of the coefficients are as expected.

Structure of District Contracts

Before we can move on to look at the effects of teacher unions on resource allocation, a number of issue associated with the structure of teacher contracts must also be resolved. One of the primary differences between this study and previous ones is our argument that part of the impact of unionization arises from interactive effects of individual articles in the contract. The majority of collective-bargaining studies, especially those focusing on wage effects, use a dichotomous union variable to introduce not only the presence but also the content and scope of collective bargaining contracts. The dummy-variable approach assumes that all collective-bargaining contracts are identical. This may suffice for wage studies, but the nonwage-

Table 5-1
Nonunion Determinants of the Allocation of District Expenditures

Independent Variables	Dependent Variables							Means
	Instruction/ Pupil	Administration/ Pupil	Benefits/ Pupil	Teacher/ Pupil	Average Salary	Salaries/ Pupil	Other	
I	10.79 (578.07)	7.33 (35.58)	9.45 (377.77)	-3.22 (133.3)	9.07 (231.9)	10.32 (398.36)	10.23 (173.07)	
OpExp pupil	.000004 (50.55)	.000005 (5.34)	.000004 (38.85)	.000001 (12.31)	.000002 (14.22)	.000004 (34.34)	.0000035 (14.00)	2,182.66
Enroll	.00001 (6.06)	.00015 (7.69)	.00013 (5.73)	-.00002 (6.61)	.00003 (7.33)	.000016 (6.34)	-.000034 (6.22)	3,467
(Enroll)²	-2.5 E-10 (3.78)	-3.41 E-9 (4.84)	-2.70 E-10 (3.16)	3.4 E-10 (4.10)	-5.3 E-10 (3.99)	-4.50 E-10 (4.86)	7.57 E-10 (3.75)	26,173,703
%Welfare	-.002 (.56)	-.10 (3.25)	.0036 (.95)	.014 (3.44)	-.008 (1.28)	-.0010 (.23)	.011 (1.27)	1.30
Dropout	-.003 (.86)	.005 (1.52)	.0013 (.28)	.002 (.57)	-.02 (3.41)	-.019 (4.01)	.0018 (1.27)	2.69
%Parents with college	.11 (3.52)	.13 (.37)	.074 (1.74)	-.006 (.15)	.09 (1.38)	.19 (4.10)	-.27 (.17)	.28
R²	.90	.34	.86	.37	.59	.85	.37	
Means (non-logs)	1,194	65.14	325.32	.051	14,833	728.82	505.13	

Note: Dependent variables in logs, t-ratios in parentheses.

[a]Dropout = number of students dropping out in grades 9-12 by the total K-12 population of the school districts.

effects literature, especially that portion pertaining to bargaining outcomes, emphasizes the importance of the scope and content of the contract. Therefore, to capture the impact of bargaining outcomes on resource allocation, the contracts must be broken down into their various components, which can then be entered into the district expenditure equations.

Previous Measures of Contract Structure. Various schemes have been suggested for indexing contracts. Kochan and Wheeler (1975), for example, score contracts for public-sector workers by assigning the provisions present in particular contracts to each of 53 predetermined categories. The total score of each contract is calculated by simply tallying the number of clauses contained in the individual contract. Recognizing that this method of scaling assigns equal weights to all terms of the agreement, Kochan and Wheeler confirm the validity of assuming equal weights by polling members and officials of the union under investigation. However, without replicating the procedure for other unions, it is unclear whether equal weights are generally applicable.

McDonnell and Pascal (1979) follow a similar classification procedure but propose another weighting scheme. Two assumptions are made in constructing their scale: (1) a more complete contract (the presence of more items) is more effective; and (2) a contract with a rare provision is stronger than a similar contract with a common provision. To capture both of these properties, a district contract is compared with the sample mean for each contract item by subtracting the district's value ("1" if present, "0" if not) from the sample mean. The scores are summed over all items within each category and divided by the corresponding number of contract provisions. McDonnell and Pascal expand the index to include the predicted probability of the appearance of a particular contract provision given such local factors as organizational resources, statutes, and other relevant demographic and locational variables.

The most fundamental problem with the Kochan-Wheeler and McDonnell-Pascal indexes, aside from the problem of determining the correct weighting scheme for the contract items, is that the impact of individual provisions cannot be isolated using either of their aggregated indexes of contract structure. We resolve this issue by viewing the structure of teacher contracts as a *hierarchy* of groups of related provisions. Using these results, we then move on to pursue the issue of the web-of-rules effect of contract structure.

Hierarchical Structure of Contracts. A hierarchical analysis of contract provisions using the Guttman scaling technique provides a solution to the problem of isolating the effect of individual provisions, as well as to the problem of determining the correct index weights. Guttman scales provide measures

of the underlying structural characteristics of three or more items that meet two basic properties.[5] First, Guttman scales are unidimensional; that is, the component items must all measure toward and away from a single underlying principle. Second, the scales are cumulative, which implies that the component items can be ordered by some criterion. In the case of contract items, districts able to obtain items that are very difficult to negotiate are also expected to obtain less difficult items.

The incremental process of contract negotiations and the cumulative principle upon which Guttman scales are constructed allows the hierarchy obtained from the Guttman analysis to be interpreted as the result of a dynamic process. Suppose that all school districts face similar financial conditions and teachers share similar preferences. The most difficult contract items to negotiate are most likely those that have not been negotiated extensively in other districts. The most easily negotiated items are the most widely accepted items. Therefore the hierarchy obtained from the Guttman analysis can be interpreted in terms of the chronology of the proliferation of particular contract items. The item at the base of the hierarchy is the first to be negotiated and over time has become the most common provision, whereas the item at the top is the path-breaking provision that is rarely present. Over time, of course, the top item may move down the hierarchy to be replaced by new path-breaking items.

Based upon previous research and the patterns of provisions in contracts for New York school districts, we selected eighteen major contract items to examine, grouped in five major categories. Both the contract items and the categories are displayed in table 5-2. The classification reflects different aspects of school district operations. The first group contains items associated with grievance and arbitration matters. These items describe procedures dealing with teacher-initiated events such as the bargaining of a contract, complaints by teachers of administrative violations of the contract, and the assessment of teacher performance based upon negotiated criteria. The second and third categories include job security and labor jurisprudence items. The reduction-in-force procedures for the most part are contingency clauses, which become constraints only when specific events external to the district occur. Items in all three categories address factors outside the control of the administrators. The last two categories, those on classroom policy and education, contain working-condition provisions that address the daily routine of classroom operations and provisions for inservice and continuing education.

Within each of the five groups the individual provisions follow a clear hierarchy, with each item extending or modifying the major objectives of that category. In some cases the language of the contract is strengthened (e.g., by replacing a reduction-in-force provision based on seniority with a provision prohibiting reductions during the term of the contract); in others

Table 5-2

Hierarchy of New York Public-School Contract Provisions[a]

	Percentage of Contracts with Items
Arbitration and grievance[b]	
Maintenance of standards (30)[d]	12
Final stage-binding arbitration (9)	83
Evaluation procedures for teachers (38)	87
c.r. = .93[c]	
Reduction in force	
No reduction during contract (56)	4
Recall to position (58)	12
Seniority clause (57)	18
Staff-reduction procedure (55)	37
c.r. = .93	
Dismissal procedures	
Severance pay (62)	2
Dismissal for just cause	
Probationary teachers only (60)	27
Tenured only (61)	38
Nontenured only (59)	39
c.r. = .99	
Classroom policy	
Number of aides specified (19)	3
Education policy committee (44)	39
Class size (40)	56
Teacher preparation provision (53)	71
c.r. = .89	
Inservice and continuing education	
Tuition reimbursement (42)	4
Summer sabbaticals (6)	16
Inservice provision (20)	40
c.r. = .92	

[a]Items are listed in order of difficulty from topmost, difficult to bottom, least difficult. Employment and fringe benefits are considered to affect primarily teacher salaries and are thus not included in the analysis.
[b]Grievance procedures are omitted since they are in 99 percent of the contracts.
[c]c.r. denotes coefficient of reproducibility. A value greater than 0.9 is generally considered to indicate a valid scale.
[d]Numbers in parentheses are codes used to identify variables in table 5-3.

the sphere of influence is broadened (e.g., by adding class-size restrictions to teacher preparation provisions). The Guttman analysis also shows that contract provisions remain independent between categories, a property we eventually exploit.

Structure as a Web of Rules. The effect of the contractual web of rules—as identified by Kerr and Siegel (1955) and Dunlop (1958)—arises not from the separate effects of individual contract provisions, but from the cumulative interaction of individual provisions. That is, the effect of a particular contract provision on administrative discretion and behavior depends in part on the number and type of other provisions in the contract. Administrators can sometimes avoid the full impact of contract constraints by substituting one resource for another or by making other adjustments. For example, administrators may attempt to reduce costs but still comply with the class-size-limitation provision by employing teacher aids in place of certified teachers. If a teacher's aide provision in the contract limits the number or duties of aides, the administrator does not have the same flexibility to substitute aides for teachers to reduce costs.

Given the hierarchical structure of teacher contracts displayed in table 5-2, we are able to perform a simple test of the web-of-rules effect using only the total number of the eighteen items present in a specific contract. With this measure we hypothesize that the sheer number of provisions in a hierarchical structure reduces administrative discretion in resource allocation and educational policy, hence is an index of contract strength.

*Teacher Contracts and the Allocation of
District Expenditures*

In this section we first examine the effect of individual contract items on resource allocations in public schools, using the hierarchical structure presented in the previous section. Again our application of the Guttman scaling technique reveals a hierarchical relationship among provisions within major functional categories, but independent among provisions in different categories. Next we test the web-of-rules effect of contract provisions on resource allocation, using the total number of provisions as one index of contract strength.

Individual Contract Items and Resource Allocation. To measure the impact of individual contract items on the allocation of resources, we enter the contract items from each category separately into the expenditure equations as interaction terms with the total budget variable. This procedure is justified by the fact that our Guttman scaling analysis established a hierarchical relation among provisions within major functional categories, but independence among provisions in different categories. Similar coefficients estimates are obtained if all provisions are entered simultaneously, but efficiency suffers.

Our estimates of the effects of individual contract provisions are pre-

sented in table 5-3. To aid in interpreting the results, we also include equations for the teacher/student ratio and average teacher salary. The eighteen contract items, identified by their corresponding number in table 5-1, are grouped by category and listed inversely by frequency of occurrence. Each coefficient represents the marginal effect of a contract provision on expenditures in a particular budget category. Each expenditure equation is estimated using the full set of independent variables that appear in table 5-1, but for brevity only the estimates of the interaction between each contract item and the total budget are presented.

As suggested earlier, contract items may have significant effects if the preferences between teachers and administrators are sufficiently diverse and if teacher-sponsored contract items are adhered to by administrators. If the divergence of preferences between the two parties is a major factor, then our results suggest that the two parties disagree more about the appropriate response to external events than they do about events of the daily routine of the district. Of the nine contract coefficients that are statistically significant at the 0.05 level for at least one dependent variable, only one is in either of the working condition categories (categories D and E, where there are seven coefficients in all), whereas two fall within the arbitration category (category A, where there are only three coefficients in all), and six within the two labor jurisprudence categories (categories B and C, where there are eight coefficients in all).

Considering each category of items, we find that items within category A, the arbitration and grievance group, appear to provide virtually no benefit to teachers in terms of nonwage budget items. The only impact appears to be in administrative costs, where districts that formally evaluate teachers (provision 38) spend more on administration and less on teacher salaries.

Items in categories B and C, the labor jurisprudence items dealing with reductions-in-force and dismissals, generally benefit teachers by protecting them from contingencies for which their preferred response differs greatly from the response preferred by administrators. Districts with a reduction-in-force procedure (55), for example, allocate more funds to instruction than districts without the clause, with the increase going primarily to an increase in teacher salaries. In addition, districts that provide severance pay (62) or have a recall provision (58) allocate more funds to instruction, at the expense of resources in the category *other*. For both provisions the increase in instructional expenses goes primarily to teacher salaries, with no significant effect on the teacher/student ratio. Some of the labor-jurisprudence contract items also address the dismissal of teachers for other than financial reasons. These just-cause dismissal provisions (59, 60, 61) identify which teachers are protected. Provisions covering tenured (61) and nontenured teachers (59) are both found to decrease the allocation of funds to administration.

Table 5-3
Impact of Individual Contract Provisions on the Allocation of District Expenditures[a]

Provision Code in Table 5-1	Instruction/ Pupil[b]	Administration/ Pupil	Benefits/ Pupil	Other/ Pupil	Salaries/ Pupil	Teacher/ Pupil[c]	Average Salary[c]
Arbitration and grievance							
30	.005 (.88)	.005 (1.45)	.006 (.34)	−.017 (.38)	−.0016 (.32)	−.0047 (.38)	.006 (.32)
9	−.010 (1.65)	−.002 (.81)	−.002 (.10)	−.003 (.22)	−.004 (.98)	−.013 (1.21)	−.009 (.50)
38	−.004 (76)	.009 (1.99)	−.0004 (.80)	−.0024 (.32)	−.009 (2.03)	.0015 (.13)	−.015 (.83)
Reduction in force							
56	−.0007 (.08)	.004 (.78)	.005 (1.82)	.0003 (.02)	.003 (.40)	−.033 (1.61)	.046 (1.39)
58	.006 (2.00)	.001 (.37)	.002 (.77)	−.106 (1.92)	.0060 (1.26)	.0001 (.005)	.040 (1.96)
57	.008 (2.00)	.001 (.51)	.00002 (.01)	.01 (1.48)	.004 (1.07)	.013 (1.28)	.025 (1.49)
55	.011 (3.03)	−.0007 (.67)	.003 (2.01)	−.020 (3.64)	.0075 (2.42)	.007 (.78)	.032 (2.43)
Dismissal procedures							
62	.018 (2.14)	.004 (.81)	.002 (.54)	−.024 (1.88)	.010 (1.36)	−.006 (.32)	.040 (1.32)
60	−.000 (.02)	−.003 (.18)	−.002 (1.16)	.003 (.50)	−.002 (.56)	.007 (.72)	.006 (.32)
61	−.002 (.51)	−.004 (2.05)	−.0013 (.99)	.004 (.73)	−.004 (1.29)	.010 (1.18)	−.004 (.31)
59	−.0009 (23.)	−.004 (2.01)	.001 (1.04)	.0024 (.45)	−.004 (1.29)	.009 (1.09)	−.002 (.17)

Table 5-3 continued

Provision Code in Table 5-1	Instruction/Pupil[b]	Administration/Pupil	Benefits/Pupil	Other/Pupil	Salaries/Pupil	Teacher/Pupil[c]	Average Salary[c]
Classroom Policy							
19	.008	−.003	−.003	.0084	.008	−.002	.008
	(.65)	(.38)	(.58)	(.45)	(.77)	(.07)	(.17)
44	.0006	−.001	.00006	−.0013	−.0002	−.009	−.006
	(.16)	(.56)	(.49)	(.24)	(.06)	(1.14)	(.45)
40	.0003	.0003	.013	−.007	.001	−.008	.004
	(.08)	(1.15)	(1.20)	(1.24)	(.44)	(1.04)	(.28)
53	.004	.0007	.00006	.0000	−.004	.001	−.013
	(1.02)	(.29)	(.04)	(.0003)	(1.17)	(.12)	(.84)
Inservice and continuing education							
42	.015	.003	.006	−.029	.012	.019	.031
	(1.96)	(.59)	(2.37)	(2.56)	(1.90)	(1.10)	(1.10)
6	.002	−.001	−.0008	.006	.0025	−.007	.013
	(.65)	(.51)	(.52)	(.87)	(.65)	(.70)	(.77)
20	.0006	.001	−.001	−.0028	−.002	.006	.003
	(.17)	(.04)	(.85)	(.52)	(.50)	(.71)	(.27)
Mean	1,194.00	65.74	325.32	505.13	728.82	.051	14,883
Coefficient of budget variable	.48	.03	.13	.18	.29	.22	.44

[a] Estimates are computed in dollar amounts and t-statistics are given in parentheses.
[b] Dependent variables entered as logs.
[c] Estimates of these categories are measured as elasticities.
[d] Refer to table 5-1 for identification of the contract provisions.

Almost none of the contract provisions in categories *D* and *E,* classroom policy and inservice and continuing education, appear to have any significant impact on resource allocation. Apparently the preferences of teachers and administrators do not differ sufficiently to result in any observable effect, or there are compensating efficiencies. Only the tuition-reimbursement item (42) yields statistically significant estimates, with more funds going to instruction and employee benefits, and fewer to the category *other.*

The total magnitude of the impact of the five functional groups of items can be measured by summing up the marginal effects. The magnitude on the various expenditure categories of these effects ranges from 0 to 30 percent, with the effects on the administration portion of the budget registering the highest values. Therefore we find the effects of contracts on budgetary allocations to be comparable in magnitude to the effects of unions on salaries as reported in chapter 4.

The hierarchical nature of contracts is further revealed by the relative magnitudes of the effects of items within a given category. The items within each of the five categories either increase the breadth of a contract or add language to the contract that strengthens the teachers' position. It follows, therefore, that items within the hierarchy should influence the allocation of resources in the same direction with varying degrees of intensity—all statistically significant coefficients are consistent with this prediction.

Number of Contract Items and Resource Allocation. As discussed earlier, our test of the web-of-rules effect of contracts depends upon the total number of contract items in a hierarchical structure as an index of contract strength. The hypothesis that the number of contract items affects the allocation of district expenditures is tested by entering the number of items into the budget equations. These estimates are presented in table 5-4. The signs and magnitudes of coefficients for all the original variables are as before, and the number of contract items has significant effects in a number of categories of expenditures. In particular, administrators who face a greater-than-average number of contract items increase the allocation of funds to instruction, employee benefits, and salaries, at the expense of the category *other.* The number of contract items does not appear to influence allocations to administrative items or to change the teacher/student ratio, although it does appear to affect average salaries. Teachers in districts with fifty contract items, for example, received about $1,900 more on average than those in districts with the minimum number of items. It appears therefore that, within a hierarchical contract structure, an increase in the number of major provisions causes administrators to reallocate funds to budget items preferred by teachers, consistent with the web-of-rules prediction.

Table 5-4
Estimates of the Effect of the Number of Contract Provisions and Other Determinants on Budget Allocation in New York Public Schools, 1976–77

Independent Variables	Dependent Variables						
	Instruction	Administration	Benefits	Other	Salaries	Teacher	Average Salary
OPEXP	.820	.660	.840	.990	.790	.310	.420
	(31.66)	(2.51)	(25.03)	(12.58)	(21.99)	(9.23)	(8.11)
Number of items	.002	.010	.002	-.007	.002	-.001	.003
	(3.99)	(1.55)	(2.11)	(3.94)	(2.05)	(1.26)	(2.44)
Enroll	.035	.519	.045	-.118	.055	-.069	.104
	(6.06)	(7.69)	(5.73)	(6.22)	(6.34)	(6.61)	(7.33)
(ENROLL)²	-.007	-.089	-.007	.020	-.012	.009	-.014
	(3.78)	(4.84)	(3.16)	(3.75)	(4.86)	(4.10)	(3.99)
Dropout	-.003	-.130	.005	.014	-.001	.018	-.010
	(.56)	(3.25)	(.95)	(1.27)	(.23)	(3.44)	(1.28)
Welfare	-.008	.014	.004	.001	-.051	.005	-.054
	(.86)	(1.52)	(.28)	(.17)	(4.01)	(.57)	(3.41)
College	.031	.036	.021	-.076	.053	-.002	.025
	(3.52)	(.37)	(1.74)	(2.65)	(4.10)	(.15)	(1.38)
R^2	.92	.34	.86	.40	.85	.37	.60

Note: t-values are in parentheses. The estimates are expressed in elasticities evaluated at the means. The total operating budget is decomposed in such a way that the dependent variables heading each column have the following relationships: (Instruction/pupil) + (Benefits/pupil) + (Other/pupil) = OPEXP; (Salaries/pupil) = (Teacher/pupil) × (Average salary). All dependent variables are entered as logs and expressed in per-pupil terms. 455 school districts are included in the sample.

Teacher Contracts and the Level of District Expenditures

Teachers' bargaining organizations can affect not only the internal allocation of funds, but also the allocation of funds within the community. Since
teachers recognize that larger budgets lead to an increase in instructional
expenses, salaries, benefits, and teaching staffs, collective-bargaining units
find it worthwhile to promote an increase in the total operating budget for
the school district. Many avenues of collective influence are open to the
teachers. They can align themselves with the administration, since both parties tend to be strong proponents of larger school budgets (except perhaps
when a superintendent is hired with a clear mandate to decrease spending).
The primary opposition to increased spending comes from school board
members who may feel that they were elected to curb spending. Teacher
unions may combat this opposition through political pressure, moral sua-
sion, or the threat of disruption of service, making the school board appear
ineffective in the management of the public schools.

Besides the influence of teacher organizations on school budgets, other
factors affect the level of spending. Families with many children find a
greater benefit per tax dollar in spending for education since their support
of public education is not directly based on the number of children in
school. Also, communities with a higher proportion of families with children also provide greater financial support for schools. The total operating
budget per pupil is also affected by state aid equalization programs and federal support of federally mandated programs.

The impact of the number of students in a district on per-pupil spending depends upon whether public education is subject to economies of scale.
Economies of scale occur in a labor-intensive service, such as education,
primarily through the specialization of certain personnel. For example,
small districts may not have sufficient demand for the full-time services of a
reading specialist and would prefer to fill that position with a part-time
teacher. However, especially when specialists are in short supply, part-time
teachers may not be available, and the district will have to employ the
teacher full time or go without the services. The latter may not be feasible
since many states require that schools provide special services to qualified
students. Larger districts on the other hand may have sufficient demand to
keep a full-time reading specialist busy. Thus the cost per pupil of the larger
district is lower than the cost per pupil in the smaller district.

We find that increases in the various sources of school revenue have different impacts on the increase of the total budget. A dollar increase in property taxes per pupil, for example, increases the total operating budget per
pupil by $0.94. A $1.00 increase in state aid per pupil increases school
spending by $0.88 per pupil, while $1.00 increase in federal aid increases
school spending by only $0.65. If each of the three sources of revenue

increased by $1.00, we would expect the total operating budget per pupil to increase by $3.00 instead of the $2.47 that we observe. The missing $0.53 can be accounted for in the substitution between the various sources. For example, a portion of the dollar per pupil received from the federal government may be used to reduce the amount of money needed from local property tax sources. The same is true for state aid but to a smaller extent.

The number of contract items has a positive effect upon the level of per-pupil spending, consistent with our evidence on the effects of the number of items on the allocation of expenditures. Districts with the minimum of four contract items spend on average $2,135 per pupil; districts with the mean number of contract items (26) increase per pupil spending by $35 to $2,171; and districts with the maximum number of contract items (50) increase their per-pupil spending by another $36 to $2,207. Clearly, teachers exercise significant influence on the size of the school budget.

Educational Policy and Practice and Teacher Contracts

The purpose of this relatively brief section is to explore some of the relationships between teacher contracts and educational policy and practice. We focus primarily on two issues—mode of instruction and extent of teacher participation in various administrative decisions (e.g., student and teacher assignments and curriculum planning). Thus, we leave consideration of the more immediate effects of teacher contracts on student achievement to chapter 6. Our data for this section come from the New York State districts and the Systems Development Corporation (SDC) national survey were discussed earlier.

Mode of Instruction and Teacher Contracts

For New York State we have information on the relative use of three different sorts of instructional modes. These are the traditional class arrangement, cluster classrooms, and open classrooms. To examine the correlation between various contract items and these instructional modes, the modes are each regressed against contract items and other factors that may determine the adoption of particular instructional modes in a district.

The empirical results are displayed in table 5–5. We find that traditional classrooms are positively related to class-size provisions and teacher-preparation provisions. Cluster classrooms are positively related to the presence of educational-policy committees, and open classrooms are inversely related to class-size provisions. For the educational policy committees and cluster arrangements, the direction of causality may be reversed. That is, districts

Table 5-5
Determinants of the Propensity of Districts in New York To Use Various Class Arrangements, 1976-1979

Explanatory Variables	Traditional	Cluster	Open
Percentage master's degree or higher	-.11	.15	-.07
	(1.87)	(1.47)	(.62)
Average total experience	.002	.0005	.002
	(.77)	(.09)	(.37)
Teacher/student ratio	-.96	-.50	2.60
	(.86)	(.26)	(1.24)
Total enrollment	4.2 E-6	5.90 E-6	1.40 E-6
	(2.57)	(2.12)	(.47)
Percentage families on welfare	.0004	-.02	-.007
	(.08)	(2.12)	(.69)
Dropout rate	.002	.002	-.009
	(.50)	(.35)	(1.04)
Operating expense/pupil	1.71 E-7	1.08 E-7	4.64 E-7
	(.93)	(.34)	(1.35)
Percentage parents college educated	-.12	.05	.17
	(2.40)	(3.00)	(1.70)
Percentage instructional expense	.38	-.74	-.83
	(2.62)	(2.94)	(3.05)
Summer sabbaticals	.01	-.03	.009
	(1.15)	(1.38)	(.03)
Release time for inservice	.006	-.09	-.05
	(.13)	(1.10)	(.62)
Payment for inservice	-.003	-.01	.04
	(.13)	(.41)	(.83)
Class-size provision	.02	-.02	-.003
	(2.67)	(1.46)	(.16)
Class-size impact	.05	-.02	.42
	(.74)	(.16)	(2.98)
Tuition reimbursement	.01	-.004	-.03
	(.47)	(.09)	(.64)
Provision for different preparations	-.004	-.01	.0007
	(.36)	(.64)	(.02)
Educational-policy committee	-.0005	.03	-.006
	(.04)	(1.72)	(.31)
Teacher-preparation provision	.02	-.009	.02
	(1.71)	(.45)	(1.10)
R^2	.09	.08	.09

Note: *t*-statistics in parentheses.

organized into cluster classrooms may require educational-policy committees to coordinate the activities of teachers. Since the remainig variables are included only as background controls, we do not discuss their coefficients.

Teacher Participation in Administrative Decisions

Based on the national SDC data, we are able to investigate differences between organized and nonorganized districts in the extent of teacher participation in various administrative decisions. The four categories we are able to consider are student assignment, teacher assignment, the planning of course content, and promoting community interaction. In each of these categories we have self-scored measures of both the importance of teacher participation and the actual extent of teacher participation. For the importance of teacher participation, the responses are scored from 1 (not important at all) to 5 (most important). For actual teacher participation, the responses are scored from 1 (administrator decision, no teacher input) to 5 (teacher decision, no administrator input). The mean values of the responses are presented in table 5-6. For all four categories, teachers appear to prefer a level of teacher participation that is higher than the level that actually occurs. However, in none of the four categories is there a significant difference between the responses of teachers covered by a contract and those not covered, even for teacher assignment.

The absence of differences in either attitudes about the importance of teacher participation or the extent of actual teacher participation might be due to other spurious differences between the two groups of teachers. To explore this possibility, we estimate the impact of collective bargaining on actual teacher participation, conditional on the importance placed on teacher participation, district enrollments, school climate, level of physical

Table 5-6
Teacher Participation by Contract Status (National SDC data)

	Contract		No Contract	
	Mean	*Std. Dev.*	*Mean*	*Std. Dev.*
Importance of teacher participation in				
Student assignment	3.45	1.18	3.24	1.24
Teacher assignment	3.42	1.17	3.31	1.20
Planning course content	4.32	.67	4.30	.69
Promoting community interaction	3.29	1.13	3.31	1.12
Actual teacher participation in				
Student assignment	2.69	1.23	2.67	1.27
Teacher assignment	1.99	1.14	1.93	1.11
Planning course content	3.54	1.17	3.56	1.19
Promoting community interaction	2.88	1.17	2.96	1.12
Number of observations	2,071		1,180	

[a]5 = Most important; 1 = Least important.
[b]5 = Teacher, No administrative input, 1 = Administrator, No teacher input.

violence, and type of community. These results, along with estimates of the links between teacher participation in administrative decisions and resource allocations, are presented in table 5-7.

The results explaining the allocation of resources per student to administrators, clerical staff and aides, and teachers show a significant link between teacher participation and resource allocation only for the teacher-assignment and course-content variables. For each of these, increased teacher participation is associated with a reduction in the number of teachers per student. The links between collective bargaining and the allocation of resources are consistent with those found in the previous section of this chapter—collective bargaining is associated with an increase in the teacher/student ratio and the administrator/student ratio, but a decrease in the number of clerical staff and teaching aides per student (again, holding a number of other factors constant, including teacher salaries).

Looking at the results for the equations explaining actual teacher participation, we find significantly positive links between the importance of participation and actual participation. The only effect of collective bargaining, however, appears to be on teacher participation in teacher assignment, and this link is only marginally significant. The results for remaining variables are generally as expected and are not discussed further here.

To summarize briefly, in none of the four categories of possible teacher participation is there a significant difference between teachers covered by collective bargaining and teachers not covered in attitudes toward the importance of teacher participation, or in the actual level of participation. All teachers, however, appear to prefer a greater degree of teacher participation in administrative decisions than actually occurs. The only link between collective bargaining and actual participation appears to be in teacher assignments, where there is a marginally significant positive link. The link between the importance placed on participation and actual participation, however, is strongly significant for all four categories of participation. Thus, desires for participation and actual participation are closely linked, regardless of union status (except perhaps for teacher assignment).

Conclusions

Our objective in this chapter was to investigate the separate and interactive effects of contract provisions in two broad areas of administrative behavior and discretion—resource allocation and educational policy and practice. First, we established a basic model, discussed some of the major nonunion determinants of expenditures, and examined the structure of contracts. For the latter we found that contract provisions follow a clear hierarchy; the presence of the various provisions is clearly ordered, within five major cate-

Table 5-7

Regressions for Teacher Participation and Contract Status (SDC Data)

(Explanatory Variables)

	Participation				
Dependent Variables	Collective Bargaining	Student Assignment	Teacher Assignment	Planning Course Content	Promoting Community Interaction
Resources (per student)					
Administrators	.179	.026	.045	.046	−.040
	(2.30)	(.91)	(1.41)	(1.56)	(1.32)
Clerical and aides	−1.21	−.281	.145	−.300	.326
	(2.65)	(1.70)	(.78)	(1.71)	(1.81)
Teachers	5.24	.242	−.546	−.330	−.068
	(12.47)	(1.60)	(3.20)	(2.06)	(.415)
Teacher participation					
Student assignment	.050				
	(1.13)				
Teacher assignment	.069				
	(1.72)				
Planning courses	−.017				
	(.404)				
Community interaction	−.062				
	(1.52)				
Salaries					
Teacher contract	.588				
	(20.75)				
Teacher supplementary	−.117				
	(1.89)				
Principal contract	1.09				
	(25.30)				
Teacher characteristics					
Experience	1.64				
	(5.80)				
Education	.098				
	((5.21)				
Length of day	−.110				
	(1.82)				

Note: *t*-statistics in parentheses. In order to conserve space, certain exogenous variables (District Enrollment, School Climate, Physical Violence, and Community Type) have been omitted from the table. The estimates of these coefficients are available from the authors upon request.

[a]The specific policy area corresponds to the dependent variable.

Salaries			Teacher Characterstics				
Teacher Contract	Teacher Supple- mental	Principal Contract	Experience	Education	Importance Placed on Participa- tion[a]	F	R^2
.060 (1.52)		−.174 (5.38)				15.16	.06
−.097 (.42)		1.36 (7.21)				22.01	.09
.418 (1.98)		.373 (2.14)				58.54	.20
					.248 (13.98)	29.72	.08
					.176 (10.18)	26.21	.07
					.289 (9.76)	21.23	.06
					.182 (10.46)	25.61	.07
			.060 (33.89)	.565 (21.26)		323.26	.50
			−.010 (2.68)	.168 (2.91)		4.04	.01
						250.44	.38
						12.22	.03
						14.29	.03
.067 (2.38)	.018 (1.11)					3.20	.21

gories, but the provisions remain independent between categories. The five categories are arbitration and grievance, reduction in force, dismissal procedures, classroom policy, and inservice and continuing education.

Our analysis of the effects of individual contract provisions within the hierarchy on resource allocation indicates a variety of significant effects, with the pattern of effects suggesting that employers and employees disagree more about the appropriate response to external events than they do about events regarding the daily routine of the district. The total magnitude of the effects of provisions within a particular contract category on expenditures varies from about 0 to 30 percent, with the largest effects on the administrative portion of the budget. Thus the effects of contract provisions on resource allocation are roughly comparable in magnitude to the effects of collective bargaining on teacher salaries and compensation found in chapter 4.

Our relatively simple test of the web-of-rules theory—the hypothesis that the effects of contract provisions are cumulative—indicated that the number of contract items, a proxy for contract strength, has significant effects on resource allocation. Administrators who face a greater-than-average number of contract items increase the allocation of funds to instruction, employee benefits, and salaries, at the expense of other budget categories. Teachers in districts with the greatest number of contract items, for example, receive about 10 to 15 percent more than those in districts with the minimum number of items.

We also found that contract provisions affect not just the internal allocation of funds but also the allocation of funds within the community, since the number of contract items present has a positive effect on the level of per-pupil expenditures. Thus districts with the minimum number of contract items spend significantly less per pupil than districts with the maximum number of contract items—which indicates that collective bargaining has a significant effect on the size of the school budget.

Finally, for our second broad topic area, educational policy and practice, we found significant links between contract provisions and mode of instruction (for example, class-size provisions are positively linked with the traditional classroom mode) but no significant differences between union and nonunion teachers in either the desired or actual level of teacher participation in a wide range of administrative decisions. Only for teacher assignment did we find a significant link between collective bargaining and actual participation. However, we did find a consistently positive link between the importance placed on participation and actual participation, regardless of coverage by a collective-bargaining contract. This suggests that desires for participation and actual participation may be closely linked even in the absence of collective bargaining. Both union and nonunion teachers, however, generally prefer a greater degree of teacher participation than actually occurs.

Notes

1. C.J. Parsley (1980) provides a survey of the effect of unions on wages. Very little work has been done on the effect of unions on management decisions. Slichter and others (1960) provide many case studies and anecdotal evidence. However, much of the empirical work in the private sector deals with the effect of unions on decisions of workers to quit and only indirectly relates to management decisions regarding hiring decisions and remuneration.

2. This two-stage allocation process implies that the expenditure equations should be estimated using two-stage least-squares (2SLS). Estimates using both OLS and 2SLS were obtained with no significant difference. Thus the OLS results are reported and the two-stage allocation model is replaced by the one-stage model.

3. Contract items can have both direct and indirect effects. These effects can be stated more explicitly by considering the various components of the change in a particular input. Consider a two-input case in which contract items are specific to only one input; that is, $\partial x_1 / \partial Q_2$ and $\partial x_2 / \partial Q_1$ are zero. The changes in inputs x_1 and x_2 are written

$$dx_1 = \left(\frac{\partial x_1}{\partial Q_1} \right) dQ_1 + \left(\frac{\partial X_1 \partial x_2}{\partial x_2 \partial Q_2} \right) dQ_2,$$

$$dx_2 = \left(\frac{\partial x_2 \partial x_1}{\partial x_1 \partial Q_1} \right) dQ_1 + \left(\frac{\partial x_2}{\partial Q_2} \right) dQ_2.$$

Notice that in this formulation, the impact of Q_2 on x_1 can come about only if x_2 is substituted for x_1 and Q_2 constrains the employment of x_2. Therefore when the impact of contract items are examined across a number of inputs, the significance of the impact of the item not directly associated with the input is due primarily to the substitution across inputs.

4. In a Tiebout model, enrollment would also be endogenous. However, we assume that school administrators treat enrollment as exogenous in determining the level and allocation of expenditures.

5. Consult Proctor (1970) for a description of the Guttman scaling technique.

6

Student Achievement
and Collective
Bargaining

In previous chapters we investigated trends in collective-bargaining contracts, major determinants of student achievement, and effects of collective bargaining for both teachers and administrators. In this chapter we attempt to bring all these diverse elements together to examine the overall impact of collective bargaining on both the level and cost of student achievement, thus providing a broad assessment of collective bargaining.

Our analysis and measurement of the potential effects of collective bargaining on levels of student achievement is decomposed into three parts. First, we measure the effects due to union-induced changes in the levels of the various *resources* going into the educational process, the determinants of student achievement emphasized in chapter 3. Second, we measure the effects due to union-induced changes in the educational *process,* differences in the educational production functions for the union and nonunion sectors. Third, we measure the effects due to interactions *between* the two types of changes, between changes in resources and changes in process. This detailed decomposition enables us both to assess the net effects of collective bargaining on student achievement and to identify some of the sources of the effects. Moreover, our results provide evidence on the question of whether the impact of collective bargaining varies for different types of students.

Our analysis and measurement of the effects of collective bargaining on the *cost* of student achievement is distinguished from previous studies by the use of national data with detailed controls for student, district, community, and regional factors, but distinguished most significantly by the use of measures of student achievement to control for quality of education. Thus we attempt to isolate the effect of collective bargaining on the costs of providing a given quality and quantity of education.

Resources, Student Achievement, and Collective Bargaining

If one views student achievement as being jointly determined by the levels of various resources (including individual student characteristics) going into

157

the educational process and by the efficiency of these resources, then changes in student achievement can be decomposed into those resulting from changes in the levels of resources, changes in the efficiency of the resources (changes in the educational process), and the interaction between the two types of changes. The sum of these three components approximates the actual change in student achievement.[1]

Differences in Educational Inputs

Our analysis of educational production functions in chapter 3 considered several dozen factors potentially important to student achievement. In this subsection we evaluate the impact on student achievement of induced differences between union and nonunion districts in the levels of these productive factors. To do this, we first compute the differences between union and nonunion districts for the factors considered in chapter 3. These differences, along with the separate union and nonunion means, are presented in table 6-1. Almost all the means differ significantly for the union and nonunion districts. Only the means for sex, race, teacher time in administrative duties, and instructional leadership by the principal are statistically the same for the two sets of districts.

We are particularly concerned with differences for those factors identified in chapter 3 as major determinants of student achievement in mathematics: teachers' instruction time, preparation time, experience, and academic degrees; principals' involvement, experience in teaching, experience in administration, and academic degrees; teacher/student ratio and administrator/student ratio. Teachers' and principal's level of education (highest degree attained) and the administrator/student ratio were found in chapter 3 to be inversely related to student achievement; all the other factors were found to be positively related. As shown in table 6-1, the union means exceed the nonunion means for all but amount of instruction time.

To assess the *net* effect of the difference in each educational input on student achievement, the impact of each difference in mean is calculated by multiplying each difference by the corresponding coefficient from the nonunion production function. Separate estimates of the nonunion coefficients are displayed in table 6-2. The calculations are displayed in the first column of table 6-3, under the column heading $\beta \Delta X$. The largest positive effects are those for economic status, teacher/student ratio, math inservice training, and pretest score; the largest negative effects are for instructional time and teachers' perception of how well-planned school programs are. The sum of all these individual effects is 1.52, about 15 percent of the average gain from the pre- to posttest score.

Many of the differences in means, however, are not actually induced by collective bargaining, so it is wrong to attribute all of the effects of the differences to collective bargaining. To get only those differences in means

Table 6–1
Means of Education Inputs by Union Status (SDC Data)

Variables	Union Means	Nonunion Means	Difference
Intercept	1.000	1.000	0.0000
Sex (male = 1)—Student	0.496	0.513	−0.0169*
Race (white = 1)—Student	0.725	0.736	−0.0103
Childhood experience—Student	1.050	1.058	−0.0084
Parental involvement—Student	1.958	1.736	0.2223*
Economic status—Student	228.970	217.937	11.0328*
Administrators/student	0.004	0.004	0.0004*
Teachers/student	0.057	0.051	0.0060*
Office staff/student	0.018	0.020	−0.0014*
Teacher time in instruction	4.830	4.992	−0.1620*
Teacher preparation time	1.425	1.371	0.0538*
Teacher time in administrative duties	0.798	0.778	0.0199
Total years teaching—Teacher	12.359	11.334	1.0254*
Highest degree—Teacher	2.477	2.444	−0.0335*
College math courses—Teacher	0.630	0.566	0.0635*
Math inservice—Teacher	6.149	9.485	−3.3361*
Principal's leadership/Teacher's perception	3.516	3.347	0.1694*
Principal's encouragement/Teacher's perception	3.124	3.244	−0.1198*
Pretest score	29.077	27.961	1.1166*
Pretest score squared	942.277	869.783	72.4938*
Highest degree of principal	2.986	3.015	−0.0290*
Total years teaching—Principal	10.602	9.464	1.1378*
Total years administration—Principal	9.129	8.408	0.7206*
Math participation—Principal	10.2295	8.9398	1.2897*
Math involvement—Principal	12.1196	11.4505	0.6691*
Instructional leadership—Principal	53.4762	53.6173	−0.1411*
Attitudes			
Well-planned—Principal	3.2050	3.3276	−0.1226*
Well-planned—Teacher	2.5423	2.6595	−0.1167*
Active leadership—Principal	3.1635	3.0456	0.1179*
Active leadership—Teacher	2.2340	2.4359	−0.2019*
Work well together—Principal	3.4545	3.3928	0.0617*
Work well together—Teacher	2.9493	3.0721	−0.1228*
Well-informed—Principal	3.3578	3.3989	−0.0411*
Well-informed—Teacher	2.2968	2.3893	−0.0925*
Conflicts identified—Principal	3.2256	3.3590	−0.1334*
Conflicts identified—Teacher	2.2237	2.3762	−0.1525*
Posttest score	39.6477	37.8411	1.8066*

*Significant at the 0.05 level.
Note: See chapter 3 for a detailed description of the variables.

Table 6-2
Educational Production Functions by Union Status (SDC Data)

Variables	Coefficients		
	Union	Nonunion	Difference
Intercept	11.71*	12.97*	1.26
Sex (male = 1)—Student	−1.85*	−1.99*	0.14
Race (white = 1)—Student	1.79*	0.98*	0.81*
Childhood experience—Student	−0.13	0.07	−0.20
Parental involvement—Student	0.13*	0.03	0.11
Economic status—Student	0.02*	0.02*	0.00
Administrators/student	−216.01*	−19.30	−196.70*
Teachers/student	17.28*	47.25*	−29.97*
Office staff/student	7.41	−26.56*	33.97*
Teacher time in instruction	0.35*	0.85*	−0.50*
Teacher preparation time	0.29*	0.64*	−0.35
Teacher time in administrative duties	0.14	−0.63*	0.77*
Total years teaching—Teacher	0.01	0.04*	−0.03
Highest degree—Teacher	−0.92*	−0.35	−0.57*
College math courses—Teacher	0.17	−0.08	0.26*
Math inservice—Teacher	−0.001	−0.32	0.32
Principal's leadership/Teacher's perception	−0.17*	0.17*	−0.33
Principal's encouragement/Teacher's perception	−0.42*	−0.15	−0.27
Pretest score	0.97*	0.71*	0.26*
Pretest score squared	−0.00165*	0.0027*	−0.00435*
Highest degree—principal	−2.27*	−0.29	−1.99*
Total years teaching—Principal	0.08*	0.02	0.05*
Total years administration—Principal	0.10*	0.13*	−0.03
Math participation—Principal	−0.05*	−0.00	−0.05*
Math involvement—Principal	0.02	0.09*	−0.07*
Instructional leadership—Principal	0.05*	−0.10*	0.16*
Attitudes			
Well-planned—Principal	−0.43	0.20	−0.64*
Well-planned—Teacher	0.04	0.06	−0.01
Active leadership—Principal	−0.11	−0.84*	0.73*
Active leadership—Teacher	0.00	0.28*	−0.28*
Work well together—Principal	0.11	−0.82*	0.93*
Work well together—Teacher	−0.08	−0.07	−0.00
Well-informed—Principal	0.45*	0.40	0.05*
Well-informed—Teacher	0.00	−0.44*	0.45*

| Variables | Coefficients | | |
	Union	Nonunion	Difference
Conflicts identified—Principal	0.18	0.61*	−0.43
Conflicts identified—Teacher	0.19*	−0.17	0.36*
R^2	.5598	.5466	
Number of observations	9,470	5,412	

Note: See chapter 3 for a detailed description of the variables.
*Significant at the 0.05 level.

attributable to collective bargaining, we return to our results in table 5-7, where the relationship between collective bargaining and major determinants of student achievement is measured with a number of other variables held constant (district enrollment, school climate, physical violence, and community type). We supplement the results in table 5-7 (for administrators per student; teachers per student; teachers' experience, degrees, time teachers spend on instruction, and time teachers spend on preparation) with similar analyses for principals' experience, degrees, and involvement (these estimates are omitted for brevity). Thus considering only the impact of the differences in means shown to be related to collective bargaining, we find a net impact of only 0.45, about 4 percent of the average gain. Hence the *net* change in student achievement resulting from union-induced changes in resources is very small—small despite a number of very substantial individual effects, since these tend to be offsetting.

Differences in Educational Production Functions

In this subsection we measure the impact on student achievement of differences in the educational production functions for union and nonunion districts. As indicated previously, separate estimates of the educational production functions for union and nonunion districts are presented in table 6-2, along with the differences in the coefficients. Over half the coefficients differ significantly between the two groups of districts, including those for race; administrators per student; teachers per student; office staff per student; teachers' instruction time, time spent in administrative duties, and degrees and college mathematics courses taken by the teacher; student pretest score; principal's degree, experience in teaching, participation, involvement, and instructional leadership; and a number of other variables related to perceptions of performance.

Table 6–3
Effects on Student Achievement of Differences between Union and
Nonunion Districts in Education Inputs and
Educational Production Functions

Variables	$\beta \Delta X$	$X \Delta \beta$	$\Delta X \Delta \beta$
Intercept	0.000	−1.264	0.000
Sex (male = 1)—Student	0.034	0.072	−0.002
Race (white = 1)—Student	−0.010	0.597	−0.008
Childhood experience—Student	−0.000	−0.209	0.002
Parental involvement—Student	0.006	0.183	0.023
Economic status—Student	0.165	0.259	0.013
Administrators/student	−0.007	−0.730	−0.073
Teachers/student	0.285	−1.519	−0.181
Office staff/student	0.037	0.670	−0.048
Teacher time in instruction	−0.138	−2.482	0.081
Teacher preparation time	0.035	−0.486	−0.019
Teacher time in administrative duties	−0.012	0.599	0.015
Total years teaching—Teacher	0.044	−0.343	−0.031
Highest degree—Teacher	−0.012	−1.387	−0.019
College math courses—Teacher	−0.005	0.145	0.016
Math inservice—Teacher	0.108	0.295	−0.104
Principal's leadership/Teacher's perception	0.028	−1.115	−0.056
Principal's encouragement/Teacher's perception	0.018	−0.880	0.032
Pretest score	0.796	7.217	0.288
Pretest score squared	0.196	−3.782	−0.315
Highest degree—principal	0.008	−5.990	0.058
Total years teaching—Principal	0.031	0.503	0.060
Total years administration—Principal	0.092	−0.257	−0.022
Math participation—Principal	−0.002	−0.447	−0.065
Math involvement—Principal	0.060	−0.746	−0.044
Instructional leadership—Principal	0.015	8.469	−0.022
Attitudes			
Well-planned—Principal	−0.025	−2.117	0.078
Well-planned—Teacher	−0.007	−0.046	0.002
Active leadership—Principal	−0.097	2.222	0.086
Active leadership—Teacher	−0.056	−0.675	0.056
Work well together—Principal	−0.051	3.159	0.057
Work well together—Teacher	0.008	−0.029	0.001
Well-informed—Principal	−0.016	0.170	−0.002

Variables	$\beta \Delta X$	$X \Delta \beta$	$\Delta X \Delta \beta$
Well-informed—Teacher	0.041	1.068	−0.041
Conflicts identified—Principal	−0.082	−1.456	0.058
Conflicts identified—Teacher	0.026	0.864	−0.055
Sum	1.5178	.5321	−.1800

Note: β refers to the coefficients of the nonunion production function in table 6-2. X refers to the nonunion means from table 6-1. The changes are calculated by subtracting the nonunion value from the corresponding union value.

To assess the impact of these differences in the educational production functions, we multiply each difference in coefficients by the nonunion mean of the corresponding variable. These products are presented in the second column of table 6-3, under the column heading $X \Delta \beta$. The largest positive effects are those for the pretest score, instructional leadership by the principal, and the principal's perception of how well teachers work together; the largest negative effects are those for instructional time, the squared term for the pretest score, principal's degree, and the principal's perception of how well-planned the school's programs are. The net impact of all the differences in coefficients is 0.53, about 5 percent of the average gain from the pre- to posttest score. Hence the impact of this second source of union-induced changes in student achievement is also very small—again small despite a number of substantial individual effects.

While our emphasis in this chapter is on the overall impact of collective bargaining rather than on all the detailed effects explored in earlier chapters, we should dwell at least a moment on one set of differences revealed in table 6-2. The coefficients for pretest score and the square of the pretest score are 0.713 and 0.0027 for nonunion districts and 0.971 and −0.0017 for union districts. The difference by union status is statistically significant in both cases. To evaluate this difference, we compute the predicted posttest score associated with a particular pretest score. Subtracting the predicted score for a student in a nonunion district from the predicted score for a student with the same pretest score in a union district, one obtains a measure of the difference in the relationship between pre- and posttest scores in union and nonunion districts.

This difference is plotted in figure 6-1 for a range of pretest scores. As the diagram illustrates, the difference in achievement scores is greatest for students near the average pretest score (about 29). This implies that union districts do relatively best with average students. For above-average stu-

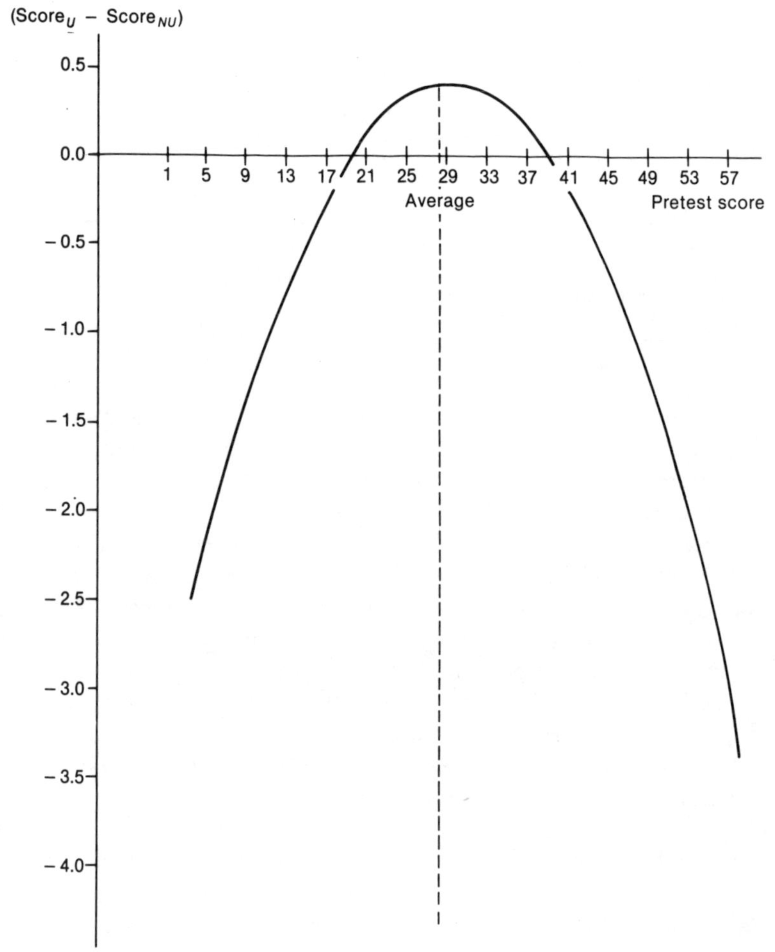

(Score$_U$ – Score$_{NU}$)

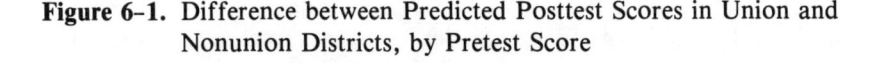

Figure 6-1. Difference between Predicted Posttest Scores in Union and
Nonunion Districts, by Pretest Score

dents, union districts tend to compress test scores toward the average, as
compared to what happens in nonunion districts. This obviously implies a
reduction in the dispersion of posttest scores for students with above-average pretest scores. For below-average students, however, just the opposite
occurs in union districts. For these students nonunion, rather than union,
districts tend to compress test scores toward the average. While we lack the

intensive case study required to explain fully why the impact of collective bargaining appears to vary for different students, we speculate that the difference results from the standardization associated with collective bargaining in most industries; for example, we already know from chapter 5 that organized districts with class-size restrictions in the contract are more likely to use standard classroom instruction as a uniform mode of instruction.

To pursue this point further, we calculate differences for union and nonunion districts in the use of special instructional modes and resources, using the national SDC data. These differences are presented in table 6–4, along with the separate union and nonunion means. Students in union districts clearly have less exposure to specialized instructional modes or resources. Since specialized modes are those typically associated with students well above or below average, these differences appear to provide one explanation for why union districts work less well for those students than for average students.

Interactive Effects

Our final component for changes in the level of student achievement attributable to collective bargaining consists of the interactions between differences in the levels of resources and in educational processes. Since we already know that the net impact on student achievement from each set of differences is small, the net impact resulting from interactions between the differences is likely to be even smaller. To calculate these interactions, we simply multiply the corresponding pairs of differences. These are displayed

Table 6–4
Instructional Modes and Resources for Mathematics in Union and Nonunion Districts (SDC Data)

Variable Description	Means		Difference
	Union	Nonunion	
Student hours spent with math specialist, class of 7 plus	2.12	3.63	−1.51 (-6.78)
Student hours spent with math aide	1.97	5.24	−3.27 (−15.57)
Student hours spent with math tutor	.96	1.29	−.33 (−3.76)
Student hours spent in independent, programmed study	3.37	5.65	−2.28 (-8.69)

Note: See chapter 3 for a description of the SDC data. The *t*-values for the difference in the means are in parentheses.

in the third column of table 6-3, under the column heading $\Delta X \Delta \beta$. The largest positive effect is that for the pretest score; the largest negative effects are those for the teacher/student ratio, teacher mathematics inservice training, and the square of the pretest score. The net effect of all the interactions is only -0.18, about 2 percent of the average gain from the pre- to posttest score.

Overall Assessment

Our results in this chapter, as well as those presented earlier in chapters 4 and 5, document numerous and profound differences between union and nonunion districts. In this chapter we find significant differences in both the levels of resources allocated to the educational process and the educational process itself. Despite this multitude of differences, however, the net effect of collective bargaining on student achievement gains (the sum of the three components discussed) is only 0.8, about 7 to 8 percent of the average gain from the pre- to posttest score. This apparent paradox is explained by the fact that, in the final analysis, the detailed differences attributable to collective bargaining tend to be offsetting in their effects on student achievement. Of course, for the harshest critics of collective bargaining, the surprise is that the net effect, if anything, is marginally positive, not significantly negative. We do find, however, that union districts tend to do best with average students, compressing test scores toward the average for above-average students, while dispersing scores away from the mean for below-average students.

Costs, Student Achievement, and Collective Bargaining

We found in the previous section that although collective bargaining significantly affects major inputs in the educational process, the effects tend to be offsetting, so that the net difference in student-achievement gains between union and nonunion schools is negligible. Stating the same result in a slightly different way, after we consider differences in the level and quality of educational resources as well as differences in the productivity of these factors, union and nonunion schools appear on average to be about equally effective.

Having found little difference in overall quality between union and nonunion schools, we now address the issue of whether union and nonunion schools produce these achievement gains at the same *cost*. We partially answered this question earlier by considering the relationship between bargaining activity and the level of district expenditures. In chapter 3, we found

that the appearance of a reduction-in-force provision increased per-pupil district expenditures, while a loss of the provision decreased expenditures. In chapter 5 we found a positive correlation between the number of provisions in the contract and the district's total operating expenditures per pupil. In this section we calculate the overall effect of collective bargaining on the cost of education, holding constant both the quantity and the quality of education provided.

The literature on the subject of teacher collective bargaining and district expenditures holds mixed views. Gallagher (1979) estimates that union districts have an approximately 9 percent larger operating budget than nonunion districts. Hall and Carroll (1973) challenge Gallagher's position and conclude that higher salaries negotiated in union districts are completely offset by larger class sizes, resulting in no significant difference in total operating expenditures between the two district types. Chambers (1977) also finds that collective bargaining reallocates resources within the district without significant increase in total operating expenditures.

None of these studies, or even our own analysis reported earlier, deal directly with the issue of overall union-nonunion cost differentials with the quality of education held constant. To do this, we estimate an expenditure equation that specifies district operating expenditures per pupil as a function of variables that reflect the quality of education, community preferences and fiscal capacity, the size of the district, and urban and geographical characteristics. Thus we rely again on the model of district expenditures developed in chapter 5.

The quality of education is measured by the district average level of student scores on the mathematics test used in the previous section and in chapter 3. An alternative measure of educational quality would be the difference between the post- and pretest scores. Since the difference in scores is considered to result from the flow of school-based educational services, the annual operating budget of districts should reflect the cost of providing these services. The level of test scores, however, is found to be a better predictor of district budgets than the change in scores, presumably due to the cumulative nature of the educational process.

We attempt to capture some of the community preferences for educational services by including the percentage of parents in the district who attended college. One would expect the level of parents' education to be positively correlated with the value placed on their children's education. The district's fiscal capacity is measured by the average income of families within the district. The assessed value of property within the district would be a better measure of fiscal capacity since the majority of district revenue comes from property taxes. However, assessed valuation was not available in our sample, and we use family income since it is highly correlated with property values. The percentage of families who own their home is also

included to account for variations in the link between property values and family income, since renters may exhibit tax illusion, the illusion that they bear no property tax burden.

Districts in our sample are drawn from different parts of the country and from different community settings; hence there may be wide variations in costs attributable to differences in labor and material costs and to differences in the students who attend these schools. To account for regional cost differences, the location of districts is identified by ten dummy variables, each representing a different geographical region in the country. Five city types are considered by including dummy variables that indicate whether the district is located in a large city, suburb, middle-size city, town, or rural area. The size of the district may also affect operating costs. District enrollment, entered in quadratic form, accounts for the possibility of economies of scale in the operation of schools and other effects one might associate with size of districts.

The difference in district expenditures per pupil attributable to collective bargaining is estimated using a dummy variable equaling one if teachers in the district are covered by a collective-bargaining agreement, and equaling zero otherwise. Staffing ratios and other district resources are not included in the equation so that both direct and indirect effects of collective bargaining on costs will be captured by the union dummy. Including staffing ratios would presumably bias downward the coefficient on the dummy variable, since collective bargaining has been shown to increase these ratios.

Effects of Collective Bargaining on Operating Costs

Estimates of the direct and indirect effects of collective bargaining on the costs of education, displayed in table 6-5, show for our national sample of districts that teacher collective bargaining increases operating costs per student by $198, about a 15 percent increase.[2] This estimate is close to what Gallagher found for a more limited sample of school districts. The estimate also lies in the middle of the range of estimates we obtained in chapter 5 for the effect of bargaining activity on the allocation of budget expenditures. More interesting, perhaps, is that the 15 percent estimate falls in the middle of the estimates obtained in chapter 4 for the effect of collective bargaining on teacher salaries. Since our estimate of the impact of collective bargaining on costs is insensitive to a number of alternative specifications (to specifying separate equations for large and small districts, for example, or for large and small cities), we conclude with some confidence that districts with collective-bargaining agreements spend about 15 percent more than districts without such agreements to achieve the same level of student performance.

Table 6–5

Estimates of the Effect of Teachers' Collective Bargaining and Student Achievement on District Operating Expenditures (SDC Data)

Variable Description	Mean	Coefficient	t-statistic
Intercept		852.82	3.81
If district covered by collective bargaining value = 1	0.65	198.00	2.94
Average district score on standardized math test	29.53	15.19	2.00
Percentage of students' parents attended college	0.28	– 387.05	1.71
Average family income in district	14,845.95	0.02	2.10
Percentage of families who own their home	0.67	– 208.82	1.35
Percentage of white students in district	0.83	– 312.72	2.66
Composite index of school climate	8.66	8.58	0.58
District enrollment (per 1000)	23.68	0.003	0.81
District enrollment squared	4,159.30	0.000	0.02
City type			
Over 200,000	0.15	– 109.65	0.89
50,000–200,000	0.15	– 27.28	0.31
Under 50,000	0.29	– 58.73	0.89
Suburb	0.10	164.77	1.61
Geographical region			
New England	0.09	157.41	1.25
Metropolitan Northeast	0.11	582.90	4.77
Mid-Atlantic	0.10	223.82	2.02
Northeast	0.13	193.47	1.68
South Central	0.12	– 62.05	0.59
Central Midwest	0.10	195.90	1.79
North Central	0.10	264.84	2.31
Pacific Southwest	0.08	311.39	2.57
Pacific Northwest	0.08	667.00	5.38

R^2: 0.46; F-ratio: 7.02; Number of observations: 205

Dependent variable: Total district expenditures per pupil, 1976–77.

Rural districts are the excluded city type; districts in the Southeast are the excluded geographical region. See chapter 3 for a description of the SDC data.

Other Factors Affecting Annual Operating Costs

Although the impact of collective bargaining on district operating costs per pupil is the primary concern of this section, results for some of the other variables also appear interesting. Aside from the coefficients associated with city type and geographic location of the school districts, only three additional variables have coefficients that are statistically significant at the 5 percent level. The quality of education, as measured by the district average of student test scores in mathematics, is positively related to per-pupil operating costs. Estimates of the educational production function, reported in chapter 3, show that the experience levels of teachers and principals and the teacher/student ratio are positively related to gains in student achievement. These inputs are costly in that more experienced staff receive higher salaries and larger staffing ratios call for larger personnel expenditures. Thus one would expect increases in quality to increase per-pupil costs.

The fiscal capacity of school districts is related to the average family income in the district. Our estimates indicate that for every $100 increase in family income, districts spend an extra $2.00 per pupil in total operating expenses. Operating budgets also differ depending upon the characteristics of students in the district. Districts with an above-average percentage of white students provide the same quality of education at lower costs than districts with a below-average percentage. Much of this cost differential may reflect the number of special programs for underpriviledged children. Since differences for districts in large cities are already accounted for, the cost differential associated with the percentage of white students does not appear to be the result of the increased cost of operating schools in large metropolitan areas.

Conclusions

We have attempted to measure the impact of collective bargaining on both the level and cost of student achievement, our broadest questions. Our results indicate that union and nonunion schools appear, on average, to be about equally effective in producing gains in student achievement, although the way in which the gains are produced differs significantly in a number of respects. Union districts appear to work best for students near the average and less well for students well above or below average. We ascribe the latter to the greater exposure of students in nonunion districts to specialized instructional modes and resources. Our results for district operating costs indicate that districts with collective-bargaining agreements spend, on average, about 15 percent more than districts without such agreements to produce the same level of student achievement. This figure falls in line with our

previous estimates of the impact of collective bargaining on salaries and on the allocation of district expenditures.

Notes

1. For an equation of the type $y = bx$, any discrete change in y can be approximately measured by the sum of $b\Delta x$, $x\Delta b$, and $\Delta b\Delta x$. For the analysis in this chapter, we use the coefficients of the nonunion production function as initial coefficients and the means of the variables for the nonunion districts as initial values for the variables. The changes are then measured by subtracting the nonunion value from the corresponding union value.

2. The estimate of 15 percent is obtained by constraining the average pretest score to be the same for both union and nonunion districts. Pretest scores of union districts, however, are 1.12 points higher than the scores in nonunion districts. Based on the value of the coefficient associated with the pretest shown in table 6–4, this difference accounts for an increase of $17 per pupil in expenditures of union districts, a percentage increase of 1 to 2 percent. The gain in student test scores is not statistically different for the union and nonunion districts, however. When gains, rather than levels, are entered into the expenditure equation, the union-nonunion cost differential turns out to be 14 percent. Thus the cost estimate is not sensitive to the way in which the quality of education is measured.

 **Conclusion**

Overall Assessment of Collective Bargaining

Teacher collective bargaining *does* affect the way public schools are run in the United States. We found that teachers covered by collective-bargaining agreements, as compared with teachers not covered, receive higher salaries, teach smaller classes, and spend slightly less time instructing students but more time preparing for classes. In addition the efficiency of a variety of factors in the educational process differs between union and nonunion districts.

Despite these significant differences in the operation of union and nonunion districts, we found very little difference in the average quality of education between the two district types. If anything, students in districts with collective bargaining may perform marginally better on standardized mathematics tests than students in districts without collective bargaining. Hence there are significant differences in the way students are taught, but not in average student achievement. The major difference we detected between union and nonunion districts is the cost of education: for the same level of educational quality, the annual operating costs per pupil in union districts is 15 percent higher than in similar nonunion districts.

These results may not be novel to many practitioners and researchers. Since the salaries of union teachers are higher than nonunion teachers, one would expect operating costs also to be higher. Previous studies have estimated cost differentials close to the values we found. The surprising result, in our opinion, is that in the face of substantial differences in the allocation of resources between union and nonunion districts, and significant differences in the structure of the educational process in the two sets of districts, the average quality of education is nearly identical. Teachers change the way in which schools are run, but the overall quality of education, as measured by the scores of average students on standardized tests, is unchanged. Very good and very poor students, however, do appear to do somewhat less well in unionized districts, presumably because of their diminished exposure to specialized instruction.

Much of what unions achieve for its members is gained at the expense of local taxpayers. One should not be surprised that union districts spend

more on education than nonunion districts. Unions would be hardpressed to attract and retain new members if they were not able to claim a greater share of the economic pie for their constituents. The obvious losers in this situation are the taxpayers. Nonetheless, their losses may be a trade-off against the possibility that fewer good teachers would have been attracted to the profession and to the taxpayers' particular district without the higher salaries and improved working conditions achieved by collective bargaining.

Detailed Effects of Collective Bargaining

A number of the detailed effects of collective bargaining for teachers, administrators, students, and taxpayers are worth repeating. For teachers, we found that employment-security provisions in collective-bargaining contracts play a key role in establishing efficient contracts, contracts in which one party can be made better off only by making the other party worse off. We also found significant compensating wage differentials, or trade-offs, among teacher and job-related attributes. The trade-off for the teacher/student ratio is particularly large, confirming the traditional emphasis on this ratio as a key element in labor contracts.

Considering the union-nonunion wage premium for teachers, we found that by the late 1970s the average union wage premium for teachers had reached a level comparable to the average union wage premium in the private sector, or about 12 to 21 percent. This result, combined with other evidence on inflationary trends and average teacher salaries, suggests that the real salaries of organized teachers tended to increase slightly during the mid to late 1970s, while those of nonorganized teachers tended to decline.

Turning to the issue of teacher attitudes and collective bargaining, we found union teachers to be less concerned about personnel policy than nonunion teachers, but more concerned about class size. This concern with class size tends to confirm the large implicit price, or compensating wage differential, found for the teacher/student ratio. Union teachers also appear to be less satisfied in general about their workplace than nonunion teachers, although this dissatisfaction may be an explanation for, rather than a consequence of, collective bargaining.

We devoted substantial attention to the nature and behavior of teacher labor markets. In general we found market forces to be robust—teachers appear to be responsive to wage differentials between teaching and other occupations, as well as to wage differentials between school districts. In fact teachers appear to be at least as responsive in this regard as other workers. In addition, we found significant erosion of market-wage differentials even within the span of one year. Both the responsiveness of teachers to wage dif-

ferentials and the erosion of wage differentials suggests that in general district monopsony power in employing teachers is not large. Finally, we found no evidence that the labor-market behavior of union teachers differs from the behavior of nonunion teachers. We did find, however, that contract provisions affect mobility. Class-size provisions increase the probability of transfers and reduce the probability of terminations, whereas seniority-based reduction-in-force provisions affect termination rates only for teachers in districts with rapidly declining enrollments.

For administrators we investigated the separate and interactive effects of contract provisions in two broad areas of administrative behavior and discretion—resource allocation and educational policy and practice. Significantly, we found that contract provisions follow a clear hierarchy: the presence of particular contract provisions tends to be clearly ordered within major categories, but the provisions remain independent between categories. Our evaluations of the effects of individual provisions indicated that employers and employees tend to disagree more about responses to external events than about events associated with the daily routine of the district. We found significant effects for a number of individual contract provisions on the allocation of district expenditures across various budget categories, with the total magnitude of the effects varying from about 0 to 30 percent. As indicated above, this range is consistent with our estimates of the effects of collective bargaining on overall costs and teachers' salaries.

Our simple test of the web-of-rules effect, the argument that the effects of contract provisions are cumulative, demonstrated that the number of contract items, which we interpret as a proxy for contract strength in the context of a hierarchical contract, has significant effects on resource allocation. We also found that the number of contract items has a positive effect on the level of per-pupil expenditures. This result reveals variations in the impact of collective bargaining even among districts already organized.

For our second broad topic area for administrators, educational policy and practice, we found significant links between contract provisions and modes of instruction (the traditional classroom mode, for example, is more likely to be used in the presence of class-size contract provisions). No significant differences were found, however, between union and nonunion teachers in either the desired level, or the actual level, of teacher participation in a wide range of administrative decisions. What we did find was a persistently positive relationship between the *desire* for participation and *actual* participation, whether or not the district is organized. Finally, both union and nonunion teachers generally prefer a greater degree of teacher participation in administrative decisions than actually occurs.

For students we found union and nonunion districts on average to be about equally effective in teaching students. However, we did find significant differences in how students are taught. In particular, union districts

appear to work best for average and near-average students, and to work less well for students well-above or well-below average. We tentatively traced this difference to the greater use of traditional classroom instruction in the union sector and to diminished use of specialists, aides, tutors, and independent programmed study. These extras are apparently crowded out of union districts by budget pressures.

For taxpayers, of course, the results are clear—teacher unions increase per-pupil operating costs significantly (our estimate is 15 percent) and presumably increase local (or state) taxes as well.

Where Does This Leave Us?

What have we learned from this examination of unions and public schools? If we cast away the paraphernalia of regression analysis and educational production functions, are there lessons to be learned for those who are concerned with education in public schools? All too often policy analysts and researchers develop their own mystiques, and administrators and politicians have a tendency to act as if they understood them. Status is frequently conferred these days on those seeming to be participants in the newest mysteries.

The purpose of this study has been to unveil some of the mysteries surrounding the role of unions in schools. In reviewing our findings, a reader must have realistic expectations. If they are too high, the results seem disappointingly modest. If our results are compared with the existing knowledge of teachers and unions, however, then their contribution is more apparent. We can say with confidence that collective bargaining changes decision making in public education in ways that affect the educational process. The influence of collective bargaining on the rate of learning is now a little less unknown than it was when McDonnell and Pascal concluded a few years ago that we knew very little.

The effects of collective bargaining on the educational process have remained a mystery for three main reasons. The first two continue to shroud our results to some extent. First, education is an imprecise activity. Unlike many technical processes in which the relationships between inputs and outputs are well known, what is involved in educating students still remains unclear. For learning to occur, there must be students able and willing to learn and teachers with sufficient knowledge and training in proximity to students. Studies of educational effectiveness cast some light on the relationships between student and community attributes, teacher characteristics, peer-group relationships, instructional methodologies, and student achievement. Yet it is accurate to say that we do not know how to package these inputs to guarantee that learning will occur. A combination of inputs

works with some students, while the same combination fails with others. Attempts to measure the impact of an event or occurrence, such as collective bargaining, on a process that itself is not well understood necessarily produces uncertain results, especially when observing behavior in the tails of the distribution of effects.

A second reason for difficulties in isolating the effects of collective bargaining in public education is that collective bargaining is just one of many factors that shape the learning process. Education occurs in a context of established routines, educational traditions, federal, state, and district laws and procedures, and immediate circumstances. Collective bargaining, except in the most extreme circumstances, affects what goes on in schools in small ways. To date, social science has not been sufficiently developed or precise to measure small differences in the operation of social institutions. The problem is further complicated by expectations of the parties involved. Union proponents believe collective bargaining substantially improves public education. They are disappointed with evidence showing that much less is actually at stake. Others may be disappointed with our results because they feel sure that collective bargaining has wrecked public school systems.

A third and important reason for why the effect of collective bargaining on the educational process has been ignored is the lack of convincing theoretical arguments for why unions *should* make a difference. The critiques of collective bargaining are almost always made on legal or financial grounds, not educational ones. Unions diminish democracy by reducing the discretion of democratically elected officials and their representatives. Unions have disproportionate power and therefore receive higher-than-optimal wages for their members and a disproportionately large allocation of public funds for public education.

Neither of these frequently heard arguments provides any insight into how collective bargaining affects the education of children. One reason the argument has not been extended to the educational process is quite clear— one cannot surmise the effect of collective bargaining on schooling by looking at the contracts alone. One has to link the bargaining activity to the determinants of the educational process. We have mapped out many of the channels through which collective bargaining can influence the educational process. To fill in the details of these channels, to explore competing interpretations of our results, and to answer important questions about the effects of collective bargaining on particular schools or children, we need to pass the baton on to researchers interested in these specific topics.

By concentrating on general trends, we have focused on average, or typical, effects of collective bargaining and indeed have found significant patterns. Unions alter the way schools are run, improve teacher compensation and working conditions, and increase operating costs but do not reduce the quality of education for most students. By tending to crowd out special-

ized instructional modes, however, they do appear to reduce achievement gains modestly for atypical students, students significantly ahead or behind the average. The results we have presented reflect long-run adjustments by teachers, administrators, and taxpayers to the bargaining environment. Unlike strikes or contract negotiations, these adjustments generally do not make headlines, but they do make lasting changes in American education.

References

Academic Collective Bargaining Information Service. 1977. *Scope of Public Sector Bargaining in 14 Selected States.* Special Report 25. Washington, D.C.

Alluto, Joseph A., and James A. Belasco. 1974. "Determinants of Attitudinal Militancy among Teachers and Nurses." *Industrial and Labor Relations Review* 27, no. 2 (January): 216–227.

Antos, Joseph, and Wesley Mellow. 1979. *The Youth Labor Market: A Dynamic Overview.* BLS Staff Paper 11, U.S. Bureau of Labor Statistics, Washington, D.C.

Antos, Joseph, and Sherwin Rosen. 1975. "Discrimination in the Market for Public School Teachers." *Journal of Econometrics* 3, no. 2 (May): 123–150.

Ashenfelter, Orley. 1972. "Racial Discrimination and Trade Unionism." *Journal of Political Economy* 80, no. 3, pt. I (May–June):435–464.

Ashenfelter, Orley, and George Johnson. 1972. "Unionism, Relative Wages, and Labor Quality in U.S. Manufacturing Industries." *International Economic Review* 13, no. 3 (October):488–508.

Baird, Robert N., and John H. Landon. 1972. "The Effect of Collective Bargaining on Public School Teachers' Salaries: Comment." *Industrial and Labor Relations Review* 25 (April):410–416.

Baugh, William H., and Joe A. Stone. 1982a. "Teachers, Unions, and Wages in the 1970s: Unionism Now Pays." *Industrial and Labor Relations Review* 35, no. 3 (April):368–376.

———. 1982b. "Mobility and Wage Equilibration in the Educator Labor Market." *Economics of Education Review* 2, no. 3 (Summer):253–274.

Becker, Gary. 1964. *Human Capital.* New York: National Bureau of Economic Research.

Belasco, James A., and Joseph A. Alluto. 1969. "Organizational Impacts of Teacher Negotiations." *Industrial Relations* 9, no. 1 (October): 67–79.

Belasco, James A., Joseph A. Alluto, and Alan Glassman. 1971. "A Case Study of Community and Teacher Expectations Concerning the Authority Structure of School Systems." *Education and Urban Society* (November):89–96.

Block, Richard N. 1978. "The Impact of Seniority Provisions on Manufacturing Quit Rates." *Industrial and Labor Relations Review* 31 (July):474–481.

Boardman, A.E., O.A. David, and P.R. Sanday. 1977. "A Simultaneous

Equations Model of the Educational Process." *Journal of Public Economics* 7, no. 1 (February):23–49.

Brandstetter, John W. 1970. "An Investigation of the Effect of Professional Negotiations on Management Functions of the Socondary School Principal." Unpublished Ed.D. dissertation, University of Houston.

Brodie, Donald, and Peg Ann Williams. 1982. *School Grievance Arbitration.* Seattle, Wash.: Butterworths.

Brookover, Wilbur, and others. 1979. *School Social Systems and Student Achievement: Schools Can Make a Difference.* New York: Praeger.

Brown, Bryon W., and Daniel M. Saks. 1975. "The Production and Distribution of Cognitive Skills within Schools." *Journal of Political Economy* 83 (June):571–595.

Brown, Charles. 1980. "Equalizing Differences in the Labor Market." *Quarterly Journal of Economics* 94 (February):113–134.

Brown, Charles, and James Medoff. 1978. "Trade Unions in the Production Process." *Journal of Political Economy* 86, no. 3 (June):355–378.

Burkhead, J., with T.G. Fox and J.W. Holland. 1967. *Input and Output in Large-City High Schools.* New York: Syracuse University Press.

Burton, John F., Jr. 1979. "The Extent of Collective Bargaining in the Public Sector," in Benjamin Aaron, Joseph R. Grodin, and James L. Stern, eds., *Public-Sector Bargaining.* Washington, D.C.: Bureau of National Affairs, pp. 1–43.

Carroll, Stephen. 1963. "Analysis of the Educational Personnel System: III. The Demand for Educational Professionalism." R-1308-HEW, Santa Monica, Calif.: The Rand Corporation.

CEPM Conference Proceedings. 1982. *The Effects of Collective Bargaining on School Administrative Leadership.* Proceedings of conference held at the Center for Educational Policy and Management, University of Oregon, July 9–10.

Chambers, Jay G. 1977. "The Impact of Collective Bargaining for Teachers on Resource Allocation in Public Shool Districts." *Journal of Urban Economics* 4, no. 3 (July):324–339.

Cohen, Elizabeth G., and Russell H. Miller. 1980. "Coordination and Control of Instruction in Schools." *Pacific Sociological Review* 23, 446–473.

Cohn, Elchanan. 1979. *The Economics of Education.* Cambridge, Mass.: Ballinger.

Coleman, James S. 1966. *Equality of Educational Opportunity.* Washington: Office of Education, U.S. Department of Health, Education, and Welfare.

Cooper, Bruce S. 1982. *Collective Bargaining, Strikes, and Financial Costs in Public Education: A Comparative Review.* Eugene, Ore.: Clearinghouse on Educational Management, University of Oregon.

Corwin, Ronald G. 1968. "Teacher Militancy in the United States: Reflections on Its Sources and Prospects." *Theory into Practice* 7 (April):96–102.

Corwin, Ronald G. 1970. *Militant Professionalism: A Study of Organizational Conflict in High Schools.* New York: Appleton-Century-Crofts.

Cresswell, Anthony, Hervey A. Juris, Leslie Nathanson, and Kathryn Tooredman. 1978. "Impacting State Labor Relations and School Finance Policies on Educational Resource Allocation." A paper presented at the American Educational Research Association Annual Meeting.

Cresswell, Anthony, and F. Spargo. 1980. "Impacts of Collective Bargaining Policy in Elementary and Secondary Education: A Review of Research. Denver, Colo.: Education Commission of the States.

Deal, T.E., and others. 1975. "Organizational Influences on Educational Innovation." in J.V. Baldridge and T.E. Deal (eds.) *Managing Change in Educational Organizations.* Berkeley, Calif.: McCutchan.

Dertouzos, John N., and John H. Pencavel. 1981. "Wage and Employment Determination under Trade Unionism: The International Typographical Union." *Journal of Political Economy* 89 (December):1162–1181.

Donley, Marshall O., Jr. 1976. *Power to the Teacher: How America's Educators Became Militant.* Bloomington: Indiana University Press.

Duckworth, Kenneth, and Wynn DeBevoise, eds. 1982. *The Effects of Collective Bargaining on School Administrative Leadership.* Proceedings of a Conference at the Center for Educational Policy and Management. Eugene, Ore.: Center for Educational Policy and Management.

Duke, Daniel, Beverly K. Showers, and Michael Imber. 1979. "Costs to Teachers of Involvement in School Decision-Making." Mimeographed paper.

Duncan, Gregory M., and Duane E. Leigh. 1980. "Wage Determination in the Union and Nonunion Sectors: A Sample Selectivity Approach." *Industrial and Labor Relations Review* 34, no. 1 (October):24–34.

Dunlop, John T. 1944. *Wage Determination under Trade Unions.* New York: Macmillan.

———. 1958. *Industrial Relations Systems.* New York: Holt.

Eberts, Randall W. 1982. "Unionism and Nonwage Effects: A Simultaneous Equations Model of Public School Teacher Collective Bargaining." Eugene, Ore.: Center for Educational Policy and Management, University of Oregon.

———. (forthcoming) "Collective Bargaining and Teacher Productivity: The Effect on the Allocation of Teacher Time." *Industrial and Labor Relations Review.*

Eberts, Randall W., and Lawrence C. Pierce. 1980. *The Effects of Collective Bargaining in Public Schools.* Final Report, NIE Grant OB-G-NIE-

81-0110-P5. Eugene, Ore.: Center for Educational Policy and Management, University of Oregon.

Eberts, Randall, and Lawrence C. Pierce. 1982. "Time in the Classroom: The Effect of Collective Bargaining on the Allocation of Teacher Time." Mimeographed. Eugene, Ore.: Center for Educational Policy and Management, University of Oregon.

Edmonds, Ronald R. 1979. "Effective Schools for the Urban Poor." *Educational Leadership* 37, 15–24.

Edmonds, Ronald. 1982. "Programs of School Improvement: An Overview." *Educational Leadership* (December):4–11.

Ehrenberg, Ronald G. 1973. "The Demand for State and Local Government Employees." *American Economic Review* 53, no. 3 (June): 378–397.

Ehrenberg, Ronald, and Ronald Oaxaca. 1976. "Unemployment Insurance, Duration of Unemployment, and Subsequent Wage Gain." *American Economic Review* 66, no. 5 (December):754–766.

Farber, Henry S., and Daniel H. Saks. 1980. "Why Doctors Want Unions: The Role of Relative Wages and Job Characteristics." *Journal of Political Economy* 88, 2 (April):349–369.

Fisher, C., et al. 1980. "Teaching Behaviors, Academic Learning Time, and Student Achievement: An Overview." In C. Denham and A. Lieverman, eds., *Time to Learn.* Sacramento: California Commission Teacher Licensing, pp. 7–32.

Freeman, Richard B. 1980. "The Exit-Voice Tradeoff in the Labor Market: Unionism, Job Tenure, Quits and Separations." *Quarterly Journal of Economics* (June):643–673.

———. 1981. "The Effect of Unionism on Fringe Benefits." *Industrial and Labor Relations Review* 34, no. 4 (July):489–509.

Freeman, Richard B., and James C. Medoff. 1979. "Two Faces of Unionism." *Public Interest* 57 (Fall):69–93.

———. 1982. "The Impact of Collective Bargaining: Can the New Facts Be Explained by Monopolicy Unionism? Working Paper no. 837. Mimeographed. Cambridge, Mass.: National Bureau of Economic Research.

Gall, Meredith D. 1983. "Using Staff Development to Improve Scholarship." *R&D Perspectives.* Eugene, Ore.: Center for Educational Policy and Management, University of Oregon (Winter).

Gallagher, Daniel G. 1979. "Teacher Negotiations, School District Expenditures, and Taxation Levels." *Educational Administration Quarterly* 15 (Winter):67–82.

Garms, Walter I., James W. Guthrie, and Lawrence G. Pierce. 1978. *School Finance: The Economics and Politics of Public Education.* Englewood Cliffs, N.J.: Prentice-Hall.

Gerhart, P.F. 1976. "Determinants of Bargaining Outcomes in Local Government Relations." *Industrial and Labor Relations Review* 29, no. 3 (April):331–351.

Gersten, Russell, and Douglas Carnine. 1981. "Administrative and Supervisory Support Functions for the Implementation of Effective Educational Programs for Low-Income Students." Eugene, Ore.: Center for Educational Policy and Management, University of Oregon.

Glass, G.V., and M.L. Smith. 1978. *Meta-analysis of Research on the Relationship of Class-size and Achievement.* San Francisco: Far West Laboratory for Educational Research and Development.

Goldschmidt, Steven M. 1982. "An Overview of the Evolution of Collective Bargaining and Its Impact on Education." Proceedings of Conference on *The Effects of Collective Bargaining on School Administrative Leadership.* Eugene, Ore.: Center for Educational Policy and Management, University of Oregon.

Greenberg, David, and John McCall. 1973. "Analysis of the Educational Personnel System: I. Teacher Mobility in San Diego." R-1071-HEW. Rand Corporation, Santa Monica, Calif.

Griffin, M.F. 1974. "The Role of the Principal in Collective Negotiations." *APSS Know How,* 25 (January):1–4.

Guthrie, James W. 1974. "Public Control of Public Schools: Can We Get It Back?" *Public Affairs Report* 15, no. 3 (June).

Hall, W. Clayton, and Norman Carroll. 1975. "The Effect of Teachers' Organizations on Salaries and Class Size." *Industrial and Labor Relations Review* 26, no. 2 (January):834–841.

Hall, Robert E., and David M. Lillien. 1979. "Efficient Wage Bargains under Uncertain Supply and Demand." *American Economic Review* (December):868–879.

Hanoch, Giora. 1967. "An Economic Analysis of Earnings and Schooling." *Journal of Human Resources* 2, no. 3 (Summer):310–329.

Hanushek, Eric. 1970. *The Value of Teachers in Teaching.* RM-6362-cc/RC. Santa Monica, Calif.: Rand Corporation.

———. 1979. "Conceptual and Empirical Issues in the Estimation of Educational Production Functions." *Journal of Human Resources* 14, 351–358.

Helsby, Robert. 1977. "The Scope of Bargaining under New York's Taylor Law." In Joseph Loewenberg and Bernard Ingster, eds., *Scope of Public Sector Bargaining.* Lexington, Mass.: Lexington Books, D.C. Heath.

Henderson, Vernon, Peter Miezskowski, and Y. Sauvageau. 1978. "Peer Group Effects and Educational Production Functions." *Journal of Public Economics,* 10, 97–106.

Herndon, T. 1976. *NEA Reporter* (April).

Kalachek, Edward, and Fredric Raines. 1976. "The Structure of Wage Differences among Mature Male Workers." *Journal of Human Resources* 11, no. 4 (Fall):484–506.

Kasper, Herschel. 1970. "The Effects of Collective Bargaining on Public Teachers' Salaries." *Industrial and Labor Relations Review* 24, no. 1 (October):417–423.

Katzman, Martin. 1971. *The Political Economy of Urban Schools.* Cambridge, Mass.: Harvard University Press.

Kay, William F. 1973. "The Need for Limitation upon the Scope of Negotiations in Public Education." *Journal of Law and Education* 2, no. 1 (January):155–175.

Keeler, B.T., and J.H. Andrews. 1973. "The Behavior of Principals, Staff Morale, and Productivity." *Alberta Journal of Educational Research* 9, 179–191.

Kerchner, Charles T., Douglas Mitchell, Gabrielle Pryor, and Wayne Erck. 1980. *The Impact of Collective Bargaining on School Management and Policy: A Preliminary Research Report.* Claremont, Calif.: Labor Relations Research Project, Claremont Graduate School.

Kerr, Clark. 1954. "The Balkanization of Labor Markets." In E. Wight Bakke et al., *Mobility and Economic Opportunity.* New York: Wiley.

Kerr, Clark, and Abraham Siegel. 1955. "The Structuring of the Labor Force in Industrial Society: New Dimensions and New Questions." *Industrial and Labor Relations Review* 8 (January):151–168.

Kochan, Thomas A. 1973. "Correlates of State Public Employment Bargaining Laws." *Industrial Relations* 12, no. 3 (October):322–337.

Kochan, Thomas A., and Richard N. Block. 1977. "An Interindustry Analysis of Bargaining Outcomes: Preliminary Evidence from Two-Digit Industries." *Quarterly Journal of Economics* (August):431–452.

Kochan, Thomas A., and Hoyt N. Wheeler. 1975. "Municipal Collective Bargaining: A Model and Analysis of Bargaining Outcomes." *Industrial and Labor Relations Review* 29, no. 1 (October):46–66.

Lee, Lung-Fei. 1978. "Unionism and Wage Rates: A Simultaneous Equations Model with Qualitative and Limited Dependent Variables." *International Economic Review* 19, no. 2 (June):415–433.

Levin, H.M. 1970. "A Cost-Effectiveness Analysis of Teacher Selection." *Journal of Human Resources* 5 (Winter):24–33.

Lewis, H. Gregg. 1963. *Unionism and Relative Wages in the United States.* Chicago: University of Chicago Press.

Lindenfeld, F. 1963. "Teacher Turnover in Public Elementary and Secondary Schools, 1959–1960." Office of Education, Circular no. 675, HEW, Washington.

Lieberman, Myron, and Michael H. Moskow. 1966. *Collective Negotiations for Teachers.* Chicago: Rand McNally.

Lillard, Lee. 1977. "Inequality: Earnings vs. Human Wealth." *American Economic Review* 67, no. 2 (March):42–53.

Lipsky, David. 1982. "The Effect of Collective Bargaining on Teacher Pay: A Review of the Evidence." *Educational Administration Quarterly* 18, no. 1 (Winter).

Lipsky, David, and John Drotning. 1973. "The Influence of Collective Bargaining on Teachers' Salaries in New York State." *Industrial and Labor Relations Review* 27, no. 1 (October):18–35.

———. 1977. "The Relationship between Teacher Salaries and the Use of Impasse Procedures under New York's Taylor Law: 1968–1972." *Journal of Collective Negotiations* 6, no. 3:230–231.

Lortie, Dan C. 1969. "Control and Autonomy of Elementary School Teachers." In A. Etzoni, ed., *The Semi-Professions*. Glencoe, Ill.: The Free Press.

Lortie, Dan C. 1977. *Schoolteacher: A Sociological Study*. Chicago: University of Chicago Press.

Mann, D. 1980. "The Politics and Administration of the Instructionally Effective School." Paper presented at the National Graduate Student Research Seminar in Educational Administration, Boston.

McDonald, Ian M., and Robert M. Solow. 1981. "Wage Bargaining and Employment." *American Economic Review* (December):896–908.

McDonnell, Lorraine, and Anthony Pascal. 1979. "Organized Teachers in American Schools." R-2407-NIE. Rand Corporation, Santa Monica, Calif.

Mellow, Wesley. 1978. "Equilibration in the Labor Market." *Southern Economic Journal* 45, no. 1 (July):192–204.

———. 1981. "Unionism and Wages: A Longitudinal Analysis." *Review of Economics and Statistics* 63, no. 1 (February):43–52.

Michelson, S. 1970. "The Association of Teacher Resourceness with Children's Characteristics." In *How Do Teachers Make A Difference?* Washington, D.C.: U.S. Department of Health, Education and Welfare, Office of Education, Bureau of Educational Personnel Development (OE-58042):55–75.

Miller, W.C. 1976. "Can a Principal's Improved Behavior Result in Higher Pupil Achievement?" *Educational Leadership* 33, 336–338.

Mincer, Jacob. 1970. "The Distribution of Labor Income: A Survey with Special Reference to the Human Capital Approach." *Journal of Economic Literature* 8 (March):1–26.

———. 1974. *Schooling, Experience and Earnings*. New York: Columbia University Press.

Mitchell, Donald, and Charles Kerchner. 1981. "The Impact of Collective Bargaining on School Management and Policy." *American Journal of Education* 89 (February):147–188.

Monk, D.H. 1980. "A Comprehensive View of Resource Allocation for Education." *Administrator's Notebook* 3, 1–4.

Moore, William J., and John Raisian. 1981. "A Time Series Analysis of the Growth and Determinants of Union/Nonunion Relative Wage Effects, 1967–77." BLS Working Paper 115, U.S. Bureau of Labor Statistics, Washington, D.C., April.

Moskow, Michael H. 1966. *Teachers and Unions.* Philadelphia: Wharton School of Finance.

Murnane, Richard J. 1975. *The Impact of School Resources on the Learning of Inner City Children.* Cambridge, Mass.: Ballinger.

———. 1981. "Interpreting the Evidence on School Effectiveness." *Teachers College Record* 83, no. 1, 19–35.

Murnane, Richard J. 1981. "Teacher Mobility Revisited." *Journal of Human Resources* 16:3–16.

National Education Association. 1957. *Status of American Public School Teachers,* Washington.

National Education Association Research Division. 1972. *Status of the American Public School Teacher, 1970–1971.* Washington.

National Education Association. 1979. *NEA Handbook.*

———. 1980. *Prices, Budgets, Salaries, and Income* (Winter).

Nerlove, Marc, and S.J. Press. 1973. "Univariate and Multivariate Log-Linear and Logistic Models." R-1306-EDA/NIH. Rand Corporation, Santa Monica, Calif.

Nicholson, E.W., and R.R. Nasstrom. 1974. "The Impact of Collective Negotiations on Principals." *NASSP Bulletin* (October):100–107.

Oaxaca, Ronald L. 1975. "Estimation of Union/Nonunion Wage Differences within Occupational/Regional Subgroups." *Journal of Human Resources* 10, no. 4 (Fall):529–537.

Parsley, C.J. 1980. "Labor Unions and Wages: A Survey." *Journal of Economic Literature* 18, no. 1 (March):1–57.

Perry, Charles R. 1979. "Teacher Bargaining: The Experience in Nine Systems." *Industrial and Labor Relations Review* 33, no. 1 (October): 3–17.

Perry, Charles R., and W.A. Wildman. 1970. *The Impact of Negotiations in Public Education: The Evidence from the Schools.* Worthington, Ohio: Jones.

Pierce, Lawrence C. 1975. "Teachers' Organizations and Bargaining: Power Imbalance in the Public Sphere." In Shelley Weinstein and Douglas E. Mitchell, eds., *Public Testimony on Public Schools.* Berkeley, Calif.: McCutchan.

Pindyck, Robert S., and Daniel L. Rubinfield. 1976. *Econometric Models and Economic Forecasts.* New York: McGraw-Hill.

Pitner, Nancy. 1980. "Training of the School Administrator: State of the

Art." Eugene, Ore.: Center for Educational Policy and Management, University of Oregon.

Proctor, C.H. 1970. "A Probablistic Formulation and Statistical Analysis of Guttman Scaling." *Psychometrika* 35:73-78.

Randles, H.E. 1975. "The Principal and Negotiated Contracts." *National Elementary Principal* (November-December):57-61.

Rees, Albert. 1962. *The Economics of Trade Unions,* 2nd ed. Chicago: University of Chicago Press.

Rosen, Sherwin. 1977. "Human Capital: A Survey of Empirical Research." In Ronald G. Ehrenberg, ed., *Research in Labor Economics.* Greenwich, Conn.: JAI Press.

Ross, Doris. 1978. *Cuebook: State Education Collective Bargaining Laws.* Denver, Colo.: Education Commission of the States.

Schmid, William W. 1971. *Retirement Systems of the American Teacher.* New York: Fleet Academic Editions.

Shapiro, David. 1978. "Relative Wage Effects of Unions in the Public and Private Sectors." *Industrial and Labor Relations Review* 31, no. 2 (January):193-204.

Slichter, Summer H., James J. Healy, and E. Robert Livernash. 1960. *The Impact of Collective Bargaining on Management.* Washington, D.C.: The Brookings Institution.

Smith, Mary Lee, and Gene Glass. 1979. *Relationship of Class-size to Classroom Processes, Teacher Satisfaction and Pupil Affect: A Meta-Analysis.* San Francisco: Far West Laboratories for Educational Research and Development.

Steele, Helen H. 1976. "A Teacher's View." *Phi Delta Kappan* (May): 590-592.

Steiber, Jack, and Benjamin Wolkinson. 1977. "Fact-Finding Viewed by Factfinders: The Michigan Experience." *Labor Law Journal* 28:89-101.

Strom, David. 1979. "Teacher Unionism: An Assessment." *Education and Urban Society* 11, no. 2 (February):152-167.

Summers, Anita, and Barbara Wolfe. 1977. "Do Schools Make a Difference?" *American Economic Review* 67, no. 4 (October):639-652.

Summers, Robert C. 1976. *Collective Bargaining and Public Benefit Conferral: A Jurisprudential Critique.* Institute of Public Employment, Monograph no. 7, Cornell University, Ithaca, N.Y.

Taubman, Paul. 1975. *Sources of Inequality in Earnings.* Amsterdam: North Holland.

Thomas, J.A. 1979. "Resource Allocation in School Districts and Classrooms." Washington, D.C.: National Institute of Education (September).

U.S. Department of Education. 1980. *Digest of Education Statistics.* Washington, D.C. National Center for Education Statistics.

U.S. Department of Labor. 1972. *Summary of State Policy Regulations for Public Sector Labor Relations: Statutes: Attorney Generals' Opinions and Selected Court Decisions.* Washington, D.C.: Labor Management Services Administration, Division of Public Employee Labor Relations.

Warner, Kenneth S., Rupert F. Chisholm, and Robert F. Unzenrider. 1978. "Motives for Unionization among State Social Service Employees." *Public Personnel Management* (May-June):181-190.

Wellington, Harry H., and Ralph K. Winter. 1969. "The Limits of Collective Bargaining in Public Employment." *Yale Law Journal* 77, no. 7 (June).

Wellisch, Jean, and others. 1978. "School Management and Organization in Successful Schools." *Sociology of Education* 51, 211-226.

Wiley, David, and Annegret Harnischfeger. 1974. "Explosion of a Myth: Quantity of Schooling and Exposure to Instruction, Major Educational Vehicles." *Education Researcher* 3 (March):7-12.

Winkler, Donald. 1975. "Education Achievement and School Peer Composition." *Journal of Human Resources* (Spring):189-204.

Yaffe, Byron, and Howard Goldblatt. 1971. *Fact Finding in Public Employment Disputes in New York State: More Promise than Illusion.* Ithaca, N.Y.: Publications Division of New York State School of Industrial and Labor Relations.

Zirkel, Perry A. 1975. "Teacher-Board Relations in Connecticut: A Summary of the Law Regarding Scope of Negotiations, Good Faith Bargaining, and Unfair Labor Practices." Preliminary Draft. *RIE* (September).

Index

Academic Collective Bargaining Information Service, 25, 27
Administrator/student ratio, 151, 158, 161, 168, 170
Administrators, 13, 18, 22, 37, 82, 108, 122, 127; and allocation of resources, 9; and collective bargaining, 1, 2, 3, 4, 9, 11, 24, 33, 41, 43, 131-155, 157, 175, 178; leadership, 9, 50-52; relationship with teachers, 11, 81, 83. *See also* Budgets; Collective bargaining; Contract provisions; Contracts; Education; Educators; School districts; Students; Teachers; Unions
Alaska, 15
American Federation of Teachers (AFT), 15, 19, 28, 32, 38
Andrews, J.H., 50
Annual Report on Certified Personnel, 98
Antos, Joseph, 96

Bargaining, collective. *See* Collective bargaining
Binding arbitration. *See* Collective bargaining, contract provisions
Block, Richard N., 131
Board of Education, Town of Huntington vs. *Associated Teachers of Huntington,* 27
Boardman, A.E., 47
Bradsletter, John W., 52
Brookover, Wilbur, 51
Brown, Bryon W., 133
Budgets, 5, 31, 32-38, 73, 132, 133, 145, 146, 147, 154, 167, 170; equations, 133-135, 142, 145. *See also* Administrators; Collective bargaining; Contract provisions; School districts; Unions; Wages
Burkhead, J., 47
Burton, John F., Jr., 19

Carnine, Douglas, 51

Carroll, Stephen, 167
CEPM, 42
Chambers, Jay G., 133, 167
Civil rights movement, 18
Class size. *See* Contract provisions
Cohen, Elizabeth G. 51
Coleman Report, 44
Collective bargaining: and administrators, 1, 2, 3, 4, 9, 11, 41, 43, 131-155, 157, 175, 178; assessment of, 173-174; bargaining and budgeting processes, 32-38; and binding arbitration, 16; *Board of Education, Town of Huntington* vs. *Associated Teachers of Huntington,* 27; and classroom, xvi, 4, 148, 149; contracts, 13-39, 120; costs, 1, 2, 3, 10, 11, 166-171; and doctrine of sovereign immunity, 14; and educational practice and policy, 3, 4, 131, 132, 148-151, 175; and educational process, 4-10; fact finding and, 16; and fringe benefits, 4, 11, 41, 65, 67, 73; legal structure of teacher, 15-17, 38, 80; literature, 2-4, 31-32; mandatory issues in, 20, 21, 27; models of, 63, 64; national trends in, 21-23; outcomes of, 30-31; and operating costs, 168-170; previous research on, 2-4; resource allocation, 131-148, 175; resources, student achievement and, 157-166; and school districts, 81-86; and students, 1, 3, 5-8, 11, 43-52, 157-171, 176; and teachers, 1, 2, 3, 4, 8, 9, 14-15, 30, 41, 63-129, 174. *See also* Administrators; Budgets; Contract provisions; Contracts; Education; Educators; Labor markets; School districts; Student achievement; Students; Teachers; Wages
Condon-Wadlin Act of 1947, 26
Consumer/producer surplus, 67
Consumer Price Index (CPI), 80

Contract curve model, 64, 65, 66, 121, 127–129

Contract provisions, 3, 11, 21, 22, 23, 24, 25, 28, 29–30, 32, 33, 38, 63–73, 81, 83, 88, 131, 132, 145, 146, 154, 174; arbitration, 16, 131, 139, 154; and class size, xvi, 3, 5, 9, 22, 32, 33, 38, 41, 43, 48, 49, 53, 58, 59, 66, 70, 83, 84, 85, 88, 115, 116, 118, 120, 122, 123, 131, 134, 154, 173, 174, 175; grievance procedures, 21, 22, 24, 29, 32, 131, 139, 154; hierarchal structure, 138–141, 145; job security, 1, 3, 4, 21, 30, 38, 65, 67, 68, 73, 118, 174; reduction-in-force, 22, 23, 33, 35, 36, 37, 38, 66, 70, 88, 116, 118, 123, 139, 142, 154, 167, 175; seniority, 72, 88, 116, 118, 123, 175; and teacher turnover, 112–120; trends in, 23, 25t, 28t; working conditions, 1, 4, 8, 18, 20, 21, 63–73, 81, 85, 131. See also Administrators; Budgets; Collective bargaining; Contracts; Education; Educators; School districts; Students; Teachers; Unions; Wages

Contracts, 3–4, 11, 22, 25, 28, 36, 63–73, 132–148, 140, 143, 146, 150, 152–153, 155; in Michigan, 29–30; in New York, 26–29. See also Administrators; Budgets; Collective bargaining; Contract provisions; Education; Educators; School districts; Students; Teachers; Unions; Wages

Cooper, Bruce S., 13, 51

Cresswell, Anthony, 3, 13

Current Population Survey (CPS), 75, 79, 91, 92, 93, 95, 97

Demand-constraint model, 63, 65, 66, 121

District Financial Categories, 135

Donley, Marshall O., Jr., 19, 81

Dunlop, John T., 13, 127, 132, 141

Eberts, Randall W., 18, 120

Education: basic models, 45–47; costs, 1, 2, 3, 10, 11, 166–171, 173; enrollment trends, 105–108, 118; inputs, 158–161; instruction, mode of, 48, 49–50, 132, 148–150, 154, 165, 175, 176; mathematics skills, 52–60; policy and practice, 3, 4, 131, 132, 148–151, 175; process, 4–10; standardized test scores, 46, 47. See also Administrators; Budgets; Collective bargaining; Contract provisions; Contracts; Educational production function; Educators; Scholastic aptitude tests; Student achievement; Students; Teachers; Unions; Wages

Educational production function, 11, 44–45, 48, 51, 59, 61, 161–165

Education Production Functions by Union Status, 160–161

Educators, 95, 97, 99, 101–102, 104–105

Ehrenberg, Ronald, 96

Enrollment. See Collective bargaining; Contract provisions; Education; School districts; Students

Fact finding, 16; and Taylor Law, 26

Farber, Henry S., 83

Freeman, Richard B., 30, 38, 131

Fringe benefits. See Collective bargaining; Contract provisions

Gallagher, Daniel G., 133, 167

Gersten, Russell, 51

Glass, G.V., 49

Governor's Committee on Public Relations (NY), 26

Greenberg, David, 88

Grievance procedures. See Contract provisions

Griffin, M.F., 51

Guttman scaling technique, 138, 139, 140

Hall, Robert E., 72, 73, 167

Hanushek, Eric, 45

Hedonic Wage Education, 69–70
Henderson, Vernon, 8, 50
Hutchinson Act, 1947, 23

Instruction Modes and Resources for
    Mathematics in Union and
    Nonunion Districts, 165
Isoprofit curve, 64–65

Job security. *See* Contract provisions

Katzman, Martin, 47
Kay, William F., 16
Keeler, B.T., 50
Kerchner, Charles T., 4, 41
Kerr, Clark, 13, 132, 141
Kochan, Thomas A., 24, 27, 35, 131,
    138

Labor market, teacher, 86–120, 122,
    123, 174, 175; characteristics of,
    86–87; interdistrict, 98–105,
    105–108; interoccupation, 91–98
Labor movement, 14, 19
Levin, H.M., 47
Lillien, David M., 72, 73

McCall, John, 88
McDonald, Ian M., 66, 127
McDonnell, Lorraine, 3–4, 13, 18, 19,
    20, 21, 22, 23, 29, 31, 42, 81, 138,
    176
Medoff, 30, 38, 131
Meet-and-confer laws, 80
Mellow, Wesley, 96
Michelson, S., 47
Michigan, 13, 15, 16, 20, 23–26, 28,
    29–30, 38, 88, 89
Michigan Education Association
    (MEA), 25
Michigan Employment Relations
    Commission (MERC), 23, 26;
    7MERC Lab. Op. 313 (1972-
    Westwood Community Schools), 24;
    Van Buren Public School District
    vs. *Wayne County Circuit Judge,* 24

Michigan Public Employee Relations
    Act (PERA), 23, 24
Minnesota, 16
Mitchell, Donald, 41
Montana, 16
Moskow, Michael H., 131
Murnane, Richard J., 8, 44, 48, 88,
    111

Nasstrom, R.R., 52
A Nation at Risk, xv
National Commission on Excellence in
    Education, xv
National Education Association
    (NEA), 15, 17, 32, 33, 38, 80, 88,
    89; and labor movement, 19
National Labor Relations Act (NLRA),
    15, 16, 20, 24
Nevada, 16, 25
New Hampshire, 15
New Jersey, 28
New York City, 19, 35, 33, 136
New York State, 13, 15, 16, 20, 25,
    26–29, 30, 34, 36, 37, 38, 116, 120,
    121, 133, 135, 139, 149
New York State Department of
    Education, 33, 68, 136
New York State Employees Fair
    Employment Act, 26
New York State United Teachers
    (NYSUT), 28, 33
Nicholson, E.W., 52

Oaxaca, Ronald, 96
Ohio, 28
Oregon, 16, 25, 99, 100, 101–102, 103,
    104–105, 106–107
Oregon Department of Education, 98

Pascal, Anthony, 3–4, 13, 18, 19, 20,
    21, 22, 23, 29, 31, 42, 81, 138, 176
Pennsylvania, 16, 25
PERA. *See* Michigan Public Employee
    Relations Act
PERB. *See* Public Employees Relations
    Board
Perry, Charles, R., 4, 51, 73, 131

Personnel policy. *See* School districts
Pierce, Lawrence C., xv–xvi
Principals, 5, 9, 43, 50, 51, 53–54, 57, 59, 60, 109, 131, 161; attitudes, 58; relationships with teachers, 8, 132. *See also* Administrators
Public Employees Relations Board (PERB), 26, 27, 29

Rand Corporation, 88, 89
Randles, H.E., 52
Reduction-in-force. *See* Budgets; Contract provisions
Rockefeller, Nelson, 26

Saks, Daniel H., 83, 133
Salary. *See* Wages
San Diego (CA) School District, 88, 89
Scholastic Aptitude Test (SAT), 47
School boards, xvi, 16, 131, 147
School districts, 2, 3, 23, 32, 41, 42, 43, 45, 87, 88, 106, 107, 120, 121, 133, 141, 144, 166; budget expenditure equation, 134–138, 142; and contract structure, 136, 137, 147–148; and collective bargaining, 81–86; expenditures, 137, 143–144, 151, 166, 167, 168, 169, 175; personnel policy, 108–120; policies and teacher turnover, 112–120. *See also* Administrators; Budgets; Collective bargaining; Contract provisions; Contracts; Education; Educators; Student achievement; Students; Teachers; Unions
Scope of bargaining trends, 20–30
Select Joint Legislative Committee on Public Employee Relations, 27
Seniority. *See* Contract provisions; Teachers
Siegel, Abraham, 13, 132, 141
Smith, Mary Lee, 49
Social Security, 88
Solow, Robert M., 66, 127
South Dakota, 25
Spargo, F., 3, 13

Standard Metropolitan Statistical Areas (SMSAs), 34, 35
Steele, Helen H., 81
Strikes, teacher, 1, 8, 16, 23, 24, 32, 178
Student achievement, 5–8, 41–62, 176; and collective bargaining, 5, 7, 157–171, 162, 169. *See also* Collective bargaining; Contract provisions; Contracts; School districts; Students; Teachers; Unions
Student/teacher ratio. *See* Teacher/ student ratio
Students, 1, 3, 5, 18, 21, 48, 136, 176; background measures and pretest scores, 55; determinants for mathematic skills, 52–60. *See also* Collective bargaining; Contract provisions; Contracts; School districts; Student achievement; Teachers; Unions
Summary of Selected Contract Provisions, 25
Summers, Anita, 8, 50, 131
Systems Development Corporation (SDC), 52, 82, 148, 151, 159, 160–161, 165

Taubman, Paul, 96
Taxpayers, 1, 3, 33, 66, 67, 127, 173, 178. *See also* School districts
Taylor, George, 26
Taylor Law, 26, 27, 29
Teacher/student ratio, 30, 33, 38, 54, 58, 59, 66, 81, 116, 121, 127, 136, 142, 145, 151, 158, 161, 168, 174
Teachers, 1, 3, 4, 10, 13, 20, 22, 38, 50, 54, 59, 83, 109, 110, 111, 137, 139, 178; assignments, 22, 32, 110, 111, 112; attitudes, 5, 17–18, 41, 43, 58, 63, 81–86, 120, 121, 174; certification requirements, 49, 87; characteristics, 8–9, 48, 53, 176; and collective bargaining, 63–129; dissatisfaction, 81, 83, 174; education achieved, 48–49, 87, 158;

instruction time, xvi, 48, 49, 53, 56,
58, 158, 161, 173; labor markets,
86–120; mobility, 8, 11, 63, 84, 87,
88, 90, 91–108, 111, 112–120; causes
for organization, 14–15;
participation in administrative
decisions, 84, 111, 132, 148,
150–151, 152–153, 154, 175;
participation by contract status,
150; relationships with
administration, 11, 37, 81, 132;
tenure, 72, 87, 94, 117, 118. *See
also* Administrators; Budgets;
Collective bargaining; Contract
provisions; Contracts; Education;
Educators; School districts; Student
achievement; Students; Unions
Teaching, job attributes, 71, 72, 73
Tenure. *See* Teachers
Terminations. *See* Teachers, mobility
Transfers. *See* Teachers, mobility
Turnover. *See* Teachers, mobility

Union, 1, 2, 3, 8, 25, 33, 63, 67, 132,
159, 160–161, 162–163, 164, 165.
See also Budgets; Collective
bargaining; Contract provisions;
Contracts; School districts; Student
achievement; Teachers
United States Bureau of Census, 91
United States Bureau of Statistics, 73
United States Congress, xv, 15
United States Department of
Education, 80
United States Department of Labor,
24, 80

United States Office of Education, 52,
88

Van Buren Public School District vs.
Wayne County Circuit Judge, 24
Vietnam War, 18

Wage-Change Regression for
Educators, 97, 104–105
Wage-Change Regressions for 1974–75
and 1977–78, 78
Wage-Level Regressions All
Occupations, 93; for Educators, 99;
for 1974 and 1977, 76
Wages, xvi, 1, 3, 4, 8, 11, 18, 20, 32,
33, 41, 65, 68, 73–81, 103, 105, 120,
121, 122, 133, 135, 142, 154, 168,
170, 173; differentials, 73–81, 91,
92, 96, 98, 103; equations, 67, 68,
69–70, 74, 77, 80, 92, 94, 121;
equilibrium, 98–105;
interoccupation mobility and,
91–98. *See also* Budgets; Collective
bargaining; Contract provisions;
Contracts; School districts; Unions
Wall Street Journal, 1, 86
Web-of-rules effect, 13, 141, 145, 154,
175
Wheeler, Hoyt N., 35, 138
Wicksell, Knut, xv
Wildman, W.A., 51
Williams, Donald, 50
Wisconsin, 15
Wisconsin Public Employee Relations
Board, 15
Wolfe, Barbara, 8, 50
Working conditions. *See* Contract
provisions

About the Authors

Randall W. Eberts received the Ph.D. in economics from Northwestern University in 1978 and is currently associate professor of economics at the University of Oregon. He has also been research associate at the Center for Educational Policy and Management at the University of Oregon and has taught economics at Texas A&M University. Dr. Eberts has received numerous federal grants to study the effects of teacher collective bargaining on public schools. His research interests also include the economics of financing public schools and other local public services and the determinants of the productivity of cities. His articles have appeared in such economic journals as *Industrial and Labor Relations Review, Journal of Labor Research,* and *Journal of Urban Economics.*

Joe A. Stone received the Ph.D. in economics from Michigan State University in 1977 and is currently associate professor of economics at the University of Oregon. He has also served as a research economist at the U.S. Bureau of Labor Statistics and as a research associate at the Center for Educational Policy and Management at the University of Oregon. Dr. Stone has received a number of grants to study teacher labor markets and the effects of collective bargaining on public schools. His research interests also include issues in industrial relations and international trade. His articles have appeared in a variety of economic journals including *The Review of Economics and Statistics, The American Economic Review, Journal of Political Economy, Industrial and Labor Relations Review,* and the *Journal of Human Resources.*